# Guardians of Power

# Guardians of Power

## The Myth of the Liberal Media

David Edwards and David Cromwell

Pluto Press

LONDON • ANN ARBOR, MI

First published 2006 by Pluto Press
345 Archway Road, London N6 5AA
and 839 Greene Street, Ann Arbor, MI 48106

www.plutobooks.com

British Library Cataloguing in Publication Data
A catalogue record for this book is available from the British Library

ISBN    0 7453 2483 5 hardback
ISBN    0 7453 2482 7 paperback

Library of Congress Cataloging in Publication Data applied for

10    9    8    7    6    5    4    3    2

Designed and produced for Pluto Press by
Chase Publishing Services Ltd, Fortescue, Sidmouth, EX10 9QG, England
Typeset from disk by Stanford DTP Services, Northampton, England
Printed and bound in the European Union by
Antony Rowe Ltd, Chippenham and Eastbourne, England

# Contents

# Acknowledgments

We would like to express our thanks to the following people for their help with this book and with the Media Lens project: Michael Albert, Gilbert Burnham, Gabriel Carlyle, Phil Chandler, Noam Chomsky, Sue Cullum, Mark Curtis, Denis Halliday, Edward Herman, Richard Keeble, Tim Llewellyn, Marianne McKiggan, Oliver Maw, Aubrey Meyer, David Miller, Milan Rai, Les Roberts, Andy Rowell, Hans von Sponeck, John Theobald and all at Pluto Press. We also gratefully acknowledge the financial support of the Barry Amiel and Norman Melburn Trust, the Lipman Miliband Trust, the Foundation de Sauve, the Marmot Trust, the Tinsley Charitable Trust and many individual donors over the years. We would like to thank our families for their love and support. David Cromwell would like to thank Foske, Sean and Stuart. We would particularly like to thank John Pilger for his encouragement and support.

# Foreword

*John Pilger*

Two epic episodes have determined how many of us in the West see the world beyond. They are the Second World War and the Cold War. As this is being written, the British are being called upon, yet again, to celebrate the 'good war' against Hitler: that 'ethical bath where the sins of centuries of conquest, slavery and exploitation were expatiated', to quote Richard Drayton on the latest crop of imperial historians like Niall Fergusson. He might as well have been referring to many 'mainstream' journalists.

'The good war', wrote Drayton, 'has underwritten sixty years of war-making. It has become an ethical blank cheque for British and American power. We claim the right to bomb, to maim, to imprison without trial on the basis of direct and implicit appeals to the war against fascism. When we fall out with such tyrant friends as Noriega, Milosevic or Saddam, we re-brand them as "Hitler". In the "good war" against them, all bad things become forgettable' (Drayton, 'An Ethical Blank Cheque', *Guardian*, May 10, 2005).

During the Cold War, the ultimate 'bad thing' was the threatened use of nuclear weapons. Declassified official files now reveal the them-and-us propaganda of the Cold War as largely fiction. British planning documents from the 1960s actually dismiss the 'Soviet threat' in Europe as exaggerated and non-existent in most of the world, even in the Middle East. The real Cold War was fought by 'our' governments, not against Russians, but expendable brown and black people, often in places of great impoverishment. This was not so much a war between East and West as between North and South, rich and poor, big and small. Indeed, the smaller the adversary, the greater the threat, because triumph by the weak might be contagious. Thus the weak, whose homelands often contained vast treasuries of oil and gas, minerals and beckoning markets, were the true goals of the West's crusaders, and still are. Western state terrorism was used from Palestine to Nicaragua, Indochina to the Congo. And when on September 11, 2001, the weak, in effect, struck back, a new mythical war, the 'War on Terror', was launched.

The latest 'bad things', such as America's and Britain's bombing of civilian targets with cluster bombs, and use of napalm and depleted uranium, in Iraq and Afghanistan, are not reported as acts of rapacious conquest but as imperfect liberation, justified by the myths of the 'good war' and the Cold War. The principal conveyer of these myths is that amorphous extension of the established order known as 'the media'. While occasionally begging to differ on tactics and political personalities, journalists know, almost instinctively or by training, or both, the true nature of their tasks, especially when the established order appears to be threatened or goes to war. Societies are to be reported in terms of their threat or usefulness to 'us'. Official enemies are to be identified and pursued. Parallels are to be drawn with the 'good war' and the Cold War, while official friends are to be treated as one views one's own government: benign, regardless of compelling evidence to the contrary.

What *has* changed is the public's perception and knowledge. No longer trusting what they read and see and hear, people are questioning as never before. A critical public intelligence is often denied by journalists, who prefer notions of an 'apathetic public' that justify their mantra of 'giving the people what they want'. These days, however, the public is well ahead of the media, refusing to accept the limits of what academics called 'the public discourse'. For example, according to the polls, a majority of the British people regard their prime minister as a liar: not one who has 'misled parliament' or 'spun the facts', but a liar. That is unprecedented.

Most of this plain-speaking has been carried on the Internet, where the media is frequently held to account for its part in the great issues of the day, such as the scandal of the invasion and occupation of Iraq. Forbidden questions are asked, such as this one: by amplifying the lies of Blair and Bush, rather than exposing them, were journalists complicit in the crime in Iraq? This has been raised many times on a remarkable British website <www.medialens.org>. The creators and editors of Media Lens, David Edwards and David Cromwell, have had such influence in a short time that, by holding to account those who, it is said, write history's draft, they may well have changed the course of modern historiography. They have certainly torn up the 'ethical blank cheque', which Richard Drayton referred to, and have exposed as morally corrupt 'the right to bomb, to maim, to imprison without trial … '. Without Media Lens during the attack on and occupation of Iraq, the full gravity of that debacle might have been consigned to oblivion, and to bad history.

They have not bothered with soft targets, such as Rupert Murdoch's *Sun*, but have concentrated on that sector of the media which prides itself on its 'objectivity', 'impartiality' and 'balance' (such as the BBC) and its liberalism and fairness (such as the *Guardian*). Not since Noam Chomsky's and Edward Herman's *Manufacturing Consent* have we had such an incisive and erudite guide through the media's thicket of agendas and vested interests. Indeed, they have done the job of true journalists: they have set the record straight.

For this reason, *Guardians of Power* ought to be required reading in every media college. It is the most important book about journalism I can remember. In the following pages, the best Media Lens 'alerts' are drawn together and cast in an historical context. They are not a source of brickbats. On the contrary, their language and tone are respectful of journalists and unfailingly polite in their often devastating analysis. They debate editors, current-affairs producers and media managers and their arguments are backed by facts and research and a sense of morality which, after a while, you realise is confined to their side.

As I write this, they are engaged with the BBC over the reporting of the American attack on the Iraqi city of Fallujah. Why, they have asked, is there a silence over the vicious assault on Fallujah in November 2004? This was a city already under siege, where only six months earlier the Americans had not denied causing 'at least' 600 deaths. On the Internet, independent journalists, such as the brave Dahr Jamail, a Lebanese–American, reported a pattern of American atrocities, such as attacks on hospitals, the arrest and shooting of staff and patients, the prevention of safe passage of medical supplies and emergency blood. Doctors told harrowing stories of US marines storming into homes and gunning down the elderly and children and people with white flags. The BBC reported none of it.

Media Lens asked the BBC why; and why its correspondents had not reported that the Americans had used napalm, which had been confirmed by Colonel James Alles, commander of Marine Air Group 11. 'We napalmed both those bridge approaches', he said, 'unfortunately, there were people there … It's no great way to die' (Alles, cited Buncombe, 'US Admits it Used Napalm Bombs in Iraq', *Independent on Sunday*, 10 August, 2003). Together with reports about cluster bombs, fire bombs, poisonous gas and other evident atrocities, this was picked up by BBC Worldwide Monitoring but not reported even as claims.

Helen Boaden, director of BBC news, disclosed to Media Lens that the corporation's 'embedded' reporter in Iraq, Paul Wood, 'did not report any of these things because he did not see any of these things'. She also wrote that a 'senior researcher' at Human Rights Watch had 'made some inquiries, but did not have any evidence to substantiate the allegations'. Media Lens asked HRW about this and was told that the human rights organisation was 'mystified' by the BBC's false claim. Like so many Media Lens 'alerts', the correspondence is continuing and illuminating, revealing why television journalism, the main source of people's information, denies so much to its viewers.

Indeed, Media Lens opened a debate that previously existed in a supine form that maintained the rules and taboos of the media 'club'. In my view, its most commendable achievement is to have broken through the defensiveness of many journalists and encouraged them to examine notions of how they are required to work, of hidden, even subliminal agendas, of censorship by omission, of why indeed they are journalists. Certainly, as a journalist, I salute the two Davids. We need their careful, tireless pursuit of truth now more than ever before.

# 1
# The Mass Media –
# Neutral, Honest, Psychopathic

Another helpful attitude is one of deep distrust. Since most of what we hear is either plainly untrue, or half true and half distorted, and since most of what we read in the newspapers is distorted interpretations served as facts, it is by far the best plan to start out with radical scepticism and the assumption that most of what one hears is likely to be a lie or a distortion. (Erich Fromm, *The Art of Being*, Continuum, 1992, p. 44)

## PULLING THE OTHER ONE – THE CORPORATE 'FREE PRESS'

Even the word 'media' is problematic. It is the plural of the word medium, which can be defined as 'the intervening substance through which impressions are conveyed to the senses'. Air, for example, acts as a medium for the transmission of sound – it is a neutral, disinterested carrier of energetic vibrations.

News organisations would have us believe that they transmit information in a similarly neutral, natural way. They represent themselves as self-evidently dispassionate windows on the world. Thus, while there is plenty of discussion about what appears in these windows, there is next to no discussion about who built them, about what their goals and values might be. One might almost think that the mass media had always existed in their current form; that they were simply facts of life, even God-given.

And yet consider two salient facts: 1) much of the contemporary world is dominated by giant, multinational corporations; 2) the media system reporting on that world is itself made up of giant corporations. Indeed, media entities are often owned by the same giant corporations they are tasked with covering.

How young would a child have to be before it failed to recognise a problem here? And yet this is a realisation that escapes close to 100 per cent of professional journalists, at least if their public utterances are to be believed.

The complacent media silence surrounding the oxymoron that is 'the corporate free press' is not indicative of an honest, rational consensus in a free society; it is symptomatic of an all-pervasive media corruption, of a deep cultural malaise. The silence, quite simply, is a lie.

In this book, we will argue that the corporate mass media – not just the right-wing Tory press, but also the most highly respected 'liberal' media – broadcasters like the BBC, and newspapers like the *Guardian*, the *Observer* and the *Independent* – constitute a propaganda system for elite interests. We will show how even the most obvious facts concerning even the most vital subjects – US–UK government responsibility for genocide, vast corporate criminality, threats to the very existence of human life – are distorted, suppressed, marginalised and ignored. In what lies ahead, readers will encounter rational mainstream discussion and forensic analysis – and then sudden, inexplicable silence. We will encounter confident, reasoned debate – and then weird irrationality.

For readers subjected to the corporate media version of the world over several decades, the above claim may well seem remarkable, even outlandish. The natural response is to insist: 'Sorry, but we *do* see honest reporting and commentary in the media. We read Robert Fisk in the *Independent*, Seumas Milne in the *Guardian* and John Pilger (and Media Lens!) in the *New Statesman*. The government *has* been widely criticised and challenged on its conduct in the build up to the Iraq war. Corporations *are* subject to robust censure and investigation – look at the Enron scandal, for goodness sake!'

Alas, all is not as it seems. As ever, the devil lies in the detail. He is also highly visible one step back from our common-sense presumptions – when we are able to recognise, with psychologist Erich Fromm, 'the pathology of normalcy'. Then we will see that the media system is less a window on the world and more a *painting* of a window on the world.

Correcting for the distorted vision of the media begins with an understanding of just how and why that vision has been distorted. It begins, in fact, with an understanding of the fundamental structure of that curious abstract entity – the corporation.

## OUTLAWING SOCIAL RESPONSIBILITY

In his book, *The Corporation*, Canadian law professor Joel Bakan notes that corporations are legally obliged to maximise returns for shareholders. Company executives are literally compelled to subordinate all considerations to profit:

The law forbids any motivation for their actions, whether to assist workers, improve the environment, or help consumers save money. They can do these things with their own money, as private citizens. As corporate officials, however, stewards of other people's money, they have no legal authority to pursue such goals as ends in themselves – only as means to serve the corporation's own interests, which generally means to maximise the wealth of its shareholders. Corporate social responsibility is thus illegal – at least when it is genuine. (Joel Bakan, *The Corporation*, Constable, 2004, p. 37)

This ban on social responsibility has been established in legal judgments over hundreds of years. In a key nineteenth-century court case, for example, Lord Bowen declared:

charity has no business to sit at boards of directors *qua* charity. There is, however, a kind of charitable dealing which is for the interest of those who practise it, and to that extent and in that garb (I admit not a very philanthropic garb) charity may sit at the board, but for no other purpose. (Quoted, ibid., pp. 38–9)

The inevitable consequence, Bakan writes, is what are known blandly as 'externalities': the routine and regular harms caused to others – workers, consumers, communities, the environment. This, Bakan notes, makes the corporation essentially a 'psychopathic creature', unable to recognise or act upon moral reasons to refrain from harming others (ibid., p. 60).

Robert Hinkley, who spent 23 years as a corporate securities attorney advising large corporations on securities offerings, mergers and acquisitions explains:

When toxic chemicals are spilled, forests destroyed, employees left in poverty, or communities devastated through plant shutdowns, corporations view these as unimportant side effects outside their area of concern. But when the company's stock price dips, that's a disaster. The reason is that, in our legal framework, a low stock price leaves a company vulnerable to takeover or means the CEO's job could be at risk. In the end, the natural result is that corporate bottom line goes up, and the state of the public good goes down. This is called privatising the gain and externalising the cost. ('How Corporate Law Inhibits Social Responsibility', *Business Ethics*, January/February 2002, <www.medialens.org/articles/the_articles/articles_2002/rh_corporate_responsibility.html>)

Businessman Robert Monks adds:

> The corporation is an externalising machine, in the same way that a shark is a killing machine ... There isn't any question of malevolence or of will; the enterprise has within it, and the shark has within it, those characteristics that enable it to do that for which it was designed. (Quoted, Bakan, *The Corporation*, p. 70)

This seems a world away, does it not, from the smiley, affable, high-tech output of the corporate media? Adverts are full of humour and fun, television presenters beam with smiles and personal warmth. Can this really be the product of some kind of psychopathic system? It is a deeply troubling notion – we grew up with the media, we are used to viewing it as a normal part of our lives.

And yet consider that the US media watch site, Fairness and Accuracy in Reporting (FAIR), described how media executives 'worry that the flood of grisly images flowing into living rooms from Iraq and elsewhere will discourage advertisers'. Sure enough, a General Motors spokesperson explained that her company 'would not advertise on a TV programme [just] about atrocities in Iraq', while an advertising executive advised 'you don't want to run a humorous commercial next to horrific images and stories' (quoted, Peter Hart and Julie Hollar, 'Fear & Favor 2004 – How Power Shapes the News', March/April 2005, <www.fair.org/index.php?page=2486>).

This helps explain why a typical half-hour US local TV news broadcast devotes 6 minutes 21 seconds to sport and weather, while a typical half-hour national newscast devotes 38 seconds to US foreign policy including the war in Iraq (*Time*, February 28, 2005).

What the West has done to Iraq is almost beyond belief – we have imposed vast slaughter and suffering on an already impoverished Third World country. And yet we see only glimpses of the truth on our TV screens because burned and blasted bodies obstruct the selling of cars and toothpaste! If that does not reflect a psychopathic set of values, what does?

## OF BIG BROTHER AND 'AUNTIE BEEB' – THE PROPAGANDA MODEL

In their seminal work *Manufacturing Consent – The Political Economy of the Mass Media* (Pantheon, 1988), Edward Herman and Noam Chomsky set out their 'propaganda model' of the media. In a subsequent article written in 1996, Edward Herman reflected on the origins of the model:

> We had long been impressed with the regularity with which the media operate within restricted assumptions, depend heavily and uncritically on elite information sources, and participate in propaganda campaigns helpful to elite interests. In trying to explain why they do this we looked for structural factors as the only possible root of systematic behaviour and performance patterns. ('The Propaganda Model Revisited', *Monthly Review*, July 1996)

This would indeed seem a highly rational response; and yet it is rejected out of hand by the mainstream media. Consider that Herman and Chomsky's propaganda model has been mentioned four times by name in British national newspapers since 1988 (including two mentions in book reviews). The much vaunted *Guardian* has mentioned the model precisely once over this period. A detailed explanation of the kind you are reading now has *never* appeared in a national British newspaper.

Herman and Chomsky were right to be impressed by patterns of media performance. As readers will discover over the course of this book, the media adhere with awesome consistency to broadly similar presumptions about the priorities and goals of Western power.

But how can this happen in a free society? Surely no conspiracy theory could account for conformity in literally thousands of journalists and media workers operating within hundreds of media organisations. The idea is outlandish in the extreme – the political mechanisms for projecting Big Brother control of this kind do not exist; a plot on such a scale would be instantly exposed by any number of whistleblowers.

Far more plausible is Herman and Chomsky's suggestion that media performance is largely shaped by market forces, by the bottom-line goals of media corporations operating within state-capitalist society. Built into the system itself, they suggest, is a range of filters that work ceaselessly to shape media output. Herman here explains with great concision:

> The crucial structural factors derive from the fact that the dominant media are firmly imbedded in the market system. They are profit-seeking businesses, owned by very wealthy people (or other companies); they are funded largely by advertisers who are also profit-seeking entities, and who want their ads to appear in a supportive selling environment. The media are also dependent

on government and major business firms as information sources, and both efficiency and political considerations, and frequently overlapping interests, cause a certain degree of solidarity to prevail among the government, major media, and other corporate businesses.

Government and large non-media business firms are also best positioned (and sufficiently wealthy) to be able to pressure the media with threats of withdrawal of advertising or TV licenses, libel suits, and other direct and indirect modes of attack. The media are also constrained by the dominant ideology, which heavily featured anticommunism before and during the Cold War era, and was mobilized often to prevent the media from criticizing attacks on small states labelled communist.

These factors are linked together, reflecting the multi-levelled capability of powerful business and government entities and collectives (e.g., the Business Roundtable; U.S. Chamber of Commerce; industry lobbies and front groups) to exert power over the flow of information. (Ibid.)

Thus, media companies are typically large conglomerates – News International, CBS (now merged with Westinghouse), Turner Broadcasting (now merged with Time-Warner) – which may belong to even larger parent corporations such as General Electric (owners of NBC).

All are tied into the stock market, all have wealthy individuals sitting on their boards, many with extensive personal and business contacts in other corporations. General Electric and Westinghouse, for example, are huge multinational companies heavily involved in weapons production and nuclear power.

It is not hard to appreciate how press neutrality is compromised by these factors. Former Murdoch editor Andrew Neil wrote of his ex-boss: 'Rupert expects his papers to stand broadly for what he believes: a combination of right-wing Republicanism from America mixed with undiluted Thatcherism from Britain' (Quoted, Alan Rusbridger, 'Sour Times – The Only Good Editor Is an Obedient Editor if You Are Rupert Murdoch', *Guardian*, October 24, 1996). Media academics Peter Golding and Graham Murdoch accept that 'media proprietors can determine the editorial line ... of the papers and broadcast stations they own' (*Mass Media and Society*, Arnold, 1996, p. 15). FAIR quote a US newspaper reporter whose bosses also own a TV station:

When the Nielsen TV ratings come out, I know I am expected to write a big story if the co-owned station's ratings are good and to bury the story if the co-owned station's ratings are down. Or another example. A few years ago,

I ran a survey asking readers what they thought of local television news programs. My general manager told me the next time I do something that might affect our sister station, I better check with him first. I got the message. I haven't done a similar project since then. (Quoted, Hart and Hollar, 'Fear & Favor 2004')

Newspapers have to attract and maintain a high proportion of advertising in order to cover the costs of production; without it, the price of any newspaper would skyrocket, which would soon spell its demise in the marketplace. Britain's most progressive broadsheet newspapers – the *Guardian*, the *Observer* and the *Independent* – are dependent on advertising for '75 per cent or more of their total take' (Peter Preston, 'War, What Is it Good For?', *Observer*, October 7, 2001).

Even the *threat* of withdrawal of advertising can affect editorial content. In April 2005, the *Independent* reported that General Motors had pulled its advertising from one of America's biggest newspapers, the *Los Angeles Times*, after it called for GM chief executive Rick Wagoner to be sacked. The car manufacturer decided to stop advertising in the west coast publication due to 'factual errors and misrepresentation' (Katherine Griffiths, 'Angry GM Withdraws Ads from LA Times', *Independent*, April 9, 2005). FAIR described how a survey of US media workers had found respondents concerned about 'pressure from advertisers trying to shape coverage' as well as 'outside control of editorial policy' (quoted, Hart and Hollar, 'Fear & Favor 2004'). In May 2005, financial giant Morgan Stanley informed key publications of new guidelines that required its adverts to be pulled if negative stories about it were published. A key section of its planned addition to advertising contracts read:

In the event that objectionable editorial coverage is planned, agency must be notified as a last-minute change may be necessary. If an issue arises after-hours or a call cannot be made, immediately cancel all Morgan Stanley ads for a minimum of 48 hours. (Jon Fine, 'Morgan Stanley Institutes New "Pull Ad" Press Policy Designed to Respond to "Objectionable" Editorial Coverage', AdAge.com, May 18, 2005)

Robert McChesney, professor of communications at the University of Illinois, notes that professional journalism relies heavily on official sources. Reporters have to talk to the PM's official spokesperson, the White House press secretary, the business association, the army general: 'What those people say is news. Their perspectives are automatically legitimate.' Whereas, McChesney notes, 'if you talk to prisoners, strikers, the homeless, or protesters, you have to paint their perspectives as unreliable, or else you've become an advocate and are no longer a "neutral" professional journalist' (interview by Robert Jensen, *Sun* magazine, Baltimore, September 2000).

Media organisations are also under intense pressure from state–corporate flak. This may take the form of letters, telegrams, phone calls, petitions, lawsuits, speeches in parliament and other modes of complaint and punitive action. Business organisations regularly come together to form flak machines.

In the summer of 2003, the British government launched an awesome flak campaign against the BBC. A year later, BBC reporter Andrew Gilligan, chairman Gavyn Davies and director general Greg Dyke had all resigned or were sacked. The BBC's director of news, Richard Sambrook, was moved sideways to a different post. All of the above happened despite the fact that those opposing the war have been overwhelmingly vindicated by events in Iraq.

Powerful interests regularly exploit dominant ideologies like anti-communism, anti-terrorism and appeals to patriotism in targeting dissent.

In May 2004, British journalists and politicians fulminated against photographs published in the *Daily Mirror* that appeared to show Iraqi prisoners being abused by British soldiers. The British military, it was claimed, now possessed incontrovertible proof that the pictures were fake. Mirror editor Piers Morgan – a fierce opponent of the war – was condemned far and wide for inciting additional hatred of British troops in Iraq, so putting their lives at risk. *Daily Mail* columnist Melanie Phillips said in a BBC interview: 'I think it's an act of treachery, actually, against the interests of this country. At a time of war, to publish a lie which puts our troops in such an appalling light is unforgivable' (*Newsnight*, BBC2, May 14, 2004). In the House of Lords, Lord Maginnis of Drumglass asked:

> Did the dishonest activity of Piers Morgan not compare with the treachery of William Joyce? Was it not high treason and should not this latter-day Lord Haw-Haw be made to feel the full rigours of the law? What action, including criminal charges, does the Government anticipate will be taken against the former editor? ('Morgan "Like traitor Lord Haw-haw"', *Express*, May 28, 2004)

Piers Morgan was sacked by his employer, Trinity-Mirror, under pressure from US shareholders. The BBC's business editor, Jeff Randall, noted: 'These companies don't actually shoot high-profile media types for fun, but they certainly don't lose any sleep over it' (*BBC News at Ten*, BBC1, May 14, 2004).

A year later, in May 2005, the Mirror's pro-war newspaper rival, the *Sun*, published photographs of Saddam Hussein in his underwear. Previously published photographs and footage of Saddam's capture and medical examination by American forces were felt by many Iraqis to be deeply disrespectful and humiliating – insurgents cited this event as a factor in motivating their decision to take up arms. George Bush's deputy press secretary, Trent Duffy, said the release of the *Sun*'s pictures violated American military regulations, and probably the Geneva Convention. He added: 'I think this could have a serious impact' (quoted, David E. Sanger and Alan Cowell, 'Hussein Photos in Tabloids Prompt US Call to Investigate', *New York Times*, May 21, 2005).

The timing of the publication of the photographs could hardly have been worse – at least 620 people, including 58 US troops, had been killed in a massive upsurge in violence since April 28, when the Iraqi prime minister, Ibrahim al-Jaafari, had announced a new Shiite-dominated government. But while a large number of political and media pundits called for the *Mirror*'s anti-war editor to be sacked for endangering British lives, the *Sun*'s managing editor, Graham Dudman, received almost no criticism at all – there was no outcry over the increased risk to British troops, no calls for Dudman to go.

## THE CONVENIENT RISE OF PROFESSIONAL JOURNALISM

It is a remarkable fact that the modern conception of 'objective' journalism is little more than 100 years old. Previously, it had been understood that journalists should both persuade and inform the public. No one worried that newspapers were partisan so long as the public were free to choose from a wide range of opinions. And no one was in any doubt that the commercial press was a mouthpiece of the wealthy individuals who owned it.

In 1863, Ferdinand Lassalle, founder of Germany's first independent labour party, identified a point when the press was transformed into a speculative enterprise whose primary aim was profit:

From that moment on, the newspaper became a highly lucrative investment for those with a talent for making money or for publishers wanting to gain a fortune ... From that moment on, then, newspapers, while still retaining the appearance of being campaigners for ideas, changed from being educators and teachers of the people into lickspittles of the wealthy and subscribing bourgeoisie and of its tastes; some newspapers thus have their hands tied by their current subscribers, others by those whom they wish to gain, but both are always shackled by the real financial foundation of the business – advertisements. (Quoted, John Theobald, *The Media and the Making of History*, Ashgate, 2004, p. 23)

The American writer Henry Adams observed in the early 1900s: 'The press is the hired agent of a moneyed system, set up for no other reason than to tell lies where the interests are concerned' (quoted, Robert McChesney, in Kristina Borjesson, ed., *Into the Buzzsaw – Leading Journalists Expose the Myth of a Free Press*, Prometheus Books, 2002, p. 366).

The kind of corporate press now glorified as a liberal standard-bearer fooled no one in the 1940s, when it was dismissed by radicals for 'carefully glossing over the sins of the banking and industrial magnates who really control the nation' (quoted, Elizabeth Fones-Wolf, *Selling Free Enterprise*, University of Illinois Press, 1994, p. 45).

Balance was provided by a thriving alternative media, including 325 newspapers and magazines published by members and supporters of the US Socialist Party, reaching 2 million subscribers.

Early last century, however, the industrialisation of the press, and the associated high cost of newspaper production, meant that wealthy capitalists backed by advertisers rapidly achieved dominance in the mass media. Unable to compete on price and outreach, the previously flourishing radical press was brushed to the margins.

Reviewing the history of the British media, James Curran and Jean Seaton write of 'a progressive transfer of ownership and control from the working class to wealthy businessmen, while dependence on advertising encouraged the absorption or elimination of the early radical press and stunted its subsequent development before the First World War' (*Power Without Responsibility – The Press and Broadcasting in Britain*, 4th edn, Routledge, 1991, p. 47). Indeed the effect on national radical papers that 'failed to meet the requirements of advertisers' was dramatic: 'They either closed down; accommodated to advertising pressure by moving up-market; stayed in a small audience ghetto with manageable losses; or accepted an alternative source of institutional patronage' (ibid., p. 43).

It is no coincidence that just as corporations achieved this unprecedented stranglehold, the notion of 'professional journalism' appeared. Robert McChesney explains: 'Savvy publishers understood that they needed to have their journalism appear neutral and unbiased, notions entirely foreign to the journalism of the era of the Founding Fathers, or their businesses would be far less profitable' (in Borjesson, *Into the Buzzsaw*, p. 367). By promoting education in formal 'schools of journalism', which did not exist before 1900 in the United States, wealthy owners could claim that trained editors and reporters were granted autonomy to make editorial decisions based on their professional judgement, rather than on the needs of owners and advertisers. As a result, owners could present their media monopoly as a 'neutral' service to the community. The claim, McChesney writes, was 'entirely bogus'.

Built in to 'neutral' professional journalism were three major biases. First, ostensibly to ensure balanced selection of stories, professional journalists decided that the actions and opinions of official sources should form the basis of legitimate news. As a result, news came to be dominated by mainstream political, business and military sources representing similar establishment interests.

The idea goes like this: journalists are neutral. Politicians are elected by voters to control the economy and military. Therefore 'neutral' journalism involves reporting the views of elected party officials and prominent public figures answerable to them. If political parties are, themselves, in reality, pre-selected by powerful state–corporate interests (including the media) working behind the scenes – so that Labour and Conservatives, Democrats and Republicans, offer a barely distinguishable range of policies benefiting the same elites – then that is not a 'neutral' media's problem. If these same parties all reflexively present self-interested realpolitik as 'humanitarian intervention', then that is also not the media's problem. In July 2004, ITV News political editor Nick Robinson wrote in *The Times* of the 2003 Iraq war:

> In the run-up to the conflict, I and many of my colleagues, were bombarded with complaints that we were acting as mouthpieces for Mr Blair. Why, the complainants demanded to know, did we report without question his warning that Saddam was a threat? Hadn't we read what Scott Ritter had said or Hans Blix? I always replied in the same way. It was my job to report what those in power were doing or thinking ... That is all someone in my sort of job can do. ('"Remember the Last Time You Shouted Like That?" I Asked the Spin Doctor', *Times*, July 16, 2004)

Second, journalists agreed that a news 'hook' – a dramatic event, official announcement or publication of a report – was required to justify covering a story. This also strongly favoured establishment interests, which were far more able to generate the required 'hook' than marginalised dissident groups.

Finally, carrot-and-stick pressures from advertisers, business associations and leading political parties had the effect of herding corporate journalists away from some issues and towards others. Newspapers dependent on corporate advertisers for 75 per cent of their revenues are, after all, unlikely to focus too intensively on the destructive impact of these same corporations on public health, the Third World and environment.

When a 2000 *Time* magazine series on environmental campaigners, sponsored by Ford Motor Company, failed to mention anti-car campaigners, *Time*'s international editor stated candidly: 'We don't run airline ads next to stories about airline crashes' (quoted, Janine Jackson and Peter Hart, 'Fear & Favor 2000 – How Power Shapes the News', Fairness and Accuracy in Reporting, <www.fair.org/ff2000. html>).

In reality, as McChesney notes, 'balanced' professional journalism continuously 'smuggles in values conducive to the commercial aims of the owners and advertisers, as well as the political aims of the owning class' (*Into the Buzzsaw*, p. 369). This 'smuggling' will become all too apparent in the chapters that follow.

## A NOTE ABOUT THE STRUCTURE OF THIS BOOK

*Guardians of Power* is structured in the hope that earlier chapters will enhance the meaning and significance of later chapters. Thus, in understanding government and media hypocrisy on East Timor, it is helpful to first discuss the government and media response to the Kosovo crisis. In understanding the later chapters on the problem of corporate media conformity, and on possible solutions rooted in compassion rather than greed, it obviously helps to have read our evidence for the existence of a problem in the early chapters, for example on Iraq, Haiti and climate change.

Having said that, we felt that we had to begin with chapters on Iraq and Afghanistan on the grounds that they concern our government's most appalling crimes against humanity in recent years. They also provide a vast wealth of insights into the propaganda function of the modern mass media.

# 2
# Iraq – The Sanctions of Mass Destruction

This is just not true ... it's saddam who's killing all the bloody children, not sanctions. Sorry. (Roger Alton, *Observer* editor, forwarded to Media Lens, March 15, 2002)

## BLAIR'S BIG BAD LIE – THE 'MORAL CASE FOR WAR'

Responding to the largest ever protest march in British history, Tony Blair said in February 2003:

> But the moral case against war has a moral answer: it is the moral case for removing Saddam ... Yes, there are consequences of war. If we remove Saddam by force, people will die, and some will be innocent. And we must live with the consequences of our actions, even the unintended ones. But there are also consequences of 'stop the war'. There will be no march for the victims of Saddam, no protests about the thousands of children that die needlessly every year under his rule, no righteous anger over the torture chambers which if he is left in power, will remain in being. ('The Price of My Conviction', *Observer*, February 16, 2003)

Two years after these words were spoken, a survey conducted by the Iraqi Planning Ministry with UN assistance found that 'almost a quarter of [Iraqi] children between the ages of six months and five years suffer from malnutrition' ('Iraqi Planning Ministry Launches First Comprehensive Survey on Living Conditions in Iraq', May 12, 2005, <www.reliefweb.int>). Barely reported by the media was the fact that this represented an actual deterioration on the already appalling pre-war figures. An October 2004 report published by the United Nations Children's Fund (UNICEF) found: 'Iraq has experienced a bigger increase in under-five mortality rates than any other country in the world and since the war there are several indications that under-five mortality has continued to rise' ('Little Progress on Child Mortality', Integrated Regional Information Networks, October 11, 2004, <www.reliefweb.int>). To be precise, UNICEF estimated an improvement in Iraqi child mortality between 1999 and 2002, when the death rate had dropped from 130 per thousand live births in 1999 to 125 in 2002. But this trend had *reversed* under the US–UK occupation. UNICEF told us: 'Since the war more children in Iraq are malnourished, fewer children are protected from immunisable diseases and there has been an increase in the incidence of diarrhoeal disease' (UNICEF Iraq Information, email to Media Lens, October 19, 2004).

On September 3, 2004, Iraq's Ministry of Health and other health professionals reported 'a chronic shortage of medicines' in a country occupied by two of the world's wealthiest nations. Intissar al-Abadi, chief pharmacist of Yarmouk hospital in Baghdad, told IRIN:

We had a programme in which cancer and growth hormone drugs were available to patients according to their needs. The ministry used to offer a certain quantity to us every year, so there could be controlled assistance to the patient, but now all that is gone. You cannot imagine what effect the shortage of such drugs has had on patients. ('Medicine Shortage Continues', Integrated Regional Information Networks, September 3, 2004, <www.reliefweb.int>)

According to a 2004 survey, nearly 1,300,000 Iraqi children, aged between eight and 16, were working. The survey revealed long working hours, with 27 per cent of children working for more than eight hours daily. Those who started working at an early stage were found to be mainly from the rural areas because of more harsh economic conditions there ('Focus on Child Labour', May 9, 2005, <www.reliefweb.int>).

A 2004 study on the condition of schools in post-invasion Iraq found that one-third of all primary schools in Iraq lacked any water supplies and almost half were without any sanitation facilities. Since March 2003, over 700 primary schools had been damaged by bombing – a third of those in Baghdad. More than 200 had been burned and over 3,000 looted ('Iraq's Schools Suffering From Neglect and War UN Children's Fund', October 15, 2004, <www.reliefweb.int>).

In June 2005, Mays Nimr, an Iraqi junior doctor, gave an indication of the scale of the country's despair:

My colleagues at work – 99.99% of them are really depressed. They want to leave the country with any chance that's given. To any other country in the world, they don't mind. Do anything there, they don't mind – they just want to leave. They're really desperate for that. (Quoted, *BBC News at Ten*, BBC1, June 7, 2005)

The cataclysm afflicting Iraq is a direct result of the illegal US–UK invasion, of the 'coalition's' incompetence in failing to plan for the occupation, and of the minimal spending on health care and public works. Bob Herbert made an obvious point in the *New York Times*: 'As for the rebuilding of Iraq, forget about it ... It's hard to believe that an administration that won't rebuild schools here in America will really go to bat for schoolkids in Iraq' ('A War Without Reason', *New York Times*, October 18, 2004).

## EFFECTIVELY TERMINATED – THE US–UK GENOCIDE IN IRAQ

Blair's 2003 mention of needless Iraqi deaths was a reference to the mass death of children under sanctions reported by the UN, human rights groups and aid agencies. In a *Newsnight* interview, Blair argued that 'because of the way he [Saddam] implements those sanctions' they are 'actually a pretty brutal policy against the Iraqi people' (*Newsnight Special*, BBC2, February 6, 2003).

Blair's mendacity on this issue would be shocking but for his comparable performance on a wide range of issues. He has, for example, said this of sanctions and suffering in Iraq:

The truth is Saddam Hussein could perfectly easily give his people the money that they need for food and medicine. You know, the sanctions regime specifically allows him to take oil revenue for food and medicine for his people and the reason why he's not doing it is because he needs them to believe ... that the reason why they're starving and have difficulties is because of the United States of America and Britain. (Kamal Ahmed, 'Tony Blair Spoke to *Observer* Political Editor Kamal Ahmed', *Observer*, October 14, 2001)

Though one would not know it from the media's response to Blair's claims, these assertions have been dismissed by the very people who set up and ran the sanctions programme in Iraq. To glance even briefly at the facts is to find that Blair was once again employing his favoured strategy – passionately 'sincere' truth-reversal.

To understand the impact of sanctions, we need to first recognise the scale of the destruction wreaked on Iraq by the 88,500 tons of allied bombs dropped during the 1991 Gulf War. Eric Hoskins, a

Canadian doctor and coordinator of a Harvard study team, reported that the allied bombardment 'effectively terminated everything vital to human survival in Iraq – electricity, water, sewage systems, agriculture, industry and health care' (quoted, Mark Curtis, *The Ambiguities of Power – British Foreign Policy since 1945*, Zed Books, 1995, p. 189).

All of Iraq's eleven major electrical power plants as well as 119 substations were destroyed – 90 per cent of electricity generation was out of service within hours; within days all power generation in the country had ceased. Eight multi-purpose dams were repeatedly hit and destroyed – this wrecked flood control, municipal and industrial water storage, irrigation and hydroelectric power. Four of Iraq's seven major water pumping stations were destroyed. Fourteen central telephone exchanges were irreparably damaged with 400,000 of the 900,000 telephone lines being destroyed. Twenty-eight civilian hospitals and 52 community health centres were hit.

Allied bombs damaged 676 schools, with 38 being totally destroyed. Historic sites were not immune – 25 mosques were damaged in Baghdad alone and 321 more around the country. Seven textile factories sustained damage, as did five construction facilities, four car assembly plants and three chlorine plants. A major hypodermic syringe factory was destroyed. All major cement plants were hit along with various clothes and cosmetic factories, and so on.

The restriction of resources as a result of sanctions made the large-scale reconstruction of this infrastructure impossible. In March 1999 an expert 'Humanitarian Panel' convened by the Security Council concluded the UN's Oil-for-Food Programme could not meet the needs of the Iraqi people, 'regardless of the improvements that might be brought about in the implementation of' the relief programme (quoted, Voices in the Wilderness website, March 2002, <www.viwuk. freeserve.co.uk>). The Panel continued:

> Regardless of the improvements that might be brought about – in terms of approval procedures, better performance by the Iraqi Government, or funding levels – the magnitude of the humanitarian needs is such that they cannot be met within the context of [the Oil-for-Food Programme] ... Nor was the programme intended to meet all the needs of the Iraqi people ... Given the present state of the infrastructure, the revenue required for its rehabilitation is far above the level available under the programme. (Ibid.)

Their conclusion: 'The humanitarian situation in Iraq will continue to be a dire one in the absence of a sustained revival of the Iraqi economy which in turn cannot be achieved solely through remedial humanitarian efforts' (ibid.).

Nevertheless, the British and US governments continued to claim that mass death in Iraq was the result, not of wrecked infrastructure, lack of funds and an economy stalled by sanctions, but of an Iraqi regime that had cruelly withheld foodstuffs and medicines from its own people.

In March 2000, we asked former UN assistant secretary-general Denis Halliday – who set up and ran the UN's Oil-for-Food Programme in Iraq – if there was any truth to the US/UK governments' assertion that Saddam had blocked the benefits of Oil-for-Food. We quoted a letter by Peter Hain, minister of state, to the *New Statesman* in 2000. Hain wrote: 'The "oil for food" programme has been in place for three years ... The Iraqi people have never seen the benefits they should have.' This was Halliday's response:

> There's no basis for that assertion at all. The Secretary-General has reported repeatedly that there is no evidence that food is being diverted by the government in Baghdad. We have 150 observers on the ground in Iraq. Say a wheat shipment comes in from god knows where, in Basra, they follow the grain to some of the mills, they follow the flour to the 49,000 agents that the Iraqi government employs for this programme, then they follow the flour to the recipients and even interview some of the recipients – there is no evidence of diversion of foodstuffs whatever *ever* in the last two years. The Secretary-General would have reported that. (interview with David Edwards, March 2000, <www.medialens.org>)

We asked Halliday about the issue of medical supplies. In January 1999, George Robertson, then defence secretary, had said, 'Saddam Hussein has in warehouses $275 million worth of medicines and medical supplies which he refuses to distribute.' Halliday responded:

> We have had problems with medical drugs and supplies, there have been delays there. There are several good reasons for that. One is that often the Iraqi government did some poor contracting; so they contracted huge orders – $5 million of aspirins or something – to some small company that simply couldn't do the job and had to re-tool and wasted three, four, five months maybe. So that was the first round of mistakes. But secondly, the Sanctions

Committee weighed in and they would look at a package of contracts, maybe ten items, and they would deliberately approve nine but block the tenth, knowing full well that without the tenth item the other nine were of no use. Those nine then go ahead – they're ordered, they arrive – and are stored in warehouses; so naturally the warehouses have stores that cannot in fact be used because they're waiting for other components that are blocked by the Sanctions Committee. (Ibid.)

We asked Halliday what he thought the motive was behind blocking the one item out of ten:

Because Washington, and to a lesser extent London, have deliberately played games through the Sanctions Committee with this programme for years – it's a deliberate ploy. For the British government to say that the quantities involved for vaccinating kids are going to produce weapons of mass destruction, this is just nonsense. That's why I've been using the word 'genocide', because this is a deliberate policy to destroy the people of Iraq. I'm afraid I have no other view at this late stage. (Ibid.)

The British government claims that Saddam was using the money from Oil-for-Food for anything other than food. Peter Hain, for example, stated: 'Over $8 billion a year should be available to Iraq for the humanitarian programme – not only for foods and medicines, but also clean water, electricity and educational material. No one should starve' (letter to *New Statesman*, March 13, 2000). Halliday responded:

Of the $20 billion that has been provided through the 'Oil for Food' programme, about a third, or $7 billion, has been spent on UN 'expenses', reparations to Kuwait and assorted compensation claims. That leaves $13 billion available to the Iraqi government. If you divide that figure by the population of Iraq, which is 22 million, it leaves some $190 per head of population per year over 3 years – that is pitifully inadequate. (interview with David Edwards, March 2000)

Both Halliday and his successor, Hans von Sponeck, resigned in protest from long careers with the UN – resignations that were unprecedented in the UN at such a senior level – but the media almost completely ignored them. When we checked in February 2003, Halliday's name, for example, had never been mentioned in the *Observer*.

Blair was able to make his outrageous case for a 'moral war' because journalists had long ignored reports from groups like Save the Children Fund UK, which had described the economic sanctions against Iraq as 'a silent war against Iraq's children' (quoted, Voices in the Wilderness UK, March 2002, <www.viwuk.freeserve.co.uk>). The Catholic Agency for Overseas Development, CAFOD, described the sanctions as 'humanly catastrophic, morally indefensible and politically ineffective. They are a failed policy and must be changed' (Milan Rai, *War Plan Iraq*, Verso, 2002, p. 175). Human Rights Watch said: 'the continued imposition of comprehensive economic sanctions is undermining the basic rights of children and the civilian population generally' and 'the [Security] Council must recognise that the sanctions have contributed in a major way to persistent life-threatening conditions in the country' (August 2000, <www. viwuk.freeserve.co.uk>). Seventy members of the US Congress signed a letter to President Clinton, appealing to him to lift the embargo and end what they called 'infanticide masquerading as policy' (quoted, *Philadelphia Enquirer*, April 1, 1999). John and Karl Mueller stated in the journal *Foreign Affairs* in May–June 1999 that the 'sanctions of mass destruction' imposed by Clinton and Blair had up to that point killed more civilians in Iraq than 'all the weapons of mass destruction in human history' (Edward Herman, 'Liberal Apologetics for Imperialism: Paul Starr and the American Prospect on Clinton's Foreign Policy', ZNet, November 21, 2000).

## MEDIA COMPLICITY – THE 'PILGER–BAATHIST LINE'

With the wholehearted complicity of the media, the US and UK governments were able to blame the Iraqi regime for the suffering. The BBC's Ben Brown said:

He [Saddam] claims UN sanctions have reduced many of his citizens to near starvation – pictures like these [of a malnourished baby and despairing mother] have been a powerful propaganda weapon for Saddam, which he'll now have to give up. (*BBC News*, June 20, 1996)

ITN's John Draper:

The idea now is targeted or 'smart' sanctions to help ordinary people while at the same time preventing the Iraqi leader from blaming the West for the hardships they're suffering. (*ITV News* at 22.30, ITN, February 20, 2001)

The *Observer*'s Nick Cohen:

> I look forward to seeing how Noam Chomsky and John Pilger manage to oppose a war which would end the sanctions they claim have slaughtered hundreds of thousands of children who otherwise would have had happy, healthy lives in a prison state (don't fret, they'll get there). ('Blair's Just a Bush Baby', *Observer*, March 10, 2002)

The 'claim', as we have seen, was not Chomsky's or Pilger's at all.

The *Observer* declared: 'The Iraqi dictator says his country's children are dying in their thousands because of the West's embargoes. John Sweeney, in a TV documentary to be shown tonight, says the figures are bogus' (Sweeney, 'How Saddam "Staged" Fake Baby Funerals', *Observer*, June 23, 2002). In his *Observer* article, Sweeney cited and dismissed one of the many sources of credible evidence of mass death:

> In 1999 UNICEF, in co-operation with the Iraqi government, made a retrospective projection of 500,000 excess child deaths in the 1990s. The projection is open to question. It was based on data from within a regime that tortures children with impunity. All but one of the researchers used by UNICEF were employees of the Ministry of Health, according to the Lancet.

In a *Spectator* article, Sweeney stooped so low as to refer to what he called 'the Pilger–Baathist line' on sanctions (Sweeney, 'The First Casualty of Pilger', *Spectator*, June 28, 2003).

We asked Hans von Sponeck, who ran the UN's Oil-for-Food Programme in Iraq, what he thought of the argument in Sweeney's *Observer* article. This was his response:

> Sweeney's article is exactly the kind of journalism that is Orwellian, double-speak. No doubt, the Iraq Government has manipulated data to suit its own purposes, every one of the protagonists unfortunately does this. A journalist should not ... This article is a very serious misrepresentation. (email to Media Lens editors, June 24, 2002)

Von Sponeck then wrote directly to Sweeney on his claims of 'bogus' UNICEF figures:

> Dear Mr. Sweeney, I have always held the 'Observer' in high regard. I am therefore even more taken aback by the article you have written on Iraq in

which you consider the mortality figures as Iraqi propaganda. Unfortunately it is very difficult to get any statistics on Iraq which are as rigorously researched as would professionally be desirable. This includes the available mortality figures. You are, however, very wrong in your assessment of the UNICEF analysis. UNICEF, of course, cooperated with the Government but methodology of analysis and the findings is UNICEF's. A large team of UNICEF professionals subjected the data to rigorous review to avoid what you have not avoided and that is a politicization of statistical material. This is not professional and disappoints. Why did you not consult with UNICEF/Baghdad and New York before you wrote your article? I am sure you did not want to play into the hands of those who want to find reason to discredit every effort that tries to portray the enormous damage that sanctions have done to Iraq in addition to the damage the Iraqi civilian population has experienced from within. But this is exactly what you have done, making a difficult situation even more difficult. Regards, Hans von Sponeck. (Copied to Media Lens editors, June 25, 2002)

As far as we know, Sweeney failed to reply.

## BURYING THE EFFECTS OF SANCTIONS

No one would deny that Saddam Hussein was a brutal and oppressive dictator, but Iraq has not always been the failed state it has become in recent years. According to the Economist Intelligence Unit's Country Report for Iraq, prior to the imposition of sanctions the Iraqi welfare state was 'among the most comprehensive and generous in the Arab world' (Iraq: Country Report 1995–96). In a December 1999 report the International Committee of the Red Cross noted: 'Just a decade ago, Iraq boasted one of the most modern infrastructures and highest standards of living in the Middle East', with a 'modern, complex health care system' and 'sophisticated water-treatment and pumping facilities' (ICRC, *Iraq: A Decade of Sanctions*, December 1999). In 1996, the Centre for Economic and Social Rights reported of pre-Gulf War Iraq:

Over 90% of the population had access to primary health-care, including laboratory diagnosis and immunisations for childhood diseases such as polio and diphtheria. During the 1970s and 80s, British and Japanese companies built scores of large, modern hospitals throughout Iraq, with advanced technologies for diagnosis, operations and treatment. Secondary and tertiary services, including surgical care and laboratory investigative support, were

available to most of the Iraqi population at nominal charges. Iraqi medical and
nursing schools emphasised education of women and attracted students from
throughout the Middle East. A majority of Iraqi physicians were trained in
Europe or the United States, and one-quarter were board-certified specialists.
(*UN Sanctioned Suffering*, May 1996 <www.cesr.org>)

The situation in Iraq under sanctions could not have been more
different. Richard Garfield, a renowned epidemiologist at Colombia
University in New York, concluded that 'most' excess child deaths
between August 1990 and March 1998 had been 'primarily associated
with sanctions' ('Morbidity and Mortality Among Iraqi Children
from 1990 Through 1998: Assessing the Impact of the Gulf War and
Economic Sanctions', March 1999, <www.nd.edu>). Garfield noted
that, in tripling since 1990, the death rate of children in Iraq was
unique, as 'there is almost no documented case of rising mortality
for children under five years in the modern world' (John Mueller
and Karl Mueller, 'The Methodology of Mass Destruction: Assessing
Threats in the New World Order', *Journal of Strategic Studies*, vol. 23,
no. 1, 2000, pp. 163–87).

These facts were utterly banished by a media system which
understood that the demonisation of Saddam Hussein and the Iraqi
regime was vital for justifying war. Also missing was even the tiniest
hint that London and Washington were responsible for the deaths
of more than a million people in Iraq – the same people that Blair
and Bush claimed to be 'liberating'.

Halliday was mentioned in 2 of the 12,366 *Guardian* and *Observer*
articles mentioning Iraq in 2003; von Sponeck was mentioned just 5
times. Halliday was mentioned in 2 of the 8,827 articles mentioning
Iraq in 2004; von Sponeck was mentioned 5 times.

In similar vein, *Channel 4 News* declared: 'The sanctions against Iraq
were always bitterly criticised for allegedly directing funds to Saddam
Hussein rather than the Iraqi people. Now it's questionable whether
some of the profits also went abroad' (*News at Noon*, Channel 4, April
22, 2004). The bitter criticism of the genocidal costs of sanctions is
not allowed to exist.

Compare this with an article in the *Daily Telegraph*: 'Critics of the
programme say it swiftly became a way for Saddam to reward his
friends in the West and manipulate the UN' (Philip Delves Broughton,
'Russian and French Politicians "Bribed to Relax UN Sanctions"', *Daily
Telegraph*, April 22, 2004).

BBC Online covered the same story making the same omissions: 'Recent media reports have accused individuals and companies from more than 40 countries, including a senior UN official, of being involved in corruption and bribery in connection with the oil sales.' The report quoted von Sponeck:

> Former UN humanitarian coordinator in Iraq Hans von Sponeck said the allegations needed to be cleared up, but denied that the world body was closely involved in corruption. 'The major part of the transactions where graft, misuse [and] kickbacks were involved by-passed United Nations officials', he told the Today programme. ('UN Orders Iraq Corruption Inquiry', *BBC News*, April 22, 2004, <http://news.bbc.co.uk/1/hi/world/middle_east/3648409.stm>)

However, no mention was made of von Sponeck's passionate denunciations of the role of sanctions in the mass killing of Iraqi people. In December 1999, for example, von Sponeck told a British audience:

> My friends, your country is trying to cage a wild tiger. But you are killing a rare and beautiful bird. In twenty years your fine universities will be using the sanctions on Iraq as an example of how *not* to pursue foreign policy. (http://no-nukes.org/voices/archive4/vfp48.html)

The *Daily Telegraph* twisted the truth out of all recognition in another article:

> There was no more bitter argument in the run-up to the war than the allegation by Left-wing activists, Arab nationalists and Muslim extremists that United Nations sanctions were 'murdering' Iraqi children by denying them food and medicine.
>
> They blamed Britain and the United States, which had maintained the sanctions in the face of growing opposition from France and Russia.
>
> Saddam's regime routinely arranged for critics of sanctions to tour hospitals and children's homes to view the suffering caused. (David Rennie, 'Saddam Cronies Grew Rich on Cash Meant for the Starving', *Daily Telegraph*, April 22, 2004)

The 'Left-wing activists' presumably included the senior UN diplomats who set up and ran the Oil-for-Food Programme, and also UN and aid agency researchers.

*The Times'* editors wrote: 'It was always obvious that the scheme was not working as intended; Iraqi children went hungry, and hospitals went without drugs, while Saddam furnished more palaces.' The programme was described as merely 'defective' in supporting the Iraqi people. Of the countless Iraqis who died and suffered terrible privations, *The Times* wrote blandly: 'The UN stands accused of rank mismanagement, if not outright complicity, in a scandal whose victims were vulnerable civilians, some of whom died for lack of medicines' (Leader, 'Food for scandal', *The Times*, April 22, 2004).

In John Sweeney's BBC documentary, *The Mother of All Ironies*, Barham Salah – then prime minister of the Patriotic Union of Kurdistan and later Iraqi deputy prime minister – said:

> The Oil-for-Food Programme is a good programme, it must continue. It is the best thing that has happened to Iraq since the foundation of the Iraqi state. By the way, not only for the Kurdish areas but also for the rest of Iraq, because we never had it so good – all Iraqis, not just Kurds. (*The Mother of All Ironies, Correspondent*, BBC2, June 23, 2002)

Supported by this wave of propaganda, journalists were able to casually pass over the West's responsibility for vast crimes against humanity. In his November 2002 BBC documentary, *Saddam: A Warning from History*, (BBC1, November 3, 2002), John Simpson limited his comments on Western responsibility for genocide in Iraq as a result of sanctions to 16 words in one sentence. For reasons known only to *Panorama*, the past tense was employed: 'They [sanctions] were indeed a savage punishment, for they chiefly hurt the ordinary people of the country.' This was as much as *Panorama* had to say on the slaughter of 1 million civilians by our government. How much more would the BBC have had to say if our government had killed 2 million people, or 3 million, or 5 million? Would they have covered the additional millions with another dozen words, or perhaps a second and third sentence? Could there ever be a level of atrocity that would lead the BBC to turn the spotlight away from officially approved enemies like Saddam and towards our own government? Simpson watered down even these 16 words by adding on sanctions: 'Saddam made sure they [the Iraqi people] suffered even more than they had to.'

Writing in the *Guardian*, Timothy Garton Ash observed: 'America has never been the Great Satan. It has sometimes been the Great Gatsby: "They were careless people, Tom and Daisy – they smashed up things and creatures and then retreated back into their money or their vast carelessness ... "' ('America on probation', *Guardian*, April 17, 2003). Tom and Daisy – Donald Rumsfeld and the US Army – have indeed smashed up things and creatures in Iraq, in this case human creatures, albeit brown-skinned ones. What could be more careless than finally terminating twelve years of sanctions that took a million innocent lives by smashing the resulting wrecked and defenceless country to bits for the second time in twelve years at a cost of 100,000 lives?

Chomsky sums up the reality of journalist performance with great accuracy:

> When you try to get someone to talk about this question, they can't comprehend what your question is. They can't comprehend that we should apply to ourselves the standards you apply to others. That is incomprehensible. There couldn't be a moral principle more elementary. All you have to do is read George Bush's favourite philosopher [Jesus]. There's a famous definition in the Gospels of the hypocrite, and the hypocrite is the person who refuses to apply to himself the standards he applies to others. By that standard, the entire commentary and discussion of the so-called War on Terror is pure hypocrisy, virtually without exception. Can anybody understand that? No, they can't understand it. (*Power and Terror*, Seven Stories Press, 2003, p. 29)

## *OBSERVER* EDITOR ROGER ALTON
## AND THE 83-YEAR-OLD WAR VETERAN

On March 15, 2002, a Media Lens reader forwarded to us an email he had sent to Roger Alton, editor of the *Observer*. Our reader told us he was an 83-year-old veteran of the Second World War (he asked to remain anonymous), an officer who had served for seven years in XIV Tank Army. In our view, he is a remarkable individual, both rational and compassionate. He told us that he wrote to Alton and *Observer* columnist Nick Cohen because he was all too familiar with the horror of war, with what it means for innocent civilians and soldiers. We feel that his letter to Alton merits reprinting in its entirety:

> I have read with some astonishment the defence you have attempted with Media Lens about your recent article and further comments about Iraq, as I had looked to you previously more as a source of enlightenment than most commentators.

There is it seems to me, (an 83 year old man and for many decades a reader of the *Observer*), a tendency on the part of so many journalists/analysts/ commentators to now go along with what they appear to assume is the line which will best ingratiate them with or not estrange them from 'the establishment', by accepting the arguments of those such as Hain, Bradshaw, Straw whose axes are continuously being ground with a view to being wielded to ensure ongoing political power. That power is looking sideways all the time to the umbrella of the hegemony of the present US government (not the American people) to forward their ambitions – such ambitions are not those of the Labour Party, (associated with which I have been for best part of 70 years) but more of those who have consigned a New role for it once they have achieved a position gained on the backs of generations of party workers.

I say with all courtesy, please examine information/facts in more depth and try and resist the temptation to assume/use the arguments of others ... hope that doesn't sound too much like the great-grand-father I am, but there is satisfaction to be had if you attempt 'From pois'nous herbs (to) extract the healing dew'. I will still look forward to your next effort ...

Sincerely,

(Name Deleted)'

The *Observer*'s editor, Roger Alton, responded with this email:

This is just not true ... it's saddam who's killing all the bloody children, not sanctions. Sorry

The callousness of Alton's response speaks for itself.

In April 2004, we wrote to reporter Andrew Buncombe of the *Independent* as follows:

Dear Andrew,

Perhaps I could ask about your article in today's Independent. You wrote that:

'The controversial Oil-for-Food programme was set up in 1996 with the aim of helping Iraqis who were suffering because of UN sanctions imposed after the 1990–91 Gulf War. The scheme allowed Iraq to sell limited amounts of oil, supposedly under tight UN supervision, to finance the purchase of food and humanitarian goods.' ('Saddam may have bribed head of UN Oil-for-Food [OFF] programme,' The Independent, April 22, 2004)

You mention that the OFF programme was 'controversial'. But why did you neglect to mention either Denis Halliday or Hans von Sponeck, former heads of that programme, who resigned in protest at the devastating effects of UN sanctions?

As you know, Denis Halliday resigned in 1998, describing the sanctions regime as 'illegal and immoral'. 'We are in the process of destroying an entire society', he said. Mr Halliday also said sanctions were bankrupt as a concept because they damaged innocent people and probably strengthened the country's leadership. He has also said that: 'I would use the term genocide to define the use of sanctions against Iraq.'

Hans von Sponeck, resigning from the same position in 2000, said the sanctions had created a 'true human tragedy'. He asked, 'For how long should the civilian population, which is totally innocent on all this, be exposed to such punishment for something they have never done?'

A 1999 UNICEF report calculated that more than half a million children had died as a direct result of sanctions.

Why was none of this deemed relevant to your report today?

I look forward to hearing from you, please.

regards,
David Cromwell (April 22, 2004)

On the same day we received this reply:

david, thank-you for your letter. it is nice to hear from you again and trust all is well with you.

my short answer to your question is that given more space and time i wd [would] not only [have] quoted halliday and van sponeck, as you suggest, but everybody else associated with the entire sanctions controversy. i wd [would] have quoted madeleine albright ('it was worth it'), ritter, etc, and wd [would] have lifted large sections from geoff simons' seminal work, targeting iraq: sanctions and boming in us policy.

as it was i had, 460 words – and 20 minutes, given the other piece i was writing yesterday morning – to write a short piece on the investigation into the alleged corruption at the UN food programme involving three of its senior officials. in my – perhaps misguided – view, i think most people are aware of the controversy surrounding the sanctions and given the limited space i had, i had to make choices on what information i used.

i don't believe that every short news piece can be, or needs to be, a complete history of every topic. that being said, if you feel the issue of sanctions and halliday's view about them has not been covered sufficiently i'll endeavour to devote some more coverage to them. i am sure this is a story i will be coming back to.

if you want an answer to why no more than 460 words was devoted to this topic when more space is devoted to such issues as david beckham's alleged infidelity, you will need to address your question to someone more senior on the newspaper than me.

does this help? have i reinforced your propoganda [sic] model view of everyone who works for the corporate-owned media?! i have actually tried to explain some of the genuine pressures and contraints of story-length and deadline – actual working pressure on journalists that often seem to be missing from your media alerts. i realise that you will selectively use parts of my response but i hope you put any remarks you choose to quote in context.

pls get back to me if there's anything else you need. i look forward to reading your piece on iraq.

best,

andrew buncombe

We were grateful to Andrew Buncombe for responding. However, the claim that space and time were lacking is remarkable. Notice that in the almost infinite media space represented by the *Independent*, the *Guardian*, *The Times*, the *Telegraph*, *Channel 4 News* and website, *BBC News* and website, and so on, there is apparently insufficient space to mention that, according to senior UN officials, Britain is complicit in genocide. Are we seriously to believe this silence is the result of a lack of space? In fact there is no shortage of space in the media – it is systematically denied, not lacking.

It is true that some readers are aware that 'controversy' surrounds the UN sanctions regime. Not many, however, will be aware that senior UN diplomats have accused the US–UK of actual genocide in Iraq for the simple reason that it has very rarely been mentioned. Even if readers were aware, the extraordinary importance of the allegation surely merits emphasis. The media, after all, never tires of reminding us of Saddam's alleged gassing of civilians at Halabja – a much smaller crime, by comparison.

### THREE REMARKABLE EMAILS FROM NICK COHEN

In March 2002, we had a series of email exchanges with the *Observer*'s Nick Cohen. There is no room to reprint the full exchanges here (links are provided below for relevant articles in our media alerts archive), but Cohen's performance was a real eye-opener for us.

On March 13, 2002, we published our media alert 'Nick Cohen of the Observer on Iraq, Chomsky and Pilger' (<www.medialens. org/alerts/02/020313_de_Guardian_Cohen.html>). We noted Nick Cohen's comments from March 10, 2002:

> I look forward to seeing how Noam Chomsky and John Pilger manage to oppose a war which would end the sanctions they claim have slaughtered hundreds of thousands of children who otherwise would have had happy, healthy lives in a prison state (don't fret, they'll get there). ('Blair's Just a Bush Baby', *Observer*, March 10, 2002)

Media Lens then received this reply from Nick Cohen on March 13, 2002:

> The problem with the sanctions cause starvation theory is that:
>
> 1. It was never used about sanctions against South Africa.
> 2. Saddam is a tyrant who has killed tens of thousands of his own people.
> 3. The sanctions regime fell apart in the mid-1990s.
> 4. And, most important, Saddam has engaged in his own version of shock-therapy capitalism to enrich himself and his cronies. As in Russia, the combination of privatisation and gangsterism has led to mortality rates collapsing.
>
> You can, if you wish, dismiss all of this and follow the UN's simple calculations. Doubtless your predecessors could find an equally convincing argument to support the thesis that the Ukranian famine was caused by the Western boycott of Bolshevism rather than dear old Uncle Joe.

We responded with some of the evidence presented in this chapter on March 15 (see <www.medialens.org/alerts/02/020315_de_Guardian_Cohen_reply.html>). Cohen responded the same day:

> Dear Serviles
>
> I would have more respect for you if you showed the smallest awareness that a tyrant bore some responsibility for tyranny. I appreciate this is difficult for you, it involves coming to terms with complexity and horribly Eurocentric principles such as justice and universality, and truly I share

your pain. But your for [sic] sake far more than mine, I'd like to know roughly how many deaths in Iraq are down to Saddam. If you admit that we're in double figures, or more, what should be done about it? Viva Joe Stalin.

We responded again on March 20 (see <www.medialens.org/alerts/02/020320_de_Observer_Cohen_reply2.html>). Finally, we received this response from Cohen on March 23, 2002:

Dear Media Lens,

Sorry to have taken the mick. The point I was trying to make in my piece, admittedly with the sinful use of humour, is that there are three possible positions to take on Iraq:

1.  There should be a war to destroy Saddam, either a direct invasion or a Western-sponsored revolt. (Bush is currently deciding between the two and Blair will do whatever Bush tells him to do.) After victory, sanctions will be dropped.
2.  There should be no war and no sanctions and Saddam should be left alone, which I guess from your email is your position.
3.  There should be no war. But sanctions, particularly sanctions directed against the arms trade, should be enforced. Foreign powers should also provide a safe haven for the Kurds and decent world opinion should support an independent Kurdistan. Foreign airforces should also provide air cover for the Shia majority in the south.

Positions one and two are far closer to each other than they are to position three, which is why I made the crack about the difficulty people like you will have in joining us in the coming struggle.

Readers can see our March 26 response here: <www.medialens.org/alerts/02/020326_de_Observer_Cohen_reply3.html>.

Cohen's emails were a real turning point for us. Less than nine months into the life of Media Lens, we began to realise the extent to which even high-profile journalists were unable to defend their arguments against rational challenge. As we wrote to Cohen (March 15, 2002):

We sent you a sincere and detailed challenge to your arguments, and in response we (and everyone who wrote to you) received a curt and dismissive response, unsupported by evidence, which made no serious attempt to answer our points. In our experience this is virtually the rule for mainstream journalism. Serious debate is not welcome in the mainstream; dissent is treated with derision and contempt, or ignored. There is no sense that ideas are to be proposed and challenged, debated and discussed – we the public are supposed simply to listen to your wise words and shut up. To dare to do anything else is deemed outrageous by journalists who seem to view themselves as celebrities to be feted, rather than public servants doing a job that demands vigorous challenge if it is to be done well.

We can't help but reflect on the fact that you are one of the most highly respected liberal commentators at the liberal extreme of the mainstream spectrum. We note also that you could hardly be addressing a more serious accusation – that our government truly is responsible for genocide in Iraq. Your performance on this vital issue is a further indication of the appalling state of the 'free press' in this country.

# 3
# Iraq Disarmed – Burying the 1991–98 Weapons Inspections

They were withdrawn because they couldn't do their job. I mean let's not be ridiculous about this, there's no point in the inspectors being in there unless they can do the job they're put in there to do. (Tony Blair, *Newsnight Special*, BBC2, February 6, 2003)

If this were argued in a court of law, the weight of evidence would go the other way. Iraq has, in fact, demonstrated over and over a willingness to cooperate with weapons inspectors. (UN weapons inspector in Iraq 1991–98, Scott Ritter, in Ritter and William Rivers Pitt, *War on Iraq*, Profile, 2002, p. 25)

## FIND ME A WAY TO DO THIS

In the run up to the invasion of Iraq, Bush and Blair promoted two key, related claims: that Iraq had refused to cooperate with UNSCOM weapons inspectors between 1991 and 1998 and that, therefore, Iraq retained deadly stockpiles of WMD that represented a 'serious and current threat' to Western interests, including British military bases on Cyprus.

The myth of non-cooperation was powerfully reinforced by the idea that Saddam Hussein had expelled weapons inspectors in December 1998. This was a vital argument because it was used to suggest that all attempts at peaceful resolution of the WMD issue had long since been exhausted and that further attempts at negotiation were futile and naive.

This argument, in turn, was important because Bush and Blair were determined to attack and occupy Iraq; a peaceful resolution was not on the agenda. Former US Treasury secretary Paul O'Neill described how the Bush administration came to office determined to topple Saddam Hussein and used the September 11 attacks as a pretext:

It was all about finding a way to do it. The president saying 'Go find me a way to do this' ... From the very beginning, there was a conviction that Saddam

Hussein was a bad person and that he needed to go. (Julian Borger, 'Bush Decided to Remove Saddam "On Day One"', *Guardian*, January 12, 2004)

O'Neill reports seeing one memorandum preparing for war dating from the first days of the administration. Another, marked 'secret' said, 'Plan for Post-Saddam Iraq'. O'Neill also saw a Pentagon document entitled 'Foreign Suitors for Iraqi Oilfield Contracts', which discussed dividing Iraq's fuel reserves up between the world's oil companies.

Although failure to secure a second UN resolution has since been presented as an obstacle preventing a peaceful outcome, in reality it represented a failure to secure legitimacy for the intended violent outcome.

## 'FUNDAMENTALLY DISARMED' BY 1998

The idea that Iraq had refused to cooperate with inspectors was pushed hard by Western leaders. Blair, for example, said: 'Before he [Saddam Hussein] kicked out the UN weapons inspectors three years ago, they had discovered and destroyed thousands of chemical and biological weapons ... As they got closer, they were told to get out of Iraq' ('The West's Tough Strategy on Iraq is in Everyone's Interests', *Daily Express*, March 6, 2002). George Bush said: 'This is a regime that agreed to international inspections – then kicked out the inspectors' (State of the Union Address, January 29, 2002, <www.whitehouse.gov>). The British foreign secretary, Jack Straw, described how 'the international community's resolve, I'm afraid, fractured rather, and Saddam Hussein was able to exploit that and expel the inspectors' (*Today*, BBC Radio 4, October 12, 2002). In a BBC interview, Bill Clinton declared how, in December 1998, 'Saddam kicked the inspectors out to try to force us to lift the sanctions' (*The Clinton Interview, A Panorama Special*, June 22, 2004).

As we will see below, these statements are entirely false. Saddam Hussein did not expel weapons inspectors and he did not refuse to cooperate with them. Blair, Straw and Clinton were all in office at the time and therefore can hardly have been ignorant of the reality.

Just prior to the Operation Desert Fox air strikes ordered by Clinton in December 1998, weapons inspectors were withdrawn from Iraq. Former UNSCOM executive chairman Richard Butler explained in his book *Saddam Defiant*:

I received a telephone call from US Ambassador Peter Burleigh inviting me for a private conversation at the US mission ... Burleigh informed me that on instructions from Washington it would be 'prudent to take measures to ensure the safety and security of UNSCOM staff presently in Iraq.' ... I told him that I would act on this advice and remove my staff from Iraq. (*Saddam Defiant*, Weidenfeld & Nicolson, 2000, p. 224)

UN secretary general Kofi Annan stated: 'I did get a call from Ambassador Burleigh saying that they are asking US personnel in the region to leave. And they had also advised chief arms inspector Richard Butler to withdraw UNSCOM, and Butler and I spoke' (Josh Friedman, 'Evacuation Delayed for 133 UN Workers', *Newsday*, December 17, 1998). Scott Ritter, chief UNSCOM weapons inspector at the time, confirmed this version of events: 'Saddam didn't kick the inspectors out. They were ordered out in December 1998 by the United States on the eve of the Operation Desert Fox bombing' (*Moral Maze*, BBC Radio 4, July 24, 2002).

Inspectors were withdrawn at a sensitive time in US politics, as Bill Clinton faced impeachment over the Monica Lewinsky affair. Clinton launched the four-day series of strikes on December 16, the day before his impeachment referendum was scheduled, and called them off two hours after the vote. Ritter noted that just prior to the strikes, 'Inspectors were sent in to carry out sensitive inspections that had nothing to do with disarmament but had everything to do with provoking the Iraqis' (Ritter and Rivers Pitt, *War on Iraq*, p. 52). In a report published on the second day of bombing, Ritter was quoted as saying: 'What [head of UNSCOM] Richard Butler did last week with the inspections was a set-up. This was designed to generate a conflict that would justify a bombing.' Ritter claimed US government sources had told him three weeks earlier that 'the two considerations on the horizon were Ramadan and impeachment'. Ritter continued:

If you dig around, you'll find out why Richard Butler yesterday ran to the phone four times. He was talking to his [US] National Security adviser. They were telling him to sharpen the language in his report to justify the bombing. (Quoted, *New York Post*, December 17, 1998)

Arguing that Butler deliberately wrote a justification for war, a UN diplomat described as 'generally sympathetic to Washington' said: 'Based on the same facts he [Butler] could have said, There were something like 300 inspections [in recent weeks] and we encountered difficulties in five' (*Washington Post*, December 17, 1998).

Following the 2003 invasion of Iraq, Ritter has been shown to be accurate (in fact conservative) in his assertion that Iraq had been 'fundamentally disarmed', with 90–95 per cent of its weapons of mass destruction 'verifiably eliminated' by the time he and the other inspectors left the country (Ritter and Rivers Pitt, *War on Iraq*, p. 23). Of the missing 5–10 per cent, Ritter said: 'It doesn't even constitute a weapons programme. It constitutes bits and pieces of a weapons programme which in its totality doesn't amount to much, but which is still prohibited' (ibid., p. 24). According to Ritter, any retained WMD would long since have been reduced to 'useless sludge' (ibid., p. 29) due to the limited 'shelf lives' of the biological and chemical agents involved (see below).

In late 1998 it emerged that CIA spies operating with arms inspectors had used information gathered to target Saddam Hussein during Desert Fox. The role of the CIA in corrupting the arms inspection regime was one of the main reasons for Ritter's resignation that year.

The basic conclusions are clear: Iraq cooperated in the 'fundamental disarmament' of its WMD. The United States nevertheless manufactured a conflict in December 1998. Inspectors were then not kicked out, as claimed, but were withdrawn by Butler to protect them from US bombing. The Iraqis subsequently refused to allow arms inspectors to return, accurately describing them as 'spies' who had used information gathered during inspections to personally target Saddam Hussein in the Desert Fox attacks.

The fallback position of Bush, Blair, Straw et al. is that while Saddam Hussein did not actually throw out weapons inspectors, he made it impossible for them to do their work. And yet Ritter describes the extent to which arms inspectors were successful in disarming Iraq. Of nuclear weapons capability, for example, Ritter says:

When I left Iraq in 1998 ... the infrastructure and facilities had been 100% eliminated. There's no doubt about that. All of their instruments and facilities had been destroyed. The weapons design facility had been destroyed. The production equipment had been hunted down and destroyed. And we had in place means to monitor – both from vehicles and from the air – the gamma rays that accompany attempts to enrich uranium or plutonium. We never found anything. (Ibid., p. 26)

Ritter explains how inspectors roamed the country monitoring Iraq's chemical, biological and nuclear facilities, installing sensitive sniffers and cameras and performing no-notice inspections: 'We blanketed Iraq – every research and development facility, every university, every school, every hospital, every beer factory ... ' (ibid., p. 38). On the potential reconstruction of Iraq's chemical weapons capability, Ritter adds:

> If no one were watching, Iraq could do this. But just as with the nuclear weapons programme, they'd have to start from scratch, having been deprived of all equipment, facilities and research. They'd have to procure the complicated tools and technology required through front companies. This would be detected. The manufacture of chemical weapons emits vented gases that would have been detected by now if they existed. We've been watching, via satellite and other means, and have seen none of this. If Iraq was producing weapons today, we'd have definitive proof, plain and simple. (Ibid., pp. 32–3)

Reviewing the years of Iraqi disarmament between 1991 and 1998, UNSCOM's executive chairman, Rolf Ekeus, stated in May 2000 that as a result of extensive Iraqi compliance 'not much is unknown about Iraq's retained proscribed weapons capabilities' and 'in all areas we have eliminated Iraq's capabilities fundamentally' (quoted, Glen Rangwala, 'A Threat to the World? The Facts about Iraq's Weapons of Mass Destruction', April 2000, <www.arabmediawatch.com/iraq>).

Greg Thielmann, an expert on Iraqi WMD and former senior foreign-service officer for 25 years, claims that key evidence presented by Colin Powell to the UN on February 5, 2003 was misrepresented and the public deceived:

> The main problem was that the senior administration officials have what I call faith-based intelligence. They knew what they wanted the intelligence to show. They were really blind and deaf to any kind of countervailing information the intelligence community would produce. I would assign some blame to the intelligence community, and most of the blame to the senior administration officials. ('The Man who Knew', October 15, 2003, <www.cbsnews.com>)

Ray McGovern, a former high-ranking CIA analyst, told John Pilger that the Bush administration demanded that intelligence be shaped to comply with political objectives: 'It was 95 per cent charade', he said (John Pilger, 'Blair's Mass Deception', *Daily Mirror*, February 3, 2004).

## PUSHED OR PULLED? THE ART OF TRUTH-REVERSAL

There are several remarkable features of media reporting of this issue. Perhaps the most amazing is that newspapers which reported and reinforced the idea that inspectors had been kicked out of Iraq had themselves reported in late 1998 and early 1999 that inspectors had *not* been kicked out.

The American media watch site, Fairness and Accuracy in Reporting (FAIR), produced a stunning report entitled: *What a Difference Four Years Makes: News Coverage of Why the Inspectors Left Iraq* (Extra! Update, October 2002, <www.fair.org>). The report consisted of ten paired examples of mainstream media reporting from 1998 and 2002, covering the withdrawal of weapons inspectors from Iraq. While the quotes from 1998 all stated that inspectors had been withdrawn, the quotes from 2002 claimed that they had been 'thrown out', or otherwise forcibly expelled. For example, in December 1998, the *Washington Post* reported: 'Butler ordered his inspectors to evacuate Baghdad, in anticipation of a military attack, on Tuesday night – at a time when most members of the Security Council had yet to receive his report' (*Washington Post*, December 18, 1998). Less than four years later, the same newspaper wrote in August 2002: 'Since 1998, when U.N. inspectors were expelled, Iraq has almost certainly been working to build more chemical and biological weapons' (Editorial, *Washington Post*, August 4, 2002. Quoted, *What a Difference Four Years Makes*).

NBC's *Today* reported in December 1998:

The Iraq story boiled over last night when the chief UN weapons inspector, Richard Butler, said that Iraq had not fully cooperated with inspectors and – as they had promised to do. As a result, the UN ordered its inspectors to leave Iraq this morning. (Katie Couric, *Today*, NBC, December 16, 1998, in *What a Difference Four Years Makes*)

Four years later, NBC's *Today* reported: 'As Washington debates when and how to attack Iraq, a surprise offer from Baghdad. It is ready to talk about re-admitting UN weapons inspectors after kicking them out four years ago' (Maurice DuBois, *Today*, NBC, August 3, 2002, in *What a Difference Four Years Makes*).

We found the same transformation in UK media coverage. In 1998, the *Guardian* reported: 'A few hours before the attack began, 125 UN personnel were hurriedly evacuated from Baghdad to Bahrain, including inspectors from the UN Special Commission on Iraq and the International Atomic Energy Agency' (Julian Borger and Ewen MacAskill, 'Missile Blitz on Iraq', *Guardian*, December 17, 1998). A year later, this version of events was still commonly reported by the UK media: 'The UN special commission charged with overseeing the destruction of Iraq's weapons of mass destruction pulled out of Iraq in mid-December, just before the US and Britain launched a series of air strikes' (David Hirst, 'Iraq Turns Down "Evil" UN Plan to Ease Sanctions', *Guardian*, December 20, 1999). And: 'The last inspectors were withdrawn to allow the four-day concentrated bombing campaign of last December' ('Russia Calls Urgent Iraq Meeting', *Guardian* staff and agencies, June 2, 1999).

And yet Brian Whitaker of the *Guardian* wrote in February 2002: '[Saddam] could still save his skin by allowing the weapons inspectors – who were thrown out of Iraq in 1998 – to return' ('Life after Saddam: The Winners and Losers', *Guardian*, February 25, 2002). The *Observer* noted in September 2002, 'the Iraqi dictator is more dangerous than he was in 1998, when the last UN inspectors were forced to leave Iraq' (Peter Beaumont and Kamal Ahmed, 'Dossier to Show Iraqi Nuclear Arms Race', *Observer*, September 22, 2002). The *Independent* reported that same month: 'Bill Clinton ... ordered Operation Desert Fox, the last big air offensive against Iraq, after the eviction of UN weapons inspectors in December 1998' (Rupert Cornwell, 'United States – President Calls for Support Inside and Outside America', *Independent*, September 5, 2002). The *Daily Telegraph* was onside: 'Saddam ... refused UN weapons-inspectors access to sites such as his presidential palaces – then expelled them from Iraq' (Editorial, 'Convince us, Mr Blair', *Daily Telegraph*, March 31, 2002). The *New Statesman*'s political editor, John Kampfner, wrote:

> Four months later came a dress rehearsal for the current crisis with Iraq. Saddam Hussein had thrown out the UN inspectors and Blair lined up behind Operation Desert Fox, another US aerial bombardment, despatching a token force from the RAF. (*New Statesman*, February 17, 2003)

The BBC's Jane Corbin stated on *Panorama* that 'the inspectors were thrown out ... and a divided UN Security Council let Saddam get away with it' (*Panorama, The Case Against Saddam*, BBC1, September 23,

2002). On the BBC's lunchtime news, James Robbins reported that inspectors were 'asked to leave' after relations with Iraq broke down (*BBC News* at 13:00, BBC1, September 17, 2002).

Did all of these journalists somehow just forget the reports they must all have seen four years earlier? Or were their memories and capacity for independent thought somehow overwhelmed by government propaganda? This points to a truly remarkable feature of media performance – that large numbers of individual journalists can come to move as an obedient herd despite easily available evidence contradicting the consensus view.

The UK media ignored or distorted much of the relevant information on WMD ahead of the war, despite having originally reported it in the late 1990s. The *Independent on Sunday* (IoS) reviewed a BBC *Newsnight* interview and debate with Blair (*Blair on Iraq – A Newsnight Special*, BBC2, February 6, 2003) answering his claims:

> Blair: The truth is the inspectors were put out of Iraq.
> IoS: No they weren't.
> Blair: They were effectively thrown out. They came back to the United Nations and said we can't carry out the work as inspectors; therefore we said you must leave.
> IoS: That's not the same thing. (Andy McSmith, 'The Paxman Dossier: Blair's Case for War', *Independent on Sunday*, February 9, 2003)

Once again, the fallback argument was allowed to go unchallenged – there was no mention of the fact that the 1991–98 inspections had been almost entirely successful, and there was no mention of US provocation and spying. This was standard right across the media, despite the available facts.

In September 2002, the *Guardian* wrote: 'The inspectors left Baghdad in December 1998, amid *Iraqi allegations* that some inspectors were spying for the United States and countercharges that Iraq was not cooperating with the teams' (Mark Oliver, 'UN Split Over Iraqi Arms Offer', *Guardian*, September 17, 2002 – our emphasis). And: 'Unlike previous inspectors, who were seconded to the UN by governments, the Unmovic staff are employed directly by the UN – a move intended to address Iraqi complaints that the earlier inspections were used as a cover for spying' (Brian Whitaker and David Teather, 'Weapons Checks Face Tough Hurdles', *Guardian*, September 18, 2002). And again: 'For its part Iraq claimed UNSCOM was full of spies' (Simon Jeffery, 'What Are Weapons Inspection Teams?', *Guardian*, September 18, 2002).

What is so remarkable about these references to 'Iraqi allegations', 'complaints' and 'claims', is that they ignore the *Guardian*'s own reporting just three years earlier. Consider this March 1999 report by Julian Borger:

> American espionage in Iraq, under cover of United Nations weapons inspections, went far beyond the search for banned arms and was carried out without the knowledge of the UN leadership, it was reported yesterday. An investigation by the Washington Post found that CIA engineers working as UN technicians installed antennae in equipment belonging to the UN Special Commission (UNSCOM) to eavesdrop on the Iraqi military. ('UN "Kept in Dark" about US spying in Iraq', *Guardian*, March 3, 1999)

Clearly this was not an 'Iraqi allegation'; it was the conclusion of an investigation carried out by a leading national US newspaper, the *Washington Post*. Earlier that year, the *Guardian* had reported another non-Iraqi source:

> United Nations arms inspectors in Iraq had secret intelligence-sharing deals not only with the United States but with four other countries, a former inspector said yesterday. Britain is likely to have been one of the four.
> Scott Ritter, a former American member of the UNSCOM weapons inspection team, said the UN body agreed to provide the five countries with information it collected in return for intelligence from their sources. His claims will fuel the controversy surrounding UNSCOM's activities, with US officials admitting it was infiltrated by American spies. (Richard Norton-Taylor, 'Arms Inspectors "Shared Iraq Data with Five States"', *Guardian*, January 8, 1999)

Again, these were US and UN claims backed up by US officials 'admitting it [UNSCOM] was infiltrated by American spies'.

In similar vein, an *Observer* overview of Western relations with Iraq since 1920 submitted this entry for 1998:

> Iraq ends all co-operation with the UN Special Commission to Oversee the Destruction of Iraq's Weapons of Mass Destruction (UNSCOM). US and Britain launch Desert Fox, a bombing campaign designed to destroy Iraq's nuclear, chemical and biological weapons programmes. ('From Friend to Foe', *Observer*, March 17, 2002)

There was no mention of claims of deliberate US provocation, of a conflict manufactured for domestic political and other reasons. Again, the infiltration of inspectors by CIA spies was airbrushed from history. There was no mention of the fact that the information gained by the spies was then used to blitz Iraq.

US military analyst William Arkin suggests that the primary goal of Operation Desert Fox was to target Saddam Hussein's internal security apparatus using information gathered specifically through UNSCOM (see Milan Rai, *War Plan Iraq*, Verso, 2002). One might think that this would be significant in an honest appraisal of why Iraq was reluctant to readmit inspectors on the basis of 'unfettered access – any time, any place, anywhere', as the US/UK had been demanding. But for our utterly compromised 'free press', truth of this kind is deemed mere pro-Iraqi propaganda, best quietly omitted.

In 2002, the words 'Iraq and inspectors' were mentioned in 736 *Guardian*/*Observer* articles. We managed to find some half a dozen articles confirming that arms inspectors had been infiltrated by CIA spies in 1998. These generally make brief mention of the presence of spies, or report that spies merely 'passed on secrets' to the US and Israel, omitting to mention that the information was used to launch a major military strike against Iraq.

This, to be sure, is only one example of how the US/UK media act as a filtering system for power, ensuring that the public is presented with the right facts and the right ideas at the right time.

## NO PARTICULAR ANSWER – MEDIA LENS AND BBC *NEWSNIGHT* EDITOR GEORGE ENTWISTLE

In researching a *New Statesman* article, David Edwards interviewed George Entwistle (March 31, 2003), then editor of the BBC's flagship current affairs programme, *Newsnight*. Part of the interview involved asking Entwistle if Scott Ritter had appeared on *Newsnight* in recent months. As discussed above, Ritter described how Iraq had been 'fundamentally disarmed' by 1998 without the threat of war, and how any retained weapons of mass destruction would likely have long since become harmless 'sludge'. He was almost completely ignored by the mainstream press ahead of the war. In 2003, the *Guardian* and *Observer* mentioned Iraq in a total of 12,356 articles. In these articles, Ritter was mentioned a total of 17 times.

David Edwards: Have you pitted Ritter against government spokespeople like Mike O'Brien and John Reid?

George Entwistle: I can't recall when we last had Ritter on.

DE: Have you had him on this year?

GE: Not this year, not in 2003, no.

DE: Why would that be?

GE: I don't particularly have an answer for that; we just haven't.

DE: Isn't he an incredibly important, authoritative witness on this?

GE: I think he's an *interesting* witness. I mean we've had ...

DE: Well, he was chief UNSCOM arms inspector.

GE: Absolutely, yeah. We've had Ekeus on, and lots of people like that.

DE: But why not Ritter?

GE: I don't have a particular answer to that ... I mean, sometimes we phone people and they're not available; sometimes they are.

DE: Well, I know he's very keen. He's forever speaking all over the place. He's travelled to Iraq and so on ...

GE: There's no particular ... there's no sort of injunction against him; we just haven't had him on as far as I'm aware.

DE: The other claim is ...

GE: David, can I ask a question of you at this stage?

DE: Yes.

GE: What's the thesis?

DE: What, sorry, on why you haven't ... ?

GE: No, I mean all these questions tend in a particular direction. Do you think that *Newsnight* is acting as a pro-government organisation?

DE: My feeling is that you tend to steer away from embarrassing the government [Entwistle laughs] in your selection of interviewees and so on. They tend to be establishment interviewees. I don't see people like Chomsky, Edward Herman, Howard Zinn, Michael Albert, you know – there's an enormous amount of dissidents ...

GE: Well, we've being trying to get Chomsky on lately, and he's not wanted to come on for reasons I can't explain. What's the guy who was the UN aid programme guy ... ?

DE: Denis Halliday?

GE: Yeah, we've had him on. I think our Blair special on BBC2 confronted him [Blair] with all sorts of uncomfortable propositions.

DE: The other thing is that UNSCOM inspectors, CIA reports and so on have said that any retained Iraqi WMD is likely to be 'sludge' – that's the word they use – because, for example, liquid bulk anthrax lasts maybe three years under ideal storage conditions. Again, I haven't seen that put to people like John Reid and Mike O'Brien.

GE: Um, I can't recall whether we have or not. Have you watched every ... episode, since when?

DE: Pretty much. This year, for example. Have you covered that?

GE: Um, I'll have to check. I mean, we've done endless pieces about the state of the WMD, about the dossier and all that stuff.

DE: Oh sure, about that, but about the fact that any retained WMD is likely to be non-lethal by now, I mean ...

GE: I'll, I can ... I'll have to have a look.

DE: You haven't covered it, have you?

GE: I honestly, I don't know; I'd have to check. I genuinely can't remember everything we've covered.

DE: Sure, but I mean it's a pretty major point, isn't it?

GE: It's an *interesting* point, but it's the kind of point that we *have* been engaging with.

DE: Well, I've never seen it.

GE: Well, I mean, I'll endeavour to get back to you and see if I can help.

Following this conversation, Entwistle wrote to Edwards by email. He provided what he considered powerful evidence that *Newsnight* *had* in fact challenged the government case for war on Iraq. He cited this exchange between *Newsnight* presenter Jeremy Paxman and Tony Blair (*Blair on Iraq – A Newsnight Special*):

Tony Blair: Well I can assure you I've said every time I'm asked about this, they have contained him up to a point and the fact is the sanctions regime was beginning to crumble, it's why it's subsequent in fact to that quote we had a whole series of negotiations about tightening the sanctions regime but the truth is the inspectors were put out of Iraq so –

Jeremy Paxman: They were not put out of Iraq, Prime Minister, that is just not true. The weapons inspectors left Iraq after being told by the American government that bombs would be dropped on the country. (The rest of the transcript followed, March 31, 2003)

We responded to Entwistle:

You mention Paxman raising the myth of inspectors being thrown out. You're right, Paxman did pick him [Blair] up on the idea that inspectors were 'put out' of Iraq, but then the exchange on the topic ended like this:

Tony Blair: They were withdrawn because they couldn't do their job. I mean let's not be ridiculous about this, there's no point in the inspectors being in

there unless they can do the job they're put in there to do. And the fact is we
know that Iraq throughout that time was concealing its weapons.
Jeremy Paxman: Right.
Right! Paxman let Blair get away with this retreat back to a second deception.
(David Edwards to Entwistle, March 31, 2003)

In fact the remarkable truth is that the 1991–98 inspections ended
in almost complete success. As we have discussed, Ritter insists
that Iraq was 'fundamentally disarmed' by December 1998, with
90–95 per cent of its weapons of mass destruction eliminated. Thus,
Entwistle's chosen example of Paxman powerfully challenging
Blair is an excellent example of him failing to make even the most
obvious challenge.

## SERIOUS AND CURRENT THREAT? – THE SLUDGE OF MASS DESTRUCTION

A further astonishing media omission relates to the fact that in the
endless discussion on Iraqi WMD there was almost zero serious
analysis of the likely condition of any retained Iraqi WMD. Bush, Blair
and others were thus allowed to spread terrifying scare stories without
significant challenge from mainstream journalists. In a BBC interview
with the much vaunted Jeremy Paxman, for example, Blair was able
to declare, without challenge: 'We still don't know, for example, what
has happened to the thousands of litres of botulism and anthrax that
were unaccounted for when the inspectors left in 1999' (*Blair on Iraq
– A Newsnight Special*). But it was entirely uncontroversial that Iraq
was only known to have produced liquid bulk anthrax, which has a
shelf life of just three years. The last known batch of liquid anthrax in
Iraq had been produced in 1991 at a state-owned factory. That factory
was blown up in 1996. Any remaining anthrax would therefore long
since have become sludge by the time of Blair's declaration.

Professor Anthony H. Cordesman of the Center for Strategic
and International Studies (CSIS) discounts the possibility that
any Iraqi anthrax produced prior to 1991 could have been
effectively weaponised:

Anthrax spores are extremely hardy and can achieve 65% to 80% lethality
against untreated patients for years. Fortunately, Iraq does not seem to have
produced dry, storable agents and only seems to have deployed wet Anthrax
agents, which have a relatively limited life. ('Claims and Evaluations of Iraq's

Proscribed Weapons', <http://middleeastreference.org.uk/iraqweaponsb. html>)

Readers will recall that Colin Powell held up a vial of dry powder anthrax in his presentation to the United Nations, referring to the anthrax attacks on the United States. This was the anthrax that Iraq 'does not seem to have produced', according to the Center for Strategic and International Studies.

Any botulinum toxin would also have been sludge. A CIA briefing in 1990 reviewed the threat from Iraq's biological weapons facilities: 'Botulinum toxin is nonpersistent, degrading rapidly in the environment ... [It is] fairly stable for a year when stored at temperatures below 27°C' ('Iraq's Biological Warfare Program: Saddam's Ace in the Hole', August 1990, <www.fas.org/irp/gulf/ cia/960702/73924_01.htm>).

The strategic dossier of the International Institute for Strategic Studies (IISS) of September 9, 2002 assessed the likelihood of Iraq retaining a stockpile of biological weapons: 'Any botulinum toxin produced in 1989–90 would no longer be useful' (ibid.).

In his interview with Blair, Paxman described how, 'Hans Blix said he saw no evidence either of weapons manufacture, or that they had been concealed.' Blair responded:

> No, I don't think again that is right. I think what he said was that the evidence that he had indicated that the Iraqis were not cooperating properly and that, for example, he thought that the nerve agent VX may have been weaponised.

Blair raised the spectre of weaponised VX nerve agent – Blix had indeed referred to 'indications' that Iraq 'had been working' on VX in the past and that that VX may have been weaponised in the past ('Statement by Hans Blix to the UN Security Council', *Guardian*, January 27, 2003). 'The real question', Ritter pointed out, was simple: 'Is there a VX nerve agent factory in Iraq today?' The answer: 'Not on your life' (Ritter and Rivers Pitt, *War on Iraq*, p. 32). UN inspectors found the factory producing VX in 1996. Having found it, they blew it up. 'With that', Ritter explained, 'Iraq lost its ability to produce VX.' The point being that VX also quickly becomes 'sludge'. The International Institute for Strategic Studies' strategic dossier of September 2002 recorded the likely status of any VX agent in Iraq: 'Any VX produced by Iraq before 1991 is likely to have decomposed over the past decade ... Any G-agent or V-agent stocks that Iraq concealed from UNSCOM inspections are likely to have deteriorated by now' (quoted, Glen Rangwala, 'US Claims of VX Nerve Agent Fall Apart', March 16, 2003, <www.cambridgeclarion. org/VX_rangwala_16mar2003.html>).

The taskforce of the US Department of Defense gave an interesting insight into how important the Iraqis viewed their own chemical warfare capability so feared by Blair. The US taskforce attributed the high level of Iraqi cooperation in revealing the scale of its chemical programme between 1991–98 to the fact that the Iraqi government realised that the nerve agents it had produced were no longer viable: 'We believe Iraq was largely cooperative on its latest declarations because many of its residual munitions were of little use – other than bolstering the credibility of Iraq's declaration – because of chemical agent degradation and leakage problems' ('Chemical Warfare Agent Issues During the Persian Gulf War', Persian Gulf War Illnesses Task Force, April 2002 <www.cia.gov/cia/publications/gulfwar/cwagents/ cwpaper1.htm>). It is these 'residual munitions ... of little use' that Blair claimed were a justification for a massive war against an impoverished Third World country.

The *Independent on Sunday* reviewed this part of the Paxman interview with Blair as follows:

> Blair: What our intelligence services are telling us, and I've no doubt what American intelligence is telling President Bush as well, is that there are weapons of mass destruction in Iraq.
>
> IoS: During his long presentation to the UN Security Council, Colin Powell produced copious evidence that the Iraqis have something which they don't want the inspectors to see, but scarcely any proof of what it was. (McSmith, 'The Paxman Dossier')

But the IoS said not a word about limited shelf lives, blown up factories, or UN arms inspectors who dismissed the claims as absurd. Ritter said in response to Powell's presentation:

> Everything in here is circumstantial, everything in here mirrors the kind of allegations the US has made in the past in regard to Iraq's weapons program ... He [Powell] just hits you, hits you, hits you with circumstantial evidence, and he confuses people – and he lied, he lied to people, he misled people. ('Ritter Dismisses Powell Report', *Kyodo News*, February 7, 2003, <www. japantoday.com>)

# 4

# Iraq – Gunning for War
# and Burying the Dead

It sickened me so that I had actually brought it up to my lieutenant, and I told him, I said, 'You know, sir, we're not going to have to worry about the Iraqis – you know, we're basically committing genocide over here, mass extermination of thousands of Iraqis' (US Marine Staff Sergeant Jimmy Massey, interview with *Democracy Now*'s Amy Goodman, 'Ex-US Marine: I killed Civilians in Iraq', May 24, 2004, <www.democracynow.org/article.pl?sid=04/05/24/148212>)

## THE MESSAGE FROM AMERICA

In late 2002 and early 2003, day after day, journalists seriously debated whether a single omission in an arms dossier, or a single failure to open a door within two hours, or the discovery of a handful of artillery shells, would justify launching a third of a million troops in a massive war against a broken Third World country. On ITN's December 19, 2002 early evening news, newsreader Katie Derham declared:

Saddam Hussein has lied to the United Nations and the world is one step closer to a war with Iraq. That's the message from America tonight, as the UN's chief weapons inspector admitted there's nothing new in Saddam's weapons dossier. The White House confirmed a short while ago that president Bush is now ramping up towards an attack. (*ITV Evening News*, ITN, December 19, 2002)

According to this kind of report, the role of the media is merely to channel the view of power. Given that this is the case, power is free to do as it pleases – the public will be told what the powerful believe is right, wrong, good and bad. With no rational challenge, with all other views ignored as irrelevant, the public is perennially in no position to contradict 'the message from America'.

Derham handed over to international editor Bill Neely, who asked, 'What's missing?' in an arms dossier presented by the Iraqi government to the UN. Neely's answer: 'Iraq doesn't account for hundreds of artillery shells filled with mustard gas that inspectors know it had. Iraq said in the past it had lost them!' There was apparently no need to question whether these missing artillery shells were being proposed in all seriousness as a reason for launching a massive war. No need to question if use of these awesome weapons – described by arms inspectors as battlefield weaponry of minimal importance – might be deterred by America's 10,600 nuclear warheads. No need to question why, if these weapons were such a dread threat, weapons inspectors had been free to come and go as they pleased in Iraq.

Speaking under a banner graphic reading, 'Timetable to War', ITN newsreader Nicholas Owen said: 'It seems the question is no longer *if* we'll attack Iraq, but *when* and *how*. So what happens next? What's the timetable to war?' All questions that might be asked by any sane individual at this critical time could safely be dumped, then, in the understanding that the coming war was now simply a fact of life to be accepted. If the powerful had decided on a course of action, then who were *we* to question or challenge what they had resolved to do? Owen continued: 'Unlike the last Gulf War, there's no option of leaving Iraq with Saddam still in power. This war *will* happen and Saddam *will* be deposed, and that message comes from the top' (ibid.).

Again, the 'message from America' – this time from the president himself – was not just war but regime change! And so Owen personally insisted that regime change was a necessity, even though regime change, like war itself, was certainly not authorised by the UN and constituted a major war crime. Much later, we learned that even the British government's chief legal advisor, the attorney general Lord Goldsmith, advised that regime change was an illegal objective under international law. Goldsmith told the government 'regime change cannot be the objective of military action. This should be borne in mind in considering the list of military targets and in making public statements about any campaign' ('Goldsmith's Legal Advice to Blair', *Guardian*, April 29, 2005).

In January 2003, Owen interviewed Air Vice Marshal Tony Mason on the subject of the discovery of eleven empty shells found in an Iraqi bunker. Owen asked if the shells constituted the 'smoking gun'. The Air Vice Marshal replied that we had first to be sure of the contents of the shells: 'The real smoking gun, of course, would be if one of those shells was still found to contain a chemical mixture.' That one shell, presumably, would have constituted a weapon of mass destruction and therefore a breach of UN Resolution 1441.

Mason then proceeded to clarify what the one shell might mean for the people of Iraq:

> I would expect the air campaign to be very intense, but this time not concentrated so much on Baghdad but on deployed forces all over the country. Previously, of course, as you know, we were concentrating in the southern area around Kuwait; now we've got to go after troops across the entire country.

The sexy phrasal verb 'go after' (other favourites include 'take out' and 'take down') refers to the blasting, puncturing and incineration of human beings.

Elsewhere, there was occasional dissent in the comment pages, asking why all of this was happening at a time when the target country had done nothing but suffer, sicken and starve for over a decade, threatening no one. But generally there was respectful silence – the media had assigned itself the role of 'weather forecaster of war', predicting if and when war would come, as though addressing an act of God.

The idea that it might be the media's job to do all in its power to challenge, or even prevent, the mass slaughter of innocents by a small group of patently cynical and ruthless men and women was dismissed as 'crusading journalism'. On this performance, it is reasonable to assert that the media would *always* adopt this servile stance no matter how corrupt the interests and goals driving war.

A further remarkable feature of media coverage is worth noting. While there was of course endless speculation on possible violent conclusions to the crisis, we saw no mention of what might have happened in the event of a peaceful resolution. What if UN investigators had given Iraq a clean bill of health on WMD? We saw no journalist asking whether non-military sanctions, or indeed all sanctions, might then be lifted. We can speculate on the reasons for this silence, but it seems clear that whereas war and the maintenance of sanctions were favoured establishment aims, the lifting of sanctions without 'regime change' was desired by no one who mattered. As Noam Chomsky has written: 'The basic principle, rarely violated, is that what conflicts with the requirements of power and privilege does not exist' (*Deterring Democracy*, Hill & Wang, 1992, p. 79).

## FALLING INTO EXECUTE MODE

With the war finally underway, the media displayed the same callous disregard for the immorality of the US–UK attack and the suffering it was causing. Thus, on ITN's April 8, 2003 *Evening News* it was Cartoon Time! From a computer-generated street in Baghdad, a radiating signal from US 'special forces' attracted a cartoon Rockwell B-1B 'Lancer' bomber circling 'on-call', like a doctor, overhead. Viewers could have been told simply that a bomber dropped four large bombs on the target, but ITN supplied a few extra details: 'The B-1 drops four 2,000-pound, satellite-guided, JDAM "bunker busting" bombs' (ITN, April 8, 2003). It was a sentence to enjoy – as with all fetishism, arousal is achieved through obsession with suggestive detail.

We saw the bombs arc down towards a computer-generated restaurant in the Mansour district of Baghdad. A couple of animated explosions flashed on the building, which vanished. There were no little cartoon people walking in the street, none sitting in the restaurant before the blast, and there were no cartoon dismembered limbs after the bombs struck.

The *Guardian* quoted the version of reality of the pilot who dropped the real bombs:

I didn't know who was there. I really didn't care. We've got 10 minutes to get the bombs on target. We've got 10 minutes to do it. We've got to make a lot of things happen to make that happen. So you just fall totally into execute mode and kill the target. (Julian Borger and Stuart Millar, '2pm: Saddam is Spotted. 2.48pm: Pilots Get Their Orders. 3pm: 60ft Crater at Target', *Guardian*, April 9, 2003)

'Special forces', B-1 'Lancers', JDAM bombs, 'on-call' aircraft, 'execute mode', 'kill the target': this is jargon fetishising the manipulation of power over people and things. Phrasal verbs are used to the same effect: 'take out', 'take down', 'go after', 'blow away' all suggest immediate, decisive, all-powerful action.

We have been made receptive to this worship of power by a hundred thousand Hollywood sermons. According to a study by the Glasgow Media Group, children can recall large sections of dialogue from the crime film *Pulp Fiction*: 'Many youngsters regard it as cool to blow people away', Greg Philo reported (*Observer*, October 26, 1997). Young people regard the two hit men in the film, Vincent and Jules, as the 'coolest' characters. A viewer explains why: 'Vincent was cool because he's not scared. He can go around shooting people without being worried.' After all, if power is possession of massive force, then ultimate power is the deployment of massive force with minimal effort and minimal emotion. This is what 'cool' means in our society: massive impact, no problem: 'So you just fall totally into execute mode and kill the target.'

During the bombing of Serbia in 1999, the leading *New York Times* commentator, Thomas Friedman, wrote:

Like it or not, we are at war with the Serbian nation (the Serbs certainly think so), and the stakes have to be very clear: Every week you ravage Kosovo is another decade we will set your country back by pulverising you. You want 1950? We can do 1950. You want 1389? We can do 1389 too. ('Stop the music', *New York Times*, April 23, 1999)

You want us to smash your country – no problem. You want us to obliterate your country – that's no problem either. The thrill of this, for Friedman, lies in discussing the devastation of a nation as if he were a salesman offering a range of services – with indifference magnifying the sense of power to near-superhuman levels.

The people Friedman was writing about, were, every one of them, born in pain and tended with devoted love by mothers and fathers over many years. Every blackened, fly-ridden corpse by the side of the road in every country bombed back to 1950, or 1389, was the apple of someone's eye, was someone's heart's desire.

## A LARGER MAN AND A STRONGER PRIME MINISTER – THE FALL OF BAGHDAD

On April 9, 2003, the media were as one in celebrating a grand 'coalition' victory as US tanks entered Baghdad. The BBC's Nicholas Witchell declared: 'It is absolutely, without a doubt, a vindication of the strategy' (*BBC News* at 18:00, April 9, 2003). BBC news reader and dance show celebrity Natasha Kaplinsky beamed as she described how Blair 'has become, again, Teflon Tony'. The BBC's Mark Mardell agreed: 'It *has* been a vindication for him' (*Breakfast* news, BBC1, April 10, 2003). 'This war has been a major success', ITN's Tom Bradby said (*ITV Evening News*, ITN, April 10, 2003). ITN's John Irvine also saw vindication in the arrival of the marines: 'A war of three weeks has brought an end to decades of Iraqi misery' (*ITV Evening News*, ITN, April 9, 2003). Words that turned sour almost the instant they

were spoken. On Channel 4, the foreign secretary, Jack Straw, told
Jon Snow that he had met with the French foreign minister that day:
'Did he look chastened?' Snow asked, wryly (*Channel 4 News*, April
9, 2003). On the same programme, reporter David Smith pointedly
ended his report from Washington with a quote from 'a leading
Republican senator': 'I'm just glad we had a commander-in-chief who
didn't listen to Hollywood, or the *New York Times*, or the French.'
The BBC's Rageh Omaar in Baghdad all but swooned at the feet of
the invading army:

> In my mind's eye, I often asked myself: what would it be like when I saw
> the first British or American soldiers, after six years of reporting Iraq? And
> nothing, nothing, came close to the actual, staggering reaction to seeing
> American soldiers – young men from Nevada and California – just rolling
> down in tanks. And they're here with us now in the hotel, in the lifts and the
> lobbies. It was a moment I'd never, ever prepared myself for. (*BBC News* at
> 18:00, BBC1, April 9, 2003)

On the BBC's *News at Ten* (April 9, 2003), Matt Frei crowed: 'For some,
these images have legitimised the war.'

As if finally liberated from the bonds of public doubt and scepticism,
the BBC's political editor, Andrew Marr, rose up to deliver a career-
defining speech to the nation from outside Downing Street: 'Frankly,
the main mood [in Downing Street] is of unbridled relief', he began.
'I've been watching ministers wander around with smiles like split
watermelons' (*BBC News at Ten*, BBC1, April 9, 2003). The fact that
Marr delivered this with his own happy smile was a portent of what
was to come. Marr was asked to describe the significance of the fall
of Baghdad. This is what he said:

> Well, I think this does one thing – it draws a line under what, before the war,
> had been a period of ... well, a faint air of pointlessness, almost, was hanging
> over Downing Street. There were all these slightly tawdry arguments and
> scandals. That is now history. Mr Blair is well aware that all his critics out
> there in the party and beyond aren't going to thank him – because they're only
> human – for being right when they've been wrong. And he knows that there
> might be trouble ahead, as I said. But I think this is very, very important for
> him. It gives him a new freedom and a new self-confidence. He confronted
> many critics.
>
> I don't think anybody after this is going to be able to say of Tony Blair
> that he's somebody who is driven by the drift of public opinion, or focus

groups, or opinion polls. He took all of those on. He said that they would be able to take Baghdad without a bloodbath, and that in the end the Iraqis would be celebrating. And on both of those points he has been proved conclusively right. And it would be entirely ungracious, even for his critics, not to acknowledge that tonight he stands as a larger man and a stronger prime minister as a result. (Marr, *BBC News at Ten*, BBC1, April 9, 2003)

One year after delivering this speech to the nation, Marr wrote in his book, *My Trade: A Short History of British Journalism*: 'Gavin Hewitt, John Simpson, Andrew Marr and the rest are employed to be studiously neutral, expressing little emotion and certainly no opinion; millions of people would says that news is the conveying of fact, and nothing more' (*My Trade*, Macmillan, 2004, p. 279).

## OUTDOING SADDAM – THE US–UK
## ARE 'ABSOLUTELY ACCOUNTABLE'

By May 2003, two months after the invasion, UNICEF reported that more than 300,000 Iraqi children were facing death from acute malnutrition – twice as many as under Saddam Hussein. Remarkably, in a few short weeks the US–UK 'coalition' had managed to double the suffering previously experienced by Iraqi children under 'one of the most sadistic regimes on the planet', as Andrew Rawnsley of the *Observer* described it in an article entitled 'The Voices of Doom Were So Wrong' (*Observer*, April 13, 2003). About this catastrophe, Western journalists had next to nothing to say.

A week after the fall of Baghdad on April 9, the Red Cross reported that 32 out of 35 hospitals in Baghdad had shut down following looting and violence – a staggering catastrophe that was reported and quickly dropped by the media.

Unable to find out what happened next from the mainstream, we turned to the internet. We managed to find some answers on the ReliefWeb site. Baghdad 'still does not have any fully functioning hospitals', Morten Rostrup, head of Médicins Sans Frontières in Iraq, reported on May 2, 2003 ('Doctors Without Borders Charges US Failed Iraq Hospitals', May 2, 2003, <www.reliefweb.int>). As a result, sufferers of chronic conditions such as diabetes, heart disease, kidney disease and epilepsy had nowhere to refill their medications. Life-threatening diseases such as tuberculosis and kala-azar, a fly-borne sickness, were 'going untreated due to lack of medicines' in Amarah,

Basra, Karbala, Nasariyah and elsewhere. Rostrup gave the kind of damning verdict that was all but banned from the still triumphal media: 'The US-led coalition was so focused on the military campaign that seeing that the health system was functioning after the war was not a priority. That was a big, big mistake. They are absolutely accountable.'

Oxfam's regional media coordinator, Alex Renton, said that Oxfam was continuing to lobby US–UK forces over their duties as an occupying power to protect civilians in the fabric of life inside Iraq: 'We believe that at this moment the occupying power is failing in those duties' ('Oxfam Sets up First Bases in Iraq since 1996, Blasts US-British forces', May 5, 2003, <www.reliefweb.int>).

It is the kind of failure that overwhelmed the residents of Al Rashad Psychiatric Hospital as Baghdad fell to US forces. Terrified, all 1,015 residents fled as looters stole medicine and equipment, then stripped the hospital of doors, windows and light fixtures. On April 25, aid worker Steve Weaver of Mennonite Central Committee (MCC) visited Al Rashad. Amid the destruction, he saw decades' worth of patient records scattered about. A lone member of staff was painstakingly sorting through the piles of papers, trying to re-file them. MCC described the bigger picture: 'This incident tells the larger story of post-war Iraq – the collapse and destruction of hospitals, water purification systems and other vital institutions, which are leaving vulnerable people in desperate straits' ('Aid Worker Provides First-hand Reports of Life in Post-war Iraq', May 12, 2003, <www. reliefweb.int>). Weaver was told that some 700 patients were still missing from Al Rashad. Staff were concerned that they might have been wandering Baghdad's lethal streets.

And consider the hell that was the sole hospital in Umm Qasr, containing twelve beds catering for around 45,000 people in May 2003. The five permanent local 'doctors' were actually students in their third and fourth years of medical school: 'There is no hygiene of any kind, no basic facilities, no fully trained medical staff, no operating theatre, no fridge – there is just nothing there', said Mark Cockburn, a paramedic with Rescue Net (IRIN, 'Huge Demand for Treatment at Tiny Hospital', May 6, 2003, <www.reliefweb.int>).

What did Blair's 'moral case for war' mean when patients undergoing basic surgery without painkillers had to 'grit their teeth, or put a piece of cloth in their mouths to bite on', as Cockburn reported? Where was the outcry in our politics and media about this fate befalling a country we were supposed to have 'liberated'? Where were the newspaper campaigns calling for the sending of medicines and other aid from British and US health services?

The deceptiveness of the British government's response was by now predictable. Tony Blair's newly appointed Special Representative to Iraq, John Sawers, claimed on *Newsnight*:

> You're focusing on problems in Baghdad. Let's put it into a bit of proportion. In major cities like Mosul and Basra, and in sensitive inter-communal places like Kirkuk, or places of religious value like Najaf and Karbala, the situation is actually quite close to getting back to normal. The situation around the country is not too bad; the problem is here in the capital. (*Newsnight*, BBC2, May 14, 2003)

On the same day that Sawers made this comment, UNICEF's Carel De Rooy reported the doubling of acute malnutrition rates in children under five in Baghdad since February 2003, adding: 'We can assume that the situation is as bad if not much worse in other urban centres throughout Iraq' (UNICEF, 'Iraq Survey Finds Slide in Child Health', May 14, 2003). This is 'close to getting back to normal', according to the British government.

Media Lens invited readers to ask the BBC and ITN why they had devoted so little coverage to the severe crises afflicting the civilian population of Iraq. One reader forwarded a copy of this letter sent to ITN's director of news, David Mannion:

> Dear David Mannion,
>
> Why have you given so little coverage to the grave crises afflicting the civilian population of Iraq? Please draw attention to UNICEF's May 14 report indicating that 300,000 Iraqi children are currently facing death from acute malnutrition – twice as many as under Saddam in February – and the suffering in Umm Qasr, where patients undergoing basic surgery without painkillers 'have to grit their teeth, or put a piece of cloth in their mouths to bite on', according to aid workers.
>
> Why are these horrors not being widely discussed? Our own government needs to take direct responsibility to relieve the suffering of the Iraqi people and the press should be bringing this to our attention.
>
> Just imagine this happening in the UK – what an outcry there would be! (Forwarded to Media Lens, May 19, 2003)

This email was close to ideal from our point of view – succinct, polite and rational. It raised issues of obviously vital humanitarian concern. And are we not forever being told that the media is desperate to engage a bored and indifferent public in political debate; to involve ordinary people in thought, discussion and democratic action in response to the vital issues of the day? So what was David Mannion's response?: 'I would be most grateful if you would cease sending me unsolicted [sic] e-mails. Thank you' (Forwarded May 19, 2003). Mannion sent the same response to several correspondents who wrote to him. Imagine if this had been sent by a politician in reply to one of his or her constituents! The difference is summed up in the title of Curran and Seaton's classic text on the British media, *Power Without Responsibility*. If Mannion felt it was not his job to respond to questions relating to his news product, he could easily have directed the emails, or emailers, elsewhere. Instead, the queries were simply rejected as 'unsolicited' and unworthy of serious reply.

What was being made visible here was the fault-line where corporate culture collides with democratic politics. The media is said to be all about serving the democratic needs of society by giving the public the information they need to make informed decisions – 'We just give them what they want!' is the perennial cry of media executives. But there is a problem – the corporate mass media, intended to supply democracy with a free flow of information, is, itself, a rigidly hierarchical structure of power. Corporations are unaccountable, totalitarian tyrannies, with power flowing strictly top-down. Employees may contribute to a 'suggestion box', but power emanates from the top – there is nothing remotely democratic about a corporation. Moreover, as we have seen, media corporations are legally obliged to prioritise shareholders' profits above all other considerations.

How can we seriously believe that greed-driven hierarchies of corporate power can provide honest information to democratic societies? How can a democratic society exist without a democratic mechanism for deciding which facts, ideas and opinions flow into society? What does democracy mean when there are two main TV broadcasters and the editor of one of them responds to queries with, effectively, 'Shut up and go away!'?

## NECESSARY 'DUD' – THE *LANCET* REPORT

On October 29, 2004, the propaganda system faced a major challenge when the prestigious scientific journal the *Lancet* published a report by researchers from the Johns Hopkins Bloomberg School of Public Health, Al-Mustansiriya University in Baghdad, and Columbia University, New York: *Mortality Before and After the 2003 Invasion of Iraq: Cluster Sample Survey* (<www.thelancet.com/journals/lancet/article/PIIS0140673604174412/fulltext>). The authors estimated that almost 100,000 more Iraqi civilians had died than would have been expected had the invasion not occurred. They wrote: 'Eighty-four percent of the deaths were reported to be caused by the actions of Coalition forces and 95 percent of those deaths were due to air strikes and artillery' (press release, 'Iraqi Civilian Deaths Increase Dramatically After Invasion', October 28, 2004, <www.jhsph.edu/Press_Room/Press_Releases/PR_2004/Burnham_Iraq.html>). Most of those killed by 'coalition' forces were women and children.

The report was met with instant government rejection and a low-key, sceptical response, or outright silence in the media. There was next to no horror, no outrage. No leaders were written pointing out that, in addition to the illegality, lies and public deception, our government was responsible for the deaths of 100,000 civilians.

Scepticism was reasonable enough, of course, but there were no debates allowing the report's authors to respond to challenges. Journalists seemed uninterested in establishing whether the government's dismissal of the report might be just one more cynical deception. Instead they were happy to move on; and just to move on in response to a mass slaughter of innocents on this scale truly is indicative of corporate psychopathy.

Our media search in November, 2004, showed that the *Lancet* report had at that time not been mentioned at all by the *Observer*, the *Telegraph*, the *Sunday Telegraph*, the *Financial Times*, the *Star*, the *Sun* and many others. The *Express* devoted 71 words to the report, but only in its Lancashire edition. We asked the *Observer* editor, Roger Alton, why his paper had failed to mention it. He replied:

Dear Mr Edwards,

Thanks for your note. The figures were well covered in the week, but also I find the methodology a bit doubtful ... (email to Media Lens, November 1, 2004)

In fact, the figures were covered in two brief *Guardian* articles (October 29 and October 30). The second of these, entitled, 'No 10 Challenges

Civilian Death Toll', focused heavily on government criticism of the report without allowing the authors to respond. The *Guardian* then dropped the story. After receiving a number of complaints from Media Lens readers, the *Observer* subsequently published a short article covering the report.

The *Independent* also published two articles on October 29 and 30. But, in contrast to the *Guardian/Observer*, these were then followed up by two articles on the subject totalling some 1,200 words in the *Independent on Sunday*. Columnist David Aaronovitch, then at the *Guardian*, told us: 'I have a feeling (and I could be wrong) that the report may be a dud' (email to Media Lens, October 30, 2004). This was the sum total of initial coverage afforded by the *Sunday Times*: 'Tony Blair, too, may have recalled Basil Fawlty when The Lancet published an estimate that 100,000 Iraqis have died since the start of the allied invasion' (Michael Portillo, 'The Queen Must Not Allow Germany to Act Like a Victim', *Sunday Times*, October 31, 2004). The *Evening Standard* managed two sentences:

> The emails came as a new study in The Lancet estimated 100,000 civilians had died since the conflict began. The Prime Minister's official spokesman ... added that the 100,000 death toll figure could not be trusted because it was based on an extrapolation. (Paul Waugh, 'Blair "Did Not Grasp Risk to Troops"', *Evening Standard*, October 29, 2004)

*The Times* restricted itself to one report on October 29. This, however, at least contradicted the growing government and media smear campaign:

> Statisticians who have analysed the data said last night that the scientists' methodology was strong and the civilian death count could well be conservative.
> They said that the work effectively disproved suggestions by US authorities that civilian bodycounts were impossible to conduct. (Sam Lister, 'Researchers Claims that 100,000 Iraqi Civilians have Died in War', *The Times*, October 29, 2004)

### OUR DATA HAVE BEEN BACK AND FORTH

The tone for the media response was set on *Channel 4 News* (October 29), by science reporter Tom Clarke, who spent 53 seconds of his 2 minute 15 second report challenging the methodology of the study: 'Today, Downing Street dismissed the report saying the researchers used an extrapolation technique, which they considered inappropriate, rather than a detailed body count' (Tom Clarke, Channel4.com, October 29, 2004).

Clarke emphasised how much higher the report's estimate of civilian deaths was than previous estimates:

> The Iraq Ministry of Health has estimated 3000 civilian deaths, but they've only been counting for six months.
>
> Another figure – over 16,000 since the conflict began – comes from a project called Iraqbodycount. Their estimate is based on reported casualties. This latest study comes up with a very different number: nearly 100,000 extra civilian deaths since war began – possibly more.

Clarke then added:

> But without bodies, can we trust the body count? Higher than average civilian casualties in Fallujah strongly distorted this study making the nationwide average well over 100,000 so families surveyed there were discounted from the final figure.
>
> The reliability of interviews must be questioned too, though four out of five families were able to produce a death certificate.

Curiously, Clarke claimed that Fallujah 'strongly distorted this study'. And yet, as he himself noted, 'families surveyed there were discounted' – so Fallujah did *not* in fact distort the report. But he then claimed the reliability of interviews must *also* be questioned – i.e., that this was a further problem in addition to the supposed distortion he had just discounted. Clarke then made his most serious claim:

> But the study's main weakness, and the one highlighted by Downing Street in dismissing today's figures, is that it multiplies a small sample across the whole of Iraq. A country at war, where people are aggrieved and displaced from their homes, makes household based surveys far less accurate.

It is remarkable that a news reporter could so casually dismiss the methodology and findings of a carefully implemented study that had been rigorously peer-reviewed for one of the world's leading scientific journals.

We asked the report's authors about the large rise in numbers of estimated civilian deaths over previous estimates, and also on the ability to make a reliable body count without bodies. Dr Gilbert Burnham responded:

> In short, we used a standard survey method that is used all over the world to estimate mortality. So bodies are not necessary to calculate mortality. In fact going to the community for household surveys on mortality is the standard method used for calculating mortality all over the world, and is probably the method used in the UK census as well, although I am not a demographer.
>
> Anyway, information collected in surveys always produces higher numbers than 'passive reporting' as many things never get reported. This is the easy explanation for the differences between iraqbodycount.net, and our survey.
>
> Further a survey can find other causes of death related to public health problems such as women dying in childbirth, children dead of infectious diseases, and elderly unable to reach a source of insulin, which body counts cannot do – since they collect information from newspaper accounts of deaths (usually violent ones). Can one estimate national figures on the basis of a sample?
>
> The answer is certainly yes (the basis of all census methods), provided that the sample is national, households are randomly selected, and great precautions are taken to eliminate biases. These are all what we did. Now the precision of the results is mostly dependent on sample size. The bigger the sample, the more precise the result. We calculated this carefully, and we had the statistical power to say what we did. Doing a larger sample size could make the figure more precise (smaller confidence intervals) but would have entailed risks to the surveyors which we did not want to take, as they were high enough already.
>
> Our data have been back and forth between many reviewers at the Lancet and here in the school (chair of Biostatistics Dept), so we have the scientific strength to say what we have said with great certainty. I doubt any Lancet paper has gotten as much close inspection in recent years as this one has! (email to David Edwards, October 30, 2004)

Channel 4's Tom Clarke made a further observation: 'The definition of civilian is also unclear. The majority of violent deaths were among young men who may – or may not – have been insurgents.' The report's lead author, Dr Les Roberts, responded to this point:

The civilian question is fair. About 25% of the population were adult males. >70% of people who died in automobile accidents were adult males. Presumably, they died more than other demographic groups because they are out and about more. 46% of people reportedly killed by coalition forces were adult males. Thus, some of them may have been combatants, some probably were not ... perhaps they were just out and about more and more likely to be in targeted areas. We reported that over half of those killed by coalition forces were women and children to point out that if there was targeting, it was not very focused. Thus, we are careful to say that about 100,000 people, perhaps far more were killed. We suspect that the vast majority were civilians, but we do not say each and every one of the approximately 100,000 was a civilian. (email to David Edwards, October 31, 2004)

Clarke concluded his Channel 4 report with a damning statement: 'Given the worsening security situation, it'll be a long time before we have an accurate picture for civilian losses in Iraq, if ever.' This suggested that flawed methodology meant the *Lancet* report could safely be dismissed as failing to provide 'an accurate picture for civilian losses in Iraq'. It meant the researchers, the *Lancet* peer reviewers and the *Lancet* editors had produced an unreliable piece of work. To reiterate the response of the report's authors: 'we have the scientific strength to say what we have said with great certainty. I doubt any Lancet paper has gotten as much close inspection in recent years as this one has!'

An October 29 Downing Street press release read:

Asked if the Prime Minister was concerned about a survey published today suggesting that 100,000 Iraqi civilians had died as a result of the war in Iraq, the PMOS [Prime Minister's Official Spokesman] said that it was important to treat the figures with caution because there were a number of concerns and doubts about the methodology that had been used. Firstly, the survey appeared to be based on an extrapolation technique rather than a detailed body count. Our worries centred on the fact that the technique in question appeared to treat Iraq as if every area was one and the same. In terms of the level of conflict, that was definitely not the case. Secondly, the survey appeared to assume that bombing had taken place throughout Iraq. Again, that was not true. It had been focussed primarily on areas such as Fallujah. Consequently, we did not believe that extrapolation was an appropriate technique to use. (<www.number-10.gov.uk/output/Page6535.asp>)

We again raised these queries with the report authors. Dr Roberts replied:

> Point 1 is true and it is not a mistake on our part. We would have had a more accurate picture if we conducted a 'stratified' sample, with some in the high violence areas and some in the low violence areas. But, that would have involved visiting far more houses and exposing the interviewers to even more risk. Secondly, we do not know how many people are in the 'high violence' areas, so this would have involved large assumptions that would now be criticized.
>
> Most samples are taken with the assumption that all the clusters are 'exchangeable' for purposes of analysis. The difference between them is considered in the interpretation of the data.
>
> Point two, assumes bombing is happening equally across Iraq. There is no such explicit assumption. There is the assumption that all individuals in Iraq had an equal opportunity to die (and if we did not, it would not be a representative sample). It happens, that the one place with a lot of bombings, Falluja, and we excluded that from our 100,000 estimate ...thus if anything, assuming that there has not been any intensive bombing in Iraq.
>
> Finally, there were 7 clusters in the Kurdish North with no violent deaths. Of those 26 randomly picked neighborhoods visited in the South, the area that was invaded, 5 had reported deaths from Coalition air-strikes. Thus, I suspect that such events are more widespread than the review suggests. (email to David Edwards, November 1, 2004)

Almost none of the above was debated anywhere in the UK press. It is clear that the Johns Hopkins researchers, the *Lancet* editors and the *Lancet*'s peer reviewers naturally took every precaution to ensure that the methodology involved could withstand the intense scrutiny a report of this kind was bound to generate. Their results point to the mass slaughter of almost 100,000 Iraqi civilians. The media is just not interested. John Pilger commented in the *New Statesman*:

> The BBC framed the report in terms of the government's 'doubts' and Channel 4 News delivered a hatchet job, based on a Downing Street briefing ... David Edwards, a MediaLens editor, asked the researchers to respond to the media criticism; their meticulous demolition can be viewed on the www.medialens. org alert for 2 November. None of this was published in the mainstream. Thus, the unthinkable that 'we' had engaged in such a slaughter was suppressed – normalised. ('Iraq: The Unthinkable Becomes Normal', *New Statesman*, November 15, 2004)

## THE CHARNEL HOUSE – A SIMPLE QUESTION
## FROM A COUPLE OF AMATEURS

Ahead of the war, almost all commentators accepted that Iraq under Saddam Hussein was one vast torture chamber for the civilian population. Journalists and politicians talked often of a 'charnel house', a 'giant Gulag' and so on.

Digby Jones, director general of the Confederation of British Industry, claimed on BBC's *Question Time* (BBC1, April 10, 2003) that Saddam had killed '3 million' people. Sir Harold Walker, former ambassador to Baghdad, declared on the BBC's main news of Saddam's regime: 'It was the most brutal tyranny, I think, in human history' (*BBC News* at 13:00, BBC1, February 3, 2003). In June 2003, the *Telegraph*'s Con Coughlin wrote: 'Another day and another mass grave is unearthed in Iraq.' He added:

> So many of these harrowing sites have been uncovered in the two months since Saddam's overthrow that even the experts are starting to lose count of just how many atrocities were committed by the Iraqi dictator's henchmen ... If this were Kosovo, the Government would be under fire for not having acted sooner to prevent the genocide.

Coughlin concluded: 'Having just returned from three weeks in post-liberation Iraq, I find it almost perverse that anyone should question the wisdom of removing Saddam from power' ('So What if Saddam's Deadly Arsenal is Never Found? The War Was Just', *Sunday Telegraph*, June 1, 2003). In October 2003, Labour MP Ann Clwyd said:

> In June this year I stood on the edge of Saddam's killing fields. I saw the skeletons of men, women and children being dug up in this enormous mass grave. I do not believe, and neither do you, that we should turn a blind eye to such atrocities. (Quoted, Paul Eastham, 'Blair Safe as Tears Wash Away Labour Rebellion over Iraq', *Daily Mail*, October 2, 2003)

*Observer* journalist Andrew Rawnsley commented casually:

> Yes, too many people died in the war. Too many people always die in war. War is nasty and brutish, but at least this conflict was mercifully short. The death toll has been nothing like as high as had been widely feared. Thousands have died in this war, millions have died at the hands of Saddam. ('The Voices of Doom Were So Wrong', *Observer*, April 13, 2003)

Timothy Garton Ash offered a similar calculation in the *Guardian*:

> The cold moral calculus of reckoning victim numbers against each other always feels inhuman: more than 100,000 Kurds killed by Saddam against perhaps as many as 10,000 Iraqi civilian casualties in this war, past v present, actual v potential, gulag v holocaust. ('America on Probation', *Guardian*, April 17, 2003)

Journalists and politicians appeared to truly believe that genocide was ongoing in Iraq immediately prior to the invasion. And yet it appeared not to have occurred to even one of them to check these claims against the findings of the *Lancet* report, which studied Iraqi deaths in periods before and after the invasion and which was based on the interviews of 8,000 people around the country.

The point is that the report produced a thorough scientific analysis of deaths for a period of time when Saddam Hussein was said to have been on a murderous rampage. It took a matter of moments for us to write to the report authors and ask them what they had found:

> Did your research uncover evidence of mass murder by Saddam Hussein's regime in the year prior to the invasion? There have been government and media claims of tens, even hundreds, of thousands murdered, whereas Amnesty International told me they estimated the figure to be in the hundreds. Did your research cast any light on that? (David Edwards to Dr Les Roberts, October 30, 2004)

The next day, we received this reply from Dr Les Roberts:

> There was one reported killing by Saddam's folks in the first days of the war (considered post-invasion) and there were a couple people who disappeared during the invasion (all adult males). We did not count disappearances as deaths. Thus, no, we have no evidence of that. That does not prove it did not happen. If it was only hundreds of deaths, our small sample probably would not have detected it. (email to David Edwards, October 31, 2004)

This tallied with information we had previously received from Amnesty International. In April 2003, we asked Amnesty for broadbrush statistics on Saddam's crimes over the previous 25 years. We were sent a report: *Human Rights Record in Iraq Since 1979*.

The crimes were indeed hideous, peaking on several occasions: thousands were killed in Halabja in 1988, with thousands more killed in the crushing of the Kurdish uprising in the north and Shi'a Arabs in the south following the Gulf War in 1991. Amnesty wrote of several hundred people, many civilians, killed and injured in southern marshes in 1993.

As for the previous ten years, Amnesty reported of 1994: 'scope of death penalty widened significantly' with 'reports of numerous people executed'. In 1995: 'hundreds of people executed'. In 1996: 'Hundreds of people executed during the year, including 100 opposition members.' In 1997, 1998, 1999 and 2000 the same words are used: 'Hundreds of executions reported.' In 2001: 'scores of people executed'. In October 2002: 'some improvement' with 'release of thousands of prisoners, abolition of certain decrees prescribing the death penalty. Jan 2003, repeal of Special Codes on branding and amputation – no longer permitted.' These were, we can guess, cynical acts of desperation by Saddam Hussein facing imminent attack.

Amnesty continued 'to receive reports of human rights violations, including arbitrary arrests and the continuing policy of expulsion of Kurds from Kirkuk to Iraqi Kurdistan'. Amnesty had also collected information on around 17,000 cases of 'disappearances' over the previous 20 years. The real figure may have been much higher.

These crimes were hideous enough, of course – Saddam *was* a murderous dictator – but notice that the numbers of killed were reported in the hundreds every year, not thousands, not hundreds of thousands, and not millions. To our knowledge, not one journalist commented on the significance of the *Lancet*'s findings for 'the moral case for war' – for the claim that Saddam Hussein had been killing and would have continued to kill countless thousands of Iraqis.

## ALL HAIL DEMOCRATIC IRAQ! – A TRAGI-COMEDY

Prior to the alleged 'transfer of sovereignty' in June 2004, the media tirelessly insisted that the 'coalition' would 'hand over power to the Iraqis' on June 30 (Laura Trevelyan, *BBC News* at 16:45, BBC1, May 23, 2004), such that 'soon the occupation will end' (Orla Guerin, *BBC News* at 19:00, BBC1, June 16, 2004). The death of one British soldier in Basra was particularly tragic, Middle East correspondent Orla Guerin noted on the BBC, because he was thereby 'the last soldier to die under the occupation' (*BBC News* at 13:00, BBC1, June 28, 2004). Washington correspondent Matt Frei declared Iraq 'sovereign and free' on 'an enormously significant day for Iraq'. It was an 'historic day', BBC anchor Anna Ford agreed on the same programme.

Even the most indolent viewer must surely have wondered how any of this could be true when hundreds of thousands of US and other troops continued to pack the country – how could the occupation end without the occupation ending? And how could an Iraqi government appointed by the invading American superpower, rather than elected by Iraqis, be declared 'free'?

On the evening news, Guerin reported how Iraqi troops participating in a ceremony 'have waited all their lives for freedom', noting that Iraqis 'feel satisfaction that power will be back in Iraqi hands' (*BBC News* at 18:00, BBC1, June 28, 2004). The sense of hidden collisions with reality was heightened by diplomatic correspondent James Robbins, who noted that the big question remained: 'Can Iraq achieve democracy?' (ibid.). So power was 'back in Iraqi hands', Iraq was 'sovereign and free', but the key question was whether Iraq could achieve democracy!

Over on ITN, senior correspondent James Mates reviled the 'determined and brutal terrorists' – he meant the insurgency, not the 'coalition' – who were threatening Iraq, which was 'now sovereign' (*ITV Evening News*, ITN, June 28, 2004). On *Channel 4 News*, Jon Snow noted that this was 'a dramatic moment in the Bush–Blair war on terror' (*Channel 4 News*, June 28, 2004). Quite why this was the case, when everyone now knew Iraq had nothing to do with September 11, had no WMD, and no links to al-Qaeda, was not explained.

Channel 4 at least managed to express some scepticism. International editor Lindsey Hilsum noted that 'the occupation ended, at least symbolically', with Snow referring to the 'new, supposedly sovereign, government'. Foreign affairs correspondent Jonathan Miller noted 'The occupation was over – at least that's how they [Bush and Blair] presented it to the world' (ibid.).

Channel 4 Washington correspondent Jonathan Rugman, however, broke all records for tragi-comic truth-reversal by commenting that unless Iraq managed to 'create some semblance of a democratic government', no one should expect any further unilateral US interventions 'anywhere else anytime soon'. Should we laugh or cry? Heaven help any Iraqi government that manages to achieve actual democracy in Iraq – a 'rogue state' and prime target for unilateral US intervention will thereby have been instantly created.

On and on, throughout the day, the broadcast media presented the government version of events as common-sense truth – there really *had* been 'a transfer of power'; Iraq was 'independent', 'sovereign' and 'free'. What was so extraordinary was that a range of journalists right across the spectrum was willing to abandon all common sense, in fact sanity, in promoting this obviously absurd argument. Writing in the hardly radical *New York Times*, the admirable Paul Krugman wrote: 'The formal occupation of Iraq came to an ignominious end yesterday ... In reality, the occupation will continue under another name, most likely until a hostile Iraqi populace demands that we leave' (Krugman, 'Who Lost Iraq?', *New York Times*, June 29, 2004). This recognition of the obvious truth was unimaginable on the main BBC and ITN news programmes on June 28, or thereafter. As Robert Fisk wrote in the *Independent*: 'Alice in Wonderland could not have improved on this. The looking-glass reflects all the way from Baghdad to Washington.' He added: 'Those of us who put quotation marks around "liberation" in 2003 should now put quotation marks around "sovereignty". Doing this has become part of the reporting of the Middle East' ('The Handover: Restoration of Iraqi Sovereignty – or Alice in Wonderland?' *Independent*, June 29, 2004).

Alas, as so often happens, Fisk's own editors provided an almost comic counterpoint to his honesty on the same day, insisting, 'the new ministers must now be left to govern as they see fit. The slightest hint that they are puppets of the former occupying powers will reinforce suspicions that the occupation never ended and fuel resistance' (Leader, 'The Violence Will Only End in Iraq if There Is a Genuine Transfer of Sovereignty', *Independent*, June 29, 2004). The 'slightest hint'? Perhaps that was provided by the quarter of a million foreign troops armed to the teeth and beyond the control of a superpower-selected Iraqi government, itself far beyond the control of the Iraqi people.

In fact the interim Iraqi government had no power even to make laws or to change laws imposed by the 'coalition'. This included a law giving US and other foreign civilian contractors legal immunity while working in Iraq. Before leaving, the coalition head, Paul Bremer, made a series of five-year appointments – interim prime minister Ayad Allawi's choice of national security and intelligence chiefs would remain in post for five years. Allawi had long worked for MI6, the CIA and twelve other intelligence agencies. Crucially, the Iraqi government had no power over the 140,000 US and 20,000 other troops occupying the country. The power of the budget continued to be largely set and paid for in Washington, and would not be in Iraqi hands – Americans would decide how the $18 billion set aside for reconstruction was spent. Journalist and author Adam Hothschild commented:

If the new Iraq-to-be is not a state, what is it? A half century ago one could talk about colonies, protectorates, and spheres of influence, but in our supposedly post-colonial world, the vocabulary is poorer. We lack a word for a country where most real power is in the hands of someone else, whether that be shadowy local militias, other nations' armies, or both. Pseudostate, perhaps. From Afghanistan to the Palestinian Authority, Bosnia to Congo, pseudostates have now spread around the globe. Some of them will even be exchanging ambassadors with Iraq. ('A Pseudostate is Born', ZNet, June 27, 2004)

## DEMOCRACY BORN AND STILL-BORN – A TALE OF TWO ELECTIONS

On the BBC's February 23 main lunchtime news, Clive Myrie reported on George Bush's 2005 State of the Union address. Bush had arranged for an American woman whose son had been killed in Iraq to embrace an Iraqi woman whose husband had been killed by Saddam Hussein. Before a national TV audience, Myrie commented: 'A woman who gave up her son so another could be free' (*BBC News* at 13:00, BBC1, February 23, 2005). This, after all the revelations about the non-existent 'threat' of Iraqi WMD, about the non-existent links to al-Qaeda, about the non-existent pre-war genocide in Iraq!

On the BBC's late news, Matt Frei insisted that the Americans were eager to leave Iraq as soon as possible. Why? Because US leaders 'don't want to outstay the welcome of their troops' (*BBC News at Ten*, BBC1, January 31, 2005). Is comment even necessary?

Competing to make the most outrageous comment on national television, the BBC's world affairs editor, John Simpson, described Iraqi insurgents as 'opponents to what they see as the foreign occupation of their country' (*Panorama – Simpson In Iraq*, BBC1, January 30, 2005). Imagine Simpson referring in 1943 to 'what the French insurgents see as the foreign occupation of their country'.

In a sane society the extremist 'mainstream' would be considered comical and irrelevant, referenced only for exotic case studies in the human capacity for self-deception in deference to individual and vested self-interest. What is currently considered the alternative media is also misnamed 'the radical media'. In fact it is the *rational* media, rooted in common sense, in genuine rather than merely proclaimed compassion for human suffering, and in a desire to solve problems rather than profit from them.

US and British journalists were all but unanimous in describing the January 30, 2005 elections in Iraq as 'democratic' and 'free'.

The *Los Angeles Times* declared that 'the world could honestly see American troops making it possible for a long-oppressed people to choose their destiny' (Leader, 'Courage Under Fire', *Los Angeles Times*, January 31, 2005). *The Times* (London) hailed 'the resounding success of Iraq's first democratic elections in half a century' in 'the latest astonishing testimony to the power of democracy' (Leader, 'The Power of Democracy', *The Times*, February 1, 2005).

The conformity in proclaiming this propaganda version of events was close to 100 per cent in Britain and the United States. The media was unanimous, for example, in immediately declaring high voter participation. The BBC reported 'a high turnout in today's election' which was 'exactly the outcome that the United States wishes for the Iraqis' (BBC, January 30, 2005. Quoted, Michel Chossudovsky, 'Iraqi Elections: Media Disinformation on Voter Turnout?' Global Research, January 31, 2005, <http://globalresearch.ca/articles>).

Beyond this mainstream consensus, it is clear that an election cannot be deemed legitimate when conducted under foreign military occupation and when run by a puppet government. Most Iraqis, after all, voted with the hope of ending the US–UK occupation. In January 2005, a pre-election poll reported in the *New York Times* found that 69 per cent of Iraq's Shias and 82 per cent of Sunnis favoured 'near-term US withdrawal'. But Blair, Rice and others have been explicit in rejecting any timetable for withdrawal. Noam Chomsky summarised the thinking in Washington and London:

> 'Uh, well, okay, we'll let them have a government, but we're not going to pay any attention to what they say.' In fact the Pentagon announced ... two days ago: we're keeping 120,000 troops there into at least 2007, even if they call for withdrawal tomorrow. ('After the Election – The Future of Iraq and the US Occupation', February 2, 2005 <www.counterpunch.org/chomsky02022005.html>)

It is also clear that the US rigged the rules to ensure US-friendly Kurds had 27 per cent of the seats in the national assembly, although they make up just 15 per cent of the population. In a rare departure from mainstream propaganda, Naomi Klein commented in the *Guardian*:

> Skewing matters further, the US-authored interim constitution requires that all major decisions have the support of two-thirds or, in some cases, three-

quarters of the assembly – an absurdly high figure that gives the Kurds the power to block any call for foreign troop withdrawal, any attempt to roll back Bremer's economic orders, and any part of a new constitution. ('Brand USA is in Trouble, so Take a Lesson from Big Mac', *Guardian*, March 14, 2005)

Ralph Nader noted that Paul Bremer had put in place rules that allowed for 'massive foreign ownership and domination of Iraqi businesses' – low corporate tax rates, immunity protection from lawsuits and not allowing workers to form trade unions ('Is the End of the Iraq War–Occupation Near?', March 30, 2005, <www.zmag.org>). Phyllis Bennis of the Institute for Policy Studies commented:

> An election cannot be legitimate when it is conducted under foreign military occupation; when the country is nominally ruled by, and the election will be officially run by, a puppet government put and kept in place by the occupying army and the election will be under the ultimate control of the occupying army; when war is raging extensively enough to prevent participation by much of the population; and when the election is designed to choose a new assembly responsible for drafting a constitution and selecting a government that will continue to function under the conditions of military occupation. ('Iraq's Elections', Institute for Policy Studies, December 20, 2004 <www. tni.org/archives/bennis/points27.htm>)

With the propaganda hullabaloo falling away as the public lost interest, the *New York Times* even managed to hint at the truth: 'The election in January, heroic though it was, will not be enough to make Iraq a functioning democracy or even ensure its future as a unified country' (Leader, 'Choosing Iraq's Prime Minister', *New York Times*, February 23, 2005).

Consider, by contrast, the media response to the spring 2005 elections in Zimbabwe, run by one of the West's official enemies – Robert Mugabe. In this case, the media regained their mental faculties and were able to identify obvious flaws in the process.

A *Guardian* editorial entitled 'Stealing Democracy' observed: 'Intimidation, gerrymandering and the use of famine relief as a weapon are just some of the many abuses that have been documented so far' in 'what looks like being an utterly flawed election' (Leader, 'Stealing Democracy', *Guardian*, March 29, 2005). The same editors had declared the Iraq process 'the country's first free election in decades', a 'landmark election' that would be 'in a way, a grand moment' (Leader, 'Vote Against Violence', *Guardian*, January 7, 2005;

Leader, 'On the Threshold', *Guardian*, January 29, 2005). There was no question that the American demolition of Iraq's third city, Fallujah, in preceding weeks, indeed the killing of 100,000 Iraqis over the previous two years, might have compromised the legitimacy of the elections. Instead: 'It is in the interests of all – Iraqis, the Arabs, the US and Britain – that something workable be salvaged from the wreckage as Iraq stands poised between imperfect democracy and worsening strife' (ibid.).

When 'we' are building 'democracy' the tone is wistful, philosophical. In essence: 'Nothing is perfect in life. But if we work with courage and optimism, some good will surely come out of it.' When officially designated 'bad guys' are involved the message changes to harsh 'realism'. Andrew Marr's comments in the *Observer* as British bombers blitzed Serbia in 1999 give an idea of the tone:

> I want to put the Macbeth option: which is that we're so steeped in blood we should go further. If we really believe Milosevic is this bad, dangerous and destabilising figure we must ratchet this up much further. We should now be saying that we intend to put in ground troops. ('Do We Give War a Chance?', *Observer*, April 18, 1999)

The *Independent*'s editors asked if Zimbabwe's elections could be considered free and fair: 'The answer is emphatically no' (Leader, 'Zimbabwe Has Been Wrecked by Mr Mugabe – and This Election Could Make Things Worse', *Independent*, March 31, 2005). As for the Iraqi elections:

> Whether it turns out that 50, 60 or more than 70 per cent of all registered Iraqis voted, a sufficient number risked the walk to the polling station to make this first attempt at a free election for half a century a credible exercise in democracy. (Leader, 'These Elections Inspire Hope for Democracy, but Cannot Vindicate a Misguided War', *Independent*, January 31, 2005)

It was no problem, then, that the elections, the media, the entire country, were being run by a superpower army that had illegally invaded the country. But why would that matter when the invading powers are 'the good guys'?

The *Daily Telegraph* wrote of Zimbabwe:

> The entire election is weighted in Mr Mugabe's favour. His cronies run the process at every level and the voters' roll is stuffed with the names of at least one million dead people. This gives the regime the leeway for outright ballot rigging. (David Blair, 'Elections are World's Freest and Fairest, says Mugabe', *Daily Telegraph*, April 1, 2005)

In a leader entitled 'Mission Accomplished', the editors reported simply that Iraqis were preparing for their 'first democratic elections' (leader, 'Mission Accomplished', *Daily Telegraph*, December 6, 2004).

The *Express* wrote: 'Few observers believe that Zimbabwe's parliamentary elections will be free or fair' (Mark Blacklock, 'Is This the Most Evil and Hated Leader in the World?', *Express*, March 31, 2005). And of the Iraqi elections: 'There has been a great deal of dreadful news coming out of Iraq since the invasion; yesterday should herald a moment of cheer. There is now a real chance that Iraq could establish itself as a democracy.' (Leader, 'Election Hope for Iraq', *Express*, January 31, 2005).

In an article entitled 'The 1M Ghost Votes of Zim; Mugabe Rigs Polls', the BBC even managed to mention problems with the free press. Reginald Matchaba-Hove, the head of Zimbabwe Election Support Network, observing the elections, told the BBC's *Focus on Africa* programme that the voting process had been 'smooth': 'But he said the atmosphere had changed in the past few weeks, when foreign observers started arriving, because previously, the opposition had little access to state media and were not free to campaign' (Mark Ellis, 'The 1M Ghost Votes of Zim; Mugabe Rigs Polls', April 1, 2005, <http://news.bbc.co.uk>). This was particularly striking to us as we saw almost no discussion of problems with press freedom in the run up to Iraq's elections.

Elsewhere, Thomas Carothers, director of the Carnegie Endowment Program on Law and Democracy, noted a 'strong line of continuity' in the US promotion of 'democracy' in the post-Cold War period. Carothers, identifies the guiding principle: 'Where democracy appears to fit in well with US security and economic interests, the United States promotes democracy. Where democracy clashes with other significant interests, it is downplayed or even ignored' (quoted, Noam Chomsky, 'Promoting Democracy in Middle East', *Khaleej Times*, March 6, 2005). Anyone with a shred of integrity and humanity can recognise that Iraq is all about the second sentence.

Alas, there is also a 'strong line of continuity' in media reporting. Where elementary common sense conflicts with the needs of elite power, journalists collapse into a Dumb and Dumber consensus. Where common sense and critical thought serve power, sanity is resurgent. Then, suddenly, issues like international law, press freedom and the impact of violence are germane to the issue of electoral legitimacy.

## 'HE WANTS DEMOCRACY' – MEDIA LENS AND BBC *NEWSNIGHT* EDITOR PETER BARRON

On the April 12, 2005 edition of the BBC's *Newsnight* programme, diplomatic editor Mark Urban discussed the significance of a lessening of Iraqi attacks on US forces since January: 'It is indeed the first real evidence that President Bush's grand design of toppling a dictator and forcing a democracy into the heart of the Middle East could work' (*Newsnight*, BBC2, April 12, 2005). We challenged *Newsnight*'s editor, Peter Barron:

> Is that really balanced reporting from the BBC? I'm sure you've studied the history of US policy in the region, current goals, and the massive flaws in the January 30 elections. It's easy to argue that genuine democracy is the last thing Bush has in mind for Iraq. Shouldn't Urban be talking in terms of Bush's 'alleged' or 'claimed' plans for democracy in the Middle East? Wouldn't that be more balanced? (David Edwards to Barron, April 12, 2005)

Barron responded:

> I think it's entirely fair reporting. We've done a huge amount of reporting on all the death, destruction and setbacks, Mark's piece tonight was full of caveats and suggestions that things could go wrong, but surely there has been in recent days a glimmer of evidence that Bush's plan could work. That's what he said. (email to Media Lens, April 12, 2005)

We wrote again:

> Thanks for that, I appreciate it. What I'm challenging is the claim that Bush's plan is for democracy in Iraq, as Urban claims. I agree it is balanced to suggest that things could go right or wrong from Bush's point of view. But surely balance also requires challenging the idea that democracy is the goal. It is not a fact, after all, but an extremely important and very contentious claim. It is simply not balanced for a regular Newsnight reporter to assume that democracy is Bush's preferred outcome. If Urban assumed that democracy

was *not* the US goal in Iraq, there would be uproar. (Edwards to Barron, April 13, 2005)

Barron replied a day later:

> David – on your point about whether Bush's aim really is democracy I'd say: While there's bound to be a debate about what kind of democracy the US is furthering in the Middle East, there can be no doubt that President Bush regards it as a foreign policy goal to install what he regards as democracy. This is evident from his deeds, in moving swiftly towards elections in countries where he toppled the previous regimes (Afghanistan and Iraq) and it is evident from his words. He has used diplomatic pressure to insist on elections in the occupied Palestinian territories. Traditional allies like Egypt and Saudi Arabia are starting their own democratic experiments, in part as a response to the President's many statements that they cannot practice business as usual, ie as they did before the 9/11 change in US foreign policy. He acknowledged these realities in his London speech of 27th November 2003: 'Now we're pursuing a different course, a forward strategy of freedom in the Middle East. We will consistently challenge the enemies of reform and confront the allies of terror. We will expect a higher standard from our friends in the region, and we will meet our responsibilities in Afghanistan and in Iraq by finishing the work of democracy we have begun.'
>
> I completely agree with you that he undoubtedly has other motives as well, but I don't think it's right to challenge the assumption that he wants democracy in Iraq.
>
> Peter (email to Edwards, April 14, 2005)

Compare Barron's response with one sent a few months earlier by the BBC's director of news, Helen Boaden:

> The Iraqi elections are the first democratic elections in Iraq for 50 years – acknowledged as a democratic opportunity. We know that the Americans and the British want the elections to be free and fair – but of course we don't yet know if that will be the case – especially bearing in mind security. But our aim is to provide impartial, fair and accurate coverage, reflecting significant strands of argument to enable our audiences to make up their own minds. (Forwarded to Media Lens, January 21, 2005)

This is staggering complacency from the BBC, which takes it for granted that the world's superpower is intent on bringing genuine democracy to the Middle East. We sent Barron's email to Noam Chomsky, who commented:

> Ever since Bush received his 'vision' from the Lord that it is his mission to bring democracy to the Middle East – oddly, just after the pretexts for the invasion had collapsed ... I've been following intellectual commentary and media reporting. Apart from the usual margin, and serious scholars (and, incidentally, the Financial Times leader after the Iraq elections), virtually 100% has ranged from rapturous awe about the President's nobility, to criticism that holds that the mission is indeed noble and generous, but perhaps beyond our means, maybe our beneficiaries are too backward, etc. I reviewed some of it in the 'afterword' to 'Hegemony or Survival,' and have updated it in recent talks and articles.
>
> Of course, the counter-evidence is overwhelming, up to the present. But irrelevant. The Dear Leader has spoken. QED.
>
> The principle is very clear: We must mimic North Korea to the best of our ability. That's a dominant norm of the intellectual culture.
>
> It's unfair to be unkind to Peter about this. He's just adopting the norm. Doubtless internalized.
>
> Noam (email to Media Lens, April 14, 2005)

# 5
# Afghanistan – Let Them Eat Grass

## NORMALISING THE UNTHINKABLE

The American media analyst Edward Herman once wrote: 'It is the function of defence intellectuals and other experts, and the mainstream media, to normalise the unthinkable for the general public' ('The Banality of Evil', <www.informationclearinghouse. info/article7278.htm>). Normalising the unthinkable is achieved by passing lightly over even the most horrendous crimes of state–corporate power, by casting doubt on the true severity of those crimes – suggesting that, anyway, the ends justify the means, that alternative courses of actions would have had even worse consequences – and by focusing laser-like on the crimes of official enemies.

Beneath these diversions lies a fundamental truth – that the suffering of impoverished, brown-skinned people in Third World countries just does not matter very much to elite corporate journalists. Moreover, as we discussed in Chapter 1, Third World suffering *cannot* matter very much – corporate media success crucially depends on positive relations with major centres of political and economic power. Like other corporate executives, journalists are legally obliged to prioritise these considerations. The art of successful mainstream journalism is to do so without the public noticing.

For much of the media, the war on Afghanistan ended with the fall of Kabul on November 13, 2001. As usual, reporting was focused on the hideous crimes of others, and on our need to destroy the Taliban and al-Qaeda. With the goal (partially) achieved, journalists declared another humanitarian victory and moved on. The war was suddenly yesterday's news, although not for the civilians being killed in the ongoing bombardment. A different story – the price of our 'victory' for the people of Afghanistan – threatened to turn the spotlight on *our* crimes and so was ignored by our media. The sheer scale of what was so casually passed over is remarkable.

A careful reader of the press might have discovered that Afghan casualties of the bombing that began on October 7, 2001 exceeded the loss of life on September 11, 2001. But this 'collateral damage' represents a small fraction of the total horror.

On September 16, the press reported that the US government had demanded that Pakistan stop the convoys of food on which much of the already starving Afghan population depended. Later that month, the UN Food and Agricultural Organisation warned that more than 7 million people were facing a crisis that could lead to widespread starvation if military action were initiated, with a likely 'humanitarian catastrophe' unless aid were immediately resumed and the threat of military action terminated. Dominic Nutt of Christian Aid warned: 'It's as if a mass grave has been dug behind millions of people. We can drag them back from it or push them in. We could be looking at millions of deaths' (Stephen Morris and Felicity Lawrence, 'Afghanistan Facing Humanitarian Disaster', *Guardian*, September 19, 2001). Imagine a Western 'coalition' launching an attack to root out terrorism in, say, Spain on the understanding that some 7 million Spanish civilians might lose their lives as a result.

Remarkably, though the media communicated these warnings of mass death, the story was then simply dropped. How many *did* die when the snows came? How many of the 7 million *were* 'pushed' into the mass grave? Certainly our government – the 'moral crusaders' of Kosovo – showed no interest in raising such questions. But the fate of millions of innocents imperilled by US–UK state policy was also a matter of indifference to our media. We can gain a sense of the moral health of our democracy from the minimal coverage that emerged.

In a media alert dated January 3, 2002 we described conditions in the Maslakh refugee camp to the west of Herat in Afghanistan, where 100 people were then dying every day. Containing 350,000 people, Maslakh had obvious significance as the largest refugee camp in the world. Four months earlier, on September 19, 2001, the *Guardian* had reported 40 deaths per day in Maslakh, 'many because they arrive too weak to survive after trying to hold out in their villages'.

One might think it would be a matter of extreme concern that the death rate had risen from 40 per day prior to bombing to 100 per day after the attack started. It seems clear that our government's actions did indeed push many thousands into a mass grave. And yet, or more accurately because this was the case, the media had little to say about civilian suffering in and around Maslakh.

Occasional reports did emerge. In January 2002, the *Guardian*'s Doug McKinlay described how refugees were dying of exposure and starvation in Maslakh. The small size of the graves in the graveyards on the edge of the camp 'is clear evidence that most of the buried are children', McKinlay noted. Ian Lethbridge, executive director of the charity Feed the Children, was quoted as saying: 'I always judge everything by what I have seen in Africa. And this is on the scale of Africa. I was shocked at the living conditions of the new arrivals' (McKinlay, 'Refugees Left in the Cold at "Slaughterhouse" Camp', *Guardian*, January 1, 2002). McKinlay reported that almost no aid was reaching Maslakh. Feed the Children had managed to fly 40 tonnes of food and shelter into Herat the previous week, but at that time just four bakeries were feeding the entire camp of 350,000 people. One woman at the camp confronted McKinlay: 'You are just taking pictures. You are not here to help. We can't eat pictures. We are dying. We need food and medicine.'

Conditions outside the camp were more horrific still. On January 4, Christian Aid reported:

> Refugees arriving at Maslakh camp near Herat have described the 'calamity conditions' their families are now living in. Heavy snowfall is making it difficult to transport humanitarian supplies to the most vulnerable areas of the mountainous Ghor province of Afghanistan … (Christian Aid website, 'Hunger Forces Families to Abandon Mountain Homes', January 4, 2002)

Hayat Fazil of Christian Aid's partner organisation NPO/RRAA (Norwegian Project Office/Rural Rehabilitation Association for Afghanistan) 'warned that rural villages are being neglected while refugee camps like Maslakh get the lion's share of aid' (ibid.).

Readers will doubtless recall the TV images of thousands of civilians fleeing the fighting and bombing in Kosovo in 1999. ITN and the BBC repeatedly showed dramatic footage of whole hillsides covered in desperate refugees, with daily on the spot reports, interviews and investigation. There was detailed and emotive coverage of the terrible human suffering.

By contrast, between September 2001 and January 2002, the *Guardian* and *Observer* mentioned the catastrophe at Maslakh five times – an average of once per month. A LexisNexis database search (May 2005) showed that Maslakh had been mentioned a grand total of 21 times between 2001 and 2005 in all UK national newspapers.

The *Guardian* and *Observer* mentioned the story of prisoners held at a US camp at Guantanamo Bay – a suitably safe and trivial issue, compared with our responsibility for the mass death of Afghan refugees – 97 times in January 2002 alone. LexisNexis figures for mentions of Guantanamo Bay were off the scale ('more than 1,000 results') for the period between May 2004 and May 2005. Also by contrast, between April and June 1999, the *Guardian* and *Observer* mentioned the plight of 65,000 Kosovan refugees stranded at Brace on Macedonia's border with Kosovo 48 times – an average of once every two days. But the scale and intensity of suffering was dwarfed by that in Afghanistan.

The vital difference is the direction in which the finger of blame was pointing. Although much of the Kosovan human flood was in response to NATO's air campaign – independent monitors, and even the US State Department, reported that the mass exodus and increased atrocities began *after* the onset of bombing (see Chapter 6) – the media chose to accept British and US claims that a Serbian 'genocide' was to blame. As a result, during the Kosovo crisis, the plight of refugees was used as powerful propaganda justifying NATO's assault.

In Afghanistan, on the other hand, it is clear that the 'war against terrorism' bore considerable responsibility for the disruption of food supplies, and for the consequent mass suffering and death, both inside and outside Afghan camps. In a report in the *Sunday Telegraph*, Christina Lamb wrote of refugees in Maslakh:

Most come from the northern provinces of Faryab, Ghor and Sar-e-Pul as well as Ghazni in central Afghanistan, mountainous places to which the World Food Programme was giving food aid but stopped because of the bombing. Now their villages cannot be reached because the passes are cut off. ('They Call This "The Slaughterhouse", *Sunday Telegraph*, December 9, 2001)

In one of the few mentions in the *Observer*, Suzanne Goldenberg noted that Maslakh had already been in crisis in the summer of 2001, but 'its population swelled after 11 September when international aid workers were evacuated from Afghanistan' in fear of bombing ('Hunger and Vengeance Haunt Afghanistan's Sprawling Tent City', *Observer*, January 27, 2002).

This, of course, was deeply damning of the US and British governments, of the 'war for civilisation', and of the establishment media supporting them. Politicians therefore did not repeatedly draw attention to the plight of refugees and, again, the media were happy to fail to do the same.

One of the *Independent*'s mentions of Maslakh was by columnist Natasha Walter who wrote:

These people are suffering from terror visited on them from the West. Yes, I know they have also suffered over the years from the evils of their fundamentalist rulers but we now share the blame for their plight. If it were not for the missiles the West has sent into Kandahar and Kunduz, these children whose faces we now see in our newspapers [sic] would not have had to take to the roads, desperately trudging the hills and deserts and sitting in tents on a bare plain. ('These Refugees Are Our Responsibility', *Independent*, November 22, 2001)

Apart from these glimpses, our responsibility for the mass suffering and death of Afghans was hidden beneath a veil of silence and indifference.

## IN THE LAND OF THE BLIND, THE ONE-EYED LION IS NEWS

To its credit, ITN did make some attempts to report the misery. On January 9, 13, 22 and 26, ITN journalists covered the story of 'Marjan the One-Eyed Lion' in Kabul zoo. Marjan's 'battered image touched people around the world', ITN told viewers on the 9th, 'his plight a symbol of maltreatment under the Taliban'. As a result, a team of vets had flown out to deliver 'much-needed help ... treatment and food' (*ITV Lunchtime News*, ITN, January 9, 2002). The concluding clip featured Marjan chewing happily on a large piece of meat.

Viewers had to read one of the *Guardian*'s rare reports on civilian suffering to discover what was being eaten elsewhere in Afghanistan that day: 'The village of Bonavash is slowly starving', Ravi Nessman wrote.

Besieged by the Taliban and crushed by years of drought, people in this remote mountain settlement have resorted to eating bread made from grass and traces of barley flour. Babies whose mothers' milk has dried up are fed grass porridge. The toothless elderly crush grass into a near powder. Many have died. More are sick. Nearly everyone has diarrhoea or a hacking cough. When the children's pain becomes unbearable, their mothers tie rags around their stomachs to try to alleviate the pressure. 'We are waiting to die. If food does not come, if the situation does not change, we will eat it [grass] ... until we die,' said Ghalam Raza, 42, a man with a hacking cough, pain in his stomach and bleeding bowels. (Nessman, 'Afghans Eat Grass as Aid Fails to Arrive', *Guardian*, January 9, 2002)

Nessman related the story of Khadabaksh, a former farm labourer, who looked on in despair at his four young daughters:

> Three weeks ago, his children had a mother and a baby sister. Both have died. Khadabaksh begs his neighbours for pinches of their small amount of home-grown barley so his family can make grass bread ... 'It is better to die in our house,' he said, 'not in some strange place with strange people.' (Ibid.)

Courtesy of political and media indifference, none of this seriously troubled the conscience of the British people.

When pressed to explain why ITN had done so little to cover the *human* catastrophe in Afghanistan while lavishing attention on a lion, Jonathan Munro, head of ITN newsgathering, responded:

> In fact, we have run several reports on the plight of the human refugees displaced by the recent events in Afghanistan ... Specifically on the lion, one of the most frequent viewer complaints is that news programmes fail to follow up on stories, and do not update viewers often enough about stories which have previously been reported.
>
> In this case there were three clear stages – first, an interview with the British vets as they left the UK; second, a piece about their first assessment of the animal; third – an update after treatment started. That completes the story, and we don't anticipate returning to the zoo again. (email to David Edwards, January 23, 2002)

In fact ITN later did return to the story, reporting that the lion had died. ITN's extraordinary indifference to the plight of human victims in Afghanistan also persisted with literally no news reports on the mass starvation and death of refugees in the same period.

By contrast, on January 18, 2002, Médecins Sans Frontières (MSF) reported one of the assorted catastrophes afflicting the Afghan population: US-dropped cluster bombs.

> Many bombs were dropped in residential and other populated areas and the Mine Action Centre is doing their best to deal with all the emergency cases. However, they do not have enough human, logistical and other necessary resources to clear the region effectively within an acceptable period of time.

MSF continued:

> In its field operations in Herat, Médecins Sans Frontières comes across many civilians who have been injured by mines or UXOs [unexploded ordnance]

(including cluster bombs). During the recent US air raids over Herat, western Afghanistan, several cluster bombs have been mistakenly dropped on residential areas causing a large number of civilian deaths and casualties ... According to official data of local de-mining organizations and the Regional Hospital in Herat, 38 deaths and an unknown number of injured people due to cluster bombs have been registered so far. However, some doctors in Herat Regional Hospital believe this number is much higher. In the village of Qala Shaker near Herat city alone, 12 people died and more than 20 were injured due to cluster bombs. (Médecins Sans Frontières, 'Cluster Bombs the Legacy to Afghan Population', January 18, 2002, <www.msf.org>)

Each cluster bomb contained 202 submunitions, of which approximately 20 per cent did not explode upon impact. The submunitions consisted of three kill mechanisms: anti-armour, anti-personnel and incendiary, comprising a lethal 'combined effects munition'. Anti-personnel fragments weighing 30 g could penetrate 6.4 mm of steel plate at a distance of 11 metres. The anti-armour submunitions could penetrate 19 cm of steel, and injure a person at 150 metres. Bomblets could be detonated by tiny changes of temperature – for example if a person's shadow fell across a bomblet lying in the sun – or by small vibrations, and even by the energy from a passing radio transmitter.

According to the Mine Action Centre, US food packages and cluster bombs were dropped in the same areas. Although different in shape and size, both were yellow in colour and 'many children pick up ... [the bomblets] thinking they contain food or other interesting items' (ibid.). To our knowledge, not one word of this appeared on either ITN or BBC TV news while the fate and progress of Marjan the one-eyed lion were being reported in detail.

## KILLING AS A FIRST RESORT

The moral sickness afflicting our society is also revealed by the contrast between the passionate intensity and extent of coverage afforded US victims of September 11 compared with Afghan victims after October 7, 2001. In early January 2002, US writer Edward Herman estimated that media coverage afforded to the death of Nathan Chapman – the first and, at that point, sole US combat casualty – had exceeded coverage afforded to *all* Afghan victims of bombing and starvation. CNN Chair Walter Isaacson is reported to have declared that it 'seems perverse to focus too much on the casualties or hardship in

Afghanistan' (Howard Kurtz, 'CNN Chief Orders "Balance" in War News', *Washington Post*, October 31, 2001).

It is an understandable aversion, given that Afghans may well have lost their lives for no good reason. Professor Victor Bulmer-Thomas of the Royal Institute of International Affairs has argued that increased security, measures against money laundering, and an increase in intelligence sharing around the world did have the power to degrade global terrorism. He has also supported an approach that addresses the causes of disaffection in the Middle East, Saudi Arabia and Iraq. But the bombing, Bulmer-Thomas argues 'has unfortunately given ammunition to many countries around the world, which is exacerbating the problem'. His conclusion is a sombre one for the grieving people of Afghanistan:

> If anyone thinks that this temporary degradation of al-Qaeda's capabilities through the elimination of terrorist training camps in Afghanistan somehow or other will reduce the risks of terrorist attacks in the future, I'm afraid they're wrong. Because terrorist training camps don't have to be in Afghanistan, they can be anywhere. And indeed the temptation now for al-Qaeda will be to site the training of its operatives in Western Europe, Canada and even in the United States. (Bulmer-Thomas, *Jonathan Dimbleby* programme, ITV, January 27, 2002)

Indeed, what is so remarkable about Western media coverage is the instant willingness to accept and justify even the most absurd arguments for the mass killing of Third World people. In April 2002, Rory Carroll of the *Guardian* wrote: 'Whoever is trying to destabilise Afghanistan is doing a good job. The broken cities and scorched hills so recently liberated are rediscovering fear and uncertainty' ('Blood-Drenched Warlord's Return', *Observer*, April 14, 2002). The broken cities and scorched hills were not 'rediscovering fear' after being 'liberated', of course. Mass starvation exacerbated by bombing and rampant warlordism ensured that fear and uncertainty were ever-present.

Two months before Carroll's comment, Refugees International reported:

> A new wave of flight from Afghanistan highlights the lack of security there. Nearly 20,000 Afghan refugees are waiting to get into Pakistan, and many more are on the way, according to the United Nations High Commissioner for Refugees (UNHCR). So far this year, more than 50,000 Afghans have

fled to Pakistan. They are trying to escape crime and fighting in their villages that are interfering with food deliveries necessitated by years of drought. ('New Refugee Flows from Afghanistan Highlight Lack of Security', Refugees International, February 25, 2002)

One month before Carroll's comment, humanitarian agencies reported on what they had seen, and asked: 'Why, eight weeks after the worst of the war in Afghanistan was over, were people still eating grass just one inch away on a highway map from the major Afghan city of Mazar-I-Sharif?' (Jonathan Frerichs, 'How Many Zarehs Are There? Finding Hunger in Afghanistan', March 7, 2002 <www.lwr.org/news/02/030702.asp>). Imagine the media of some superpowerful foreign coalition describing how British people subsisting on grass had been 'liberated' by their bombs from fear, uncertainty and chaos.

The reality is not allowed to interfere with the key propaganda messages to be absorbed, namely: 1) Western military action freed Afghanistan from fear, uncertainty and chaos, but meddlesome Afghans are now undermining our good work; and 2) The US and UK act benignly, and 'humanitarian' military assault is beneficial.

In reality, two possible options were immediately obvious in the aftermath of the atrocities of September 11, 2001. Western leaders could have sought to identify and address the real and perceived grievances that lay behind the attacks; or they could have exploited the tragedy to reinforce, or extend, existing policies and practices.

But the media refusal to seek out the true motives behind the attacks on New York and the Pentagon was almost complete. As the first anniversary of the atrocity approached, the BBC's Tom Carver talked of 'anti-Americanism' as America's 'image problem'. Thinking hard on the roots of this antipathy, Carver cited 'envy' and 'unrequited love' as possible causes: 'people hate America for not paying them more attention', he declared mysteriously (Newsnight, BBC2, September 5, 2002). On the BBC's Newsnight, Peter Marshall observed that many who hated America were 'jealous of the US role in the world' (Newsnight, BBC2 February 11, 2003). Tom Carver added further sage comments on the same programme, noting that Americans 'try to think the best of people, and nations, even to the point of naivety'. And yet, in a September 19, 2001 appearance on the David Letterman show, ABC journalist John Miller stated that bin Laden had listed his top three grievances in an interview several years earlier. These were: 'the US military presence in Saudi Arabia; US support for Israel; and US policy toward Iraq'.

And as for the appropriate response to al-Qaeda's attacks, in an interview with playwright Arthur Miller, *Newsnight's* Jeremy Paxman asked:

> You live in New York City ... you must vividly recall what happened on September 11. In the world in which we live now, isn't some sort of pre-emptive strike the only defensive option available to countries like the United States? (*Newsnight*, BBC2, February 18, 2003)

Noam Chomsky reflects on the idea that this kind of pre-emptive strike might have been the best or only 'defensive option' available in dealing with, say, the conflict in Northern Ireland:

> One choice would have been to send the RAF to bomb the source of their finances, places like Boston, or to infiltrate commandos to capture those suspected of involvement in such financing and kill them or spirit them to London to face trial. (Chomsky, *9–11*, Seven Stories Press, 2001, pp. 62–3)

Another, sane possibility, Chomsky comments, is 'to consider realistically the background concerns and grievances, and try to remedy them, while at the same time following the rule of law to punish criminals' (ibid.).

## BOMBING IT BETTER

On January 7, 2003, Media Lens published a media alert 'Moral Dark Age? Millions of Suffering Iraqis – A "Blip" in the Global Economy?', <www.medialens.org> in response to a comment piece in the *Independent* by economics correspondent Hamish McRae. We wrote to McRae on January 2, 2003:

> Dear Hamish McRae,
>
> I read your January 1st article in The Independent ('A year when more realistic expectations should not lead to disappointment'). 'Last year seemed dispiriting', you wrote, 'because so few of the problems of the beginning of the year were solved', but you added that at least the 'war in Afghanistan' was successful 'in military terms'. That the 'war' could be more accurately described as a 'massacre', with likely more than 5,000 Afghans killed under

the bombing and perhaps 20,000 more dead from the effects of the bombing (starvation, disease), is not mentioned. Why not?

Also, you correctly recognise that 'the chief quarry remains at large and the terrorist threat continues', surely contradicting your claim that the 'war' was 'successful in military terms', since removing bin Laden and the al-Qaeda threat were the stated war aims of Washington and London.

I would be interested in hearing your response.

yours sincerely,

David Cromwell (email to Hamish McRae, January 2, 2003)

Reply from Hamish McRae, 2 January, 2003:

Dear Mr Cromwell.

Thank you for your email. I deliberately used the phrase 'in military terms' because, as you correctly point out, there were high costs in human terms. I would not, however, accept your term 'massacre'. I think it would be reasonable to argue that in the years to come, the Afghan people (especially women) will have a much better life than they would have had under the Taliban. Those humanitarian gains have to be taken into account. If I did not expand on the human costs, I equally did not also stress these human gains. This was an article of a wide compass about the threat to the world in the coming year, not one specifically looking back at that particular war. Had I been writing at more length I would have sought to maintain this balance, though of course I would not expect people who feel strongly on either side of the argument to agree with me.

As for the success or otherwise of the attack, I think it reasonable to argue [it] was successful in the sense that it helped remove the regime that had given shelter to Osama bin Laden and has clearly disrupted the al-Qaeda network. The terrorist training camps, for example, are no longer operating – so the threat is surely less now than it would have been had the attack not taken place.

I hope this helps.

My regards and thanks for your interest.

Sincerely,

Hamish McRae

For the full exchange, including a follow-up challenge to Hamish McRae, see the media alert 'Bombing it Better – Iraq, the Bombing of Afghanistan and Segregated Compassion', January 20, 2003 <www.medialens.org/alerts>. A crucial feature of the propaganda system, then, is that well-placed journalists will prattle of supposed 'humanitarian gains' arising from brutal Western attacks on Third World countries, thereby echoing the rhetoric of Western politicians. In tandem with this endless proclamation of Western virtue is the mainstream labelling of dissidents as fantasists who bash on about media conspiracies. Consider the following example from the *Guardian*.

On December 8, 2001, Media Lens issued a media alert: Dissidents Dismissed as Angry, Deluded Egotists (www.medialens.org). The alert focused on an article written by Rory Carroll of the *Guardian* concerning the dissident novelist Gore Vidal (Carroll, 'We Don't Know Where We're Going', *Guardian*, 6 December, 2001). We sent the alert to Carroll and received this reply on January 11, 2002:

Dear David

Thanks for the email and sorry about tardy reply, just out of five weeks in Afghanistan where I'd no access to this email address. Some of your points about the corporate nature of media and how that corrodes independence I agree with. Some of the coverage out of Afghanistan and Pakistan since September [2001] has been shameful. But your main point, that the Vidal piece I wrote fits into a broader conspiracy [sic] to smear such intellectuals, is wrong. No one told me what to write nor was there an unspoken agenda or expectation on the part of the commissioning editor that I knew of. What I wrote matched what I thought of the man. You appear to share many of Vidal's views, I don't, and that came across in the piece since I'm paid partly to report my impressions. But I also reported his views accurately. You're entitled to consider my opinions dumb and naive but dismissing them as part of a corporate smear sails close to what you accuse me of.

Best

Rory

We agree that 'Some of the coverage out of Afghanistan and Pakistan since September has been shameful', but believe the comment has little meaning – no matter how honest and accurate media performance might be, personal opinion will always ensure that individuals find some coverage 'shameful'.

What is meaningful is analysis of media performance as a whole based on comparisons of reasonably well-matched examples. The *Guardian*, including Carroll, has produced some informative reports on events in Afghanistan. However, when the *Guardian*'s coverage of civilian victims in Afghanistan is compared with coverage of civilian victims in Kosovo, a very different picture emerges.

As discussed above, the *Guardian* has afforded a tiny fraction of the coverage it gave to victims in Kosovo to Afghan victims of a disaster for which the West bears considerable responsibility. But this is no isolated case. On the one hand, the *Guardian*, like the rest of the corporate media, consistently, over many years, provides massive coverage of the crimes of 'enemies': Nazi Germany, Cambodia under the Khmer Rouge, Iraq under Saddam (in the 1990s), Serbia under Milosevic. On the other hand, these same media have provided minimal coverage of crimes for which we bear some or all responsibility: those committed in Chile under Pinochet, Guatemala under Armas, Indonesia under Suharto, Iran under the Shah, Iraq under Saddam (in the 1980s), Afghanistan now, Turkey now, Colombia now, etc. Individual 'shameful' articles aside, this basic pattern reveals that the 'liberal' *Guardian*, like the corporate mainstream generally, functions as a *de facto* propaganda system promoting and protecting state–corporate interests.

But this absolutely does *not* mean that we are proposing any kind of conspiracy. Carroll wrote that we were accusing him of producing a piece that 'fits into a broader conspiracy to smear such intellectuals'. He even suggested that we imagined he might have been fed a line on what was wanted, or that the commissioning editor might have had expectations based on some hidden agenda. All we can say is that we find such suggestions completely outlandish; we made no mention of a conspiracy in our media alert and none will be found anywhere in our writing. This is Carroll's own (mistaken) interpretation of what we wrote.

We regularly meet this 'straw man' dismissal of our work. As US media analyst Edward Herman has noted:

Left criticisms of the media have always drawn the accusation of conspiracy theory, because media personnel and defenders of the media establishment are either too lazy to examine closely the case made by left analysts, can't understand it, or are pleased to resort to a smear tactic. ('Nuggets from a Nuthouse', *Z Magazine*, November 2001)

When Media Lens interviewed Channel 4 presenter Jon Snow in 2001, he said of our arguments:

> It's so much easier for hacks to be able to blame some corporate conspiracy that prevents them from discussing these matters ... I can tell you if somebody rings me up from Pepsi-Cola – and I must say I don't think I've ever been rung by any corporation, would that I was! – I'd give them short shrift! (interview with David Edwards, January 1, 2001, <www.medialens.org/articles_2001/de_Jon_Snow_interview.htm>)

When we assured Snow that we didn't believe for a moment that media bias was a conspiracy, or even conscious, he replied: 'Well, I'm sorry to say, it either happens or it doesn't happen. If it does happen, it's a conspiracy; if it doesn't happen, it's not a conspiracy.' A salient example of what Herman calls, 'comic book level analysis' (Herman, 'Nuggets from a Nuthouse'). Similarly, in the famous 'Rumble in the Media Jungle' encounter, in which the former *Independent* editor Andrew Marr interviewed Noam Chomsky, Marr said: 'The idea that Orwell's warning [about thought control and propaganda] is still relevant may seem bizarre' (*The Big Idea*, BBC2, February 14, 1996). Marr asked his audience to consider whether it were possible that the media was 'designed to limit how you imagine the world'. Yet Chomsky's whole point is that thought control in democratic societies does *not* happen through conspiratorial, Big Brother-style mechanisms, but is the result of free market forces. Marr continued: 'What I don't get is that all of this suggests ... people like me are self-censoring.' Chomsky disagreed: 'I don't say you're self-censoring. I'm sure you believe everything you're saying. But what I'm saying is, if you believed something different you wouldn't be sitting where you're sitting.'

What Marr, like Carroll, 'doesn't get' is that dissident arguments do not depend on conspiratorial self-censorship, but on a filter system maintained by free market forces – bottom-line pressures, owner influence, parent company goals and sensitivities, advertiser needs, business-friendly government influence and corporate PR 'flak' – which introduce bias by marginalising alternatives, providing incentives to conform and costs for failure to conform.

This is all we are suggesting of Rory Carroll – we are sure he is sincere in what he writes; we don't believe for a moment that he is dishonest, or conforming to a conspiracy. We are not trying to smear him. We are suggesting that he is part of a corporate media system that strongly selects for certain editors, certain journalists, certain beliefs, certain facts, certain victims and certain crimes against humanity. This system has selected *for* Hamish McRae, Rory Carroll, Timothy Garton-Ash, Jay Rayner, Jon Snow, David Rieff, Charles Jennings, Joe Joseph et al. All we're saying is, if they believed something different they wouldn't be sitting where they're sitting.

## OUTSIDE LOOKING IN – MEDIA LENS AND THE BBC'S DIRECTOR OF NEWS, RICHARD SAMBROOK

From Richard Sambrook, January 21, 2002:

Dear Mr Cromwell,

Thank you for your email about our coverage of Afghanistan. I am sorry you feel we have paid insufficient attention to the plight of refugees. However, we have not ignored the suffering of Afghan civilians. You may not have had a chance to see last night's BBC2 Correspondent programme The Dispossessed. Taghi Amirani gained rare access to Makaki, a refugee camp near the Afghan–Iran border. He wanted to hear the voices of ordinary Afghans, see the war against terrorism through their eyes, and find out what life is really like in a refugee camp. The programme included footage of Abdol Sattar Sharifi, a driver from Kabul saying 'If one American dies the whole world hears about it. But Afghans die everyday and nobody pays any attention. No one will ask who was killed and how. Look at me; I have lost my wife and my child and now live in dirt, and no one cares.'

Just this morning the Today programme on Radio 4 carried a report by Andrew Gilligan from Kabul about the scale of the aid needed. It was followed by an interview with Clare Short, the International Development Secretary about what the international community is doing to help.

Jonathan Charles reported on the suffering of Afghan people on this Saturday's BBC1 Television News (19th January). He said 'this is why the money's needed so desperately. The streets of south Kabul lie in ruins after shelling. Many people live a miserable existence amongst the rubble. This man lost a leg when a bomb landed. He hopes foreign aid will give Afghans a better future. He says winter's here, people urgently need their houses rebuilt to escape the cold.'

Ishbel Mattheson has also reported from Kabul for BBC TV News about terrible state of women's health.

Afghanistan remains a very dangerous place and it is dificult to travel outside of the capital. David Loyn who has reported from the country for many years is planning to go with an aid aeroplane to a refugee camp in Maslach, but the timing is in the hands of the aid agencies. BBC News has a long history of covering Afghanistan, even when other broadcasters were not reporting from the country. The BBC Bureau in Kabul was opened in 1989. When the most recent Correspondent Kate Clark was expelled in March 2001 she was the only western correspondent in Kabul.

Although that does not mean we can report every day on what is happening there, it is a commitment we will maintain in the future. I hope that these examples help to allay your concern that BBC News is ignoring the plight of Afghan civilians. Thank you for taking the time to contact me with your comments.

Yours sincerely

Richard Sambrook

## Media Lens reply, January 22, 2002:

Dear Mr Sambrook,

Many thanks for kindly responding so promptly. I did, in fact, watch Correspondent on Sunday night. It was moving but fell short on describing the true horror of conditions in Afghanistan. Taghi Amirani reported in conclusion that 3500 Afghan civilians had lost their lives, failing to specify the cause of death. As we know, this is a conservative estimate of victims of the bombing alone. Yet, on January 3, The Guardian reported conditions facing 350,000 Afghan refugees in the Maslakh camp, 30 miles west of Herat city. Doug McKinlay described how 100 of these refugees were dying every day of exposure and starvation (a disaster on the scale of September 11 every month. On January 9, The Guardian reported that dying villagers in Bonavash were subsisting on a diet of grass – this suffering was immeasurably worse than anything portrayed in Amirani's film.

Prior to the onset of bombing, aid agencies consistently warned that even the threat of an assault would imperil as many as 7.5 million Afghan civilians. Since the commencement of the assault, those agencies have confirmed that the chaos and terror caused by bombing have indeed been responsible for immense additional suffering and in fact the mass death of Afghans. There was no reference to this in Amirani's film, as there has been none on BBC TV and ITN news this year.

You point to a small number of reports that have dealt with the plight of Afghan civilians. But the coverage pales into insignificance compared to the coverage the BBC (rightly) lavished on refugees during the Kosovo crisis in 1999. Then, there were daily reports of the horrors facing refugees; now there is next to nothing. The contrast could not be more dramatic. How do you account for the difference? The difficulty of filming inside Afghanistan neither explains nor excuses this. At the very least, the BBC could have devoted more coverage to Afghan refugees who had crossed the border into Pakistan.

In your speech last December to the Royal Television Society, you said: 'News viewing across all channels is now down 25 per cent for the under 45s ... there is a new political divide: no longer "left" and "right"; it's now "us and them", with "them" being politicians, the establishment and the broadcasters and media ... some 40 per cent of the audience feel they are outside looking in, offered few real choices.' [David Lister, '"Time Bomb" of Fewer Viewers Watching the Television News', *Independent*, December 5, 2001].

It is entirely reasonable that the BBC should be largely regarded by the public as being part of 'them' – the establishment. The BBC news coverage on Afghanistan – as on other important issues – demonstrates clearly that the BBC looks with favour upon western institutions of power. It is hard to avoid the impression that the BBC's performance can be in large part explained by the fact that the suffering of Kosovar refugees was used as a powerful propaganda tool supporting UK government policy [the suffering could be blamed on the Serbs] in 1999, whereas the suffering of Afghan refugees is a very real embarrassment to the British government now.

We believe that BBC reporting is profoundly distorted by its lack of independence from government influence and ideology, particularly where foreign policy is concerned. Sadly, the BBC's poor coverage of the mass death of Afghan refugees has added great strength to the argument that our 'free press' is, in fact, a sham.

When Media Lens tried to ask Mr. Amirani his views on the minimal BBC coverage of Afghan suffering this year – indicating, as examples, the unreported catastrophes at Maslakh and Bonavash – all our arguments questioning the BBC's performance were censored [this is not too strong a word] by Correspondent's online staff. This is what remained of our attempt to engage in open and honest debate:

'I was deeply impressed by the courage and compassion of your film. It was extremely heartening to see the people of Afghanistan, including the

Taliban, presented as human beings. The suffering of the Afghan people is a terrible tragedy. Sincerest thanks for the humanity of your film. Let's hope it helps bring some relief to the people you met.

David Edwards, England'

The congratulatory introduction and conclusion were allowed to remain, but not one word of dissent. Do you wonder that, as you said in your speech last December, 'the audience feel they are outside looking in' and that they sense that they are 'offered few real choices.'

Yours sincerely,

David Cromwell
Co-Editor, Media Lens

Richard Sambrook did not respond.

# 6
# Kosovo – Real Bombs, Fictional Genocide

## IRAQ AND KOSOVO – THE FORBIDDEN PARALLELS

The truth about the invasion of Iraq in 2003 was perhaps best summed up by Ray McGovern, one of the CIA's most senior analysts: 'It was 95 per cent charade. And they all knew it: Bush, Blair, Howard' (quoted, John Pilger, 'Universal Justice Is not a Dream', ZNet, March 23, 2004). One might think that exposés of this kind would lead the media to take a fresh look at some of the US–UK governments' earlier claims justifying war. In what follows, we consider the 78-day NATO assault on Serbia from March 24 until June 10, 1999, said to have been launched to protect the Albanian population of Kosovo.

In the wake of the war against Iraq, what is so striking about the US–UK government case for war against Serbia is the familiarity of the propaganda used. In a key, pre-war speech on Iraq in 2003, Blair said: 'Looking back over 12 years, we have been victims of our own desire to placate the implacable … to hope that there was some genuine intent to do good in a regime whose mind is in fact evil' ('Tony Blair's Speech', *Guardian*, March 18, 2003). Blair similarly described the war with Serbia as 'a battle between good and evil; between civilisation and barbarity; between democracy and dictatorship' (quoted, Philip Hammond and Edward S. Herman (eds), *Degraded Capability, The Media and the Kosovo Crisis*, Pluto Press, 2000, p. 123).

In discussing Iraq, Blair referred in 2003 to the lessons of 'history':

> We can look back and say: there's the time; that was the moment; for example, when Czechoslovakia was swallowed up by the Nazis – that's when we should have acted.
>
> But it wasn't clear at the time. In fact at the time, many people thought such a fear fanciful. Worse, put forward in bad faith by warmongers. ('Tony Blair's Speech' *Guardian*, March 18, 2003)

Four years earlier, in March 1999, the British defence secretary, George Robertson, insisted that intervention in Kosovo was vital to stop 'a regime which is bent on genocide' (quoted, John Pilger's introduction to Phillip Knightley, *First Casualty – The War Correspondent as Hero and Myth-maker from the Crimea to Kosovo*, Prion Books, 2000, p. xii). A year later, Robertson also conjured up the ghost of Nazism to justify NATO's action:

> We were faced with a situation where there was this killing going on, this cleansing going on – the kind of ethnic cleansing we thought had disappeared after the second world war. You were seeing people there coming in trains, the cattle trains, with refugees once again. (*Jonathan Dimbleby* programme, ITV, June 11, 2000)

President Clinton also talked of 'deliberate, systematic efforts at ... genocide' in Kosovo (quoted, Pilger in Knightley, *First Casualty*, p. xii). The US defence secretary, William Cohen, said during the war: 'We've now seen about 100,000 military-aged men missing ... They may have been murdered' (quoted, Hammond and Herman, *Degraded Capability*, p. 139). Two weeks later, David Scheffer, the US ambassador at large for war crimes, announced that as many as '225,000 ethnic Albanian men aged between 14 and 59' may have been killed (quoted, John Pilger, *The New Rulers of the World*, Verso, 2001, p. 144). In a speech in Illinois in April 1999, Blair alluded to Kosovo:

> But the principle of non-interference must be qualified in important respects. Acts of genocide can never be a purely internal matter. When oppression produces massive flows of refugees which unsettle neighbouring countries then they can properly be described as threats to international peace and security. (Colin Brown, 'War in the Balkans: Blair's Vision of Global Police', *Independent*, April 23, 1999)

This rhetoric depicting 'genocide', even a kind of Holocaust, in Kosovo certainly merits comparison with the claim that British bases in Cyprus were under threat from Iraqi weapons of mass destruction that could be launched within 45 minutes of an order being given.

So how did the keen and critical intellects of the 'free press', backed up by massive research and investigative resources, respond? Did they scrutinise and challenge these extraordinary claims as they later so patently failed to do with regard to the Iraqi WMD 'threat'?

## LIGHTS OUT IN BELGRADE – THE MEDIA LINE UP

Reviewing UK media performance, British historian Mark Curtis wrote of the Kosovo war: 'The liberal press – notably the *Guardian* and the *Independent* – backed the war to the hilt (while questioning the tactics used to wage it) and lent critical weight to the government's arguments' (*Web of Deceit*, Vintage, 2003, pp. 134–5). In so doing, the media 'revealed ... how willingly deceived it generally is by government rhetoric on its moral motives' (ibid., p. 135).

Thus, Jonathan Freedland wrote in the *Guardian*: 'the prize is not turf or treasure but the frustration of a plan to empty a land of its people'. It was 'a noble goal', he insisted (Freedland, 'No Way to Spin a War', *Guardian*, April 21, 1999). A Guardian editorial described the war as nothing less than 'a test for our generation' (leader, *Guardian*, March 26, 1999). The attack was intended to stop 'something approaching genocide', Timothy Garton Ash opined ('Imagine no America', *Guardian*, September 19, 2002). The *Mirror* referred to 'Echoes of the Holocaust' (quoted, Pilger, *The New Rulers of the World*, p. 144). The *Sun* urged us to 'Clobba Slobba' and 'Bomb, Bomb, Bomb'. As British bombs rained on Serbia, a breathless Andrew Marr wrote articles in the *Observer* entitled: 'Brave, Bold, Visionary. Whatever Became of Blair the Ultra-Cautious Cynic?' (*Observer*, April 4, 1999) and 'Hail to the Chief. Sorry, Bill, but This Time We're Talking About Tony' (*Observer*, May 16, 1999). Marr declared himself in awe of Blair's 'moral courage', adding: 'I am constantly impressed, but also mildly alarmed, by his utter lack of cynicism' (*Observer*, April 4, 1999). A 2002 BBC documentary on the alleged Serbian genocide, *Exposed* (BBC2, January 27, 2002), was billed as a programme marking Holocaust Memorial Day, no less.

There were no holds barred. In an article with the title, 'Stop the Music', Thomas Friedman wrote in the *New York Times*:

> [I]f NATO's only strength is that it can bomb forever, then it has to get every ounce out of that. Let's at least have a real air war. The idea that people are still holding rock concerts in Belgrade, or going out for Sunday merry-go-round rides, while their fellow Serbs are 'cleansing' Kosovo, is outrageous. It should be lights out in Belgrade: every power grid, water pipe, bridge, road and war-related factory has to be targeted. ('Stop the Music', *New York Times*, April 23, 1999)

## PURE INVENTION – THE KOSOVO 'GENOCIDE'

So how real was the Serbian genocide in Kosovo compared, say, to the threat of Iraqi WMD? And did this alleged mass abuse of human rights justify the 78 days of NATO bombing that claimed

500 Yugoslav civilian lives and caused an estimated $100 billion in damage? NATO bombs crashed through 33 hospitals, 344 schools, 144 major industrial plants, through hotels, libraries, housing estates, theatres, museums, farms (setting fields alight), a mosque in Djakovica, a Basilica in Nis, a church in Prokuplje, trains, tractors, power stations, and so on. According to Yugoslav authorities, civilian targets comprised 60 per cent of the total hit by NATO bombs.

Amnesty International claimed that during the bombing: 'NATO forces ... committed serious violations of the laws of war leading in a number of cases to the unlawful killings of civilians' (Amnesty International press release, 'NATO Violations of the Laws of War During Operation Allied Force Must Be Investigated', June 7, 2000). Amnesty focused in particular on the April 23 bombing of the headquarters of Serbian state radio and television, which left 16 civilians dead, describing it as 'a deliberate attack on a civilian object', which therefore 'constitutes a war crime'. The report also noted that the requirement that NATO aircraft fly above 15,000 feet to provide maximum protection for aircraft and pilots 'made full adherence to international humanitarian law virtually impossible' (ibid.).

In February 1999, one month before the start of NATO bombing, a report released by the German Foreign Office noted that 'the often feared humanitarian catastrophe threatening the Albanian civil population has been averted'. In the larger cities 'public life has since returned to relative normality' (quoted, Curtis, *Web of Deceit*, p. 136).

Another German report, exactly one month before the bombing, refers to the CIA-backed Kosovo Liberation Army (KLA) seeking independence for Kosovo from Serbia:

> Events since February and March 1998 do not evidence a persecution program based on Albanian ethnicity. The measures taken by the [Serbian] armed forces are in the first instance directed towards combating the KLA and its supposed adherents and supporters. (Ibid., p. 136)

Following the war, NATO sources reported that 2,000 people had been killed in Kosovo on all sides in the year prior to bombing. George Robertson testified before the House of Commons that until mid January 1999, 'the Kosovo Liberation Army was responsible for more deaths in Kosovo than the Serbian authorities had been' (quoted, Noam Chomsky, *Hegemony or Survival – America's Quest for Global Dominance*, Routledge, 2003, p. 56). This is supported by Nicholas Wheeler of the University of Wales who estimates that Serbs killed

500 Albanians before the NATO bombing, implying that 1,500 had been killed by the KLA. The KLA had openly declared that their strategy was to provoke Serbian forces into retaliatory action that would generate Western public support for NATO intervention.

Far from averting a humanitarian crisis, it is clear that NATO bombing caused a major escalation of killings and expulsions. The flood of refugees from Kosovo, for example, began immediately *after* NATO launched its attack. Prior to the bombing, and for the following two days, the United Nations High Commissioner for Refugees (UNHCR) reported no data on refugees. On March 27, three days into the bombing, UNHCR reported that 4,000 had fled Kosovo to the neighbouring countries of Albania and Macedonia. By April 5, the *New York Times* reported 'more than 350,000 have left Kosovo since March 24' (Carlotta Gall, 'Misery and Disease Sweep Macedonian Camp', *New York Times*, April 5, 1999).

A study by the Organisation for Security and Cooperation in Europe (OSCE) recorded 'a pattern of expulsions and the vast increase in lootings, killings, rape, kidnappings and pillage once the NATO air war began on March 24' and that 'the most visible change in the events was *after* NATO launched its first air strikes' (Curtis, *Web of Deceit*, p. 137, our emphasis). A House of Commons Foreign Affairs Committee investigating the war concluded:

It is likely that the NATO bombing did cause a change in the character of the assault upon the Kosovo Albanians. What had been an anti-insurgency campaign – albeit a brutal and counter-productive one – became a mass, organised campaign to kill Kosovo Albanians or drive them from the country. (Ibid., pp. 137–8)

The media response was to exactly *reverse* cause and effect suggesting that bombing was justified as a way of halting the flood of refugees it had in fact created. Philip Hammond of South Bank University comments:

the refugee crisis became NATO's strongest propaganda weapon, though logically it should have been viewed as a damning indictment of the bombing ... The hundreds of thousands of Serbs who fled the bombing were therefore determinedly ignored by British journalists. (Hammond and Herman, *Degraded Capability*, p. 126–7)

Robert Hayden of the University of Pittsburgh reports that the casualties among Serb civilians in the first three weeks of the war were higher than all of the casualties on both sides in Kosovo in the three months that led up to the war. And yet, Hayden points out, 'those three months were supposed to be a humanitarian catastrophe' (quoted, Noam Chomsky, *The New Military Humanism*, Pluto Press, 1999, p. 20). Hammond indicates the awesome scale of the truth buried by the media:

> We may never know the true number of people killed. But it seems reasonable to conclude that while people died in clashes between the KLA and Yugoslav forces ... the picture painted by NATO – of a systematic campaign of Nazi-style genocide carried out by Serbs – was pure invention. (Hammond and Herman, *Degraded Capability*, p. 129)

In other words, the US–UK assault on Serbia, like the assault on Iraq, was made possible by audacious government manipulation of a public denied access to the truth by an incompetent and structurally corrupt media. Every major British newspaper, except the *Independent on Sunday*, took a pro-war line in its editorial column. Journalists, indeed, were so utterly fooled by government propaganda that they proudly proclaimed their role in supporting the 'humanitarian intervention'.

Responding to Blair's press spokesman Alastair Campbell's accusation of press cynicism over the Kosovo attack (another familiar theme from the 2003 Iraq war), Channel 4 correspondent Alex Thomson declared: 'If you want to know why the public supported the war, thank a journalist, not the present government's propagandist-in-chief' (quoted, Charles Glass, 'Hacks Versus Flacks', *Z Magazine*, August, 1999). The *Guardian*'s Maggie O'Kane agreed: 'But Campbell should acknowledge that it was the press reporting of the Bosnian war and the Kosovar refugee crisis that gave his boss the public support and sympathy he needed to fight the good fight against Milosevic' (ibid.). As did John Simpson of the BBC: 'Why did British, American, German, and French public opinion stay rock-solid for the bombing, in spite of NATO's mistakes? Because they knew the war was right. Who gave them the information? The media' (ibid.).

So much for 'neutral and 'objective' reporting. As a result, Blair has been able to use the lie of Kosovo to justify more recent killing. In a speech in 2004, Blair said of the Iraq war:

The real point is that those who disagree with the war, disagree fundamentally with the judgement that led to war. What is more, their alternative judgement is both entirely rational and arguable. Kosovo, with ethnic cleansing of ethnic Albanians, was not a hard decision for most people; nor was Afghanistan after the shock of September 11; nor was Sierra Leone. ('Tony Blair's Speech', *Guardian*, March 5, 2004)

Kosovo was 'not a hard decision for most people' because awkward facts pointing to something other than a 'battle between good and evil' were kept well out of sight.

To be sure, the alliance of state violence and media servility does not *always* result in tragedy, death and disaster – sometimes there are happy endings. While covering the Kosovo crisis, CNN's leading foreign correspondent, Christiane Amanpour, married James Rubin, chief public relations official of the US State Department. Amanpour had announced that her future husband's war was for 'the first time ... a war fought for human rights'. And, after all, 'only a fraction of 1 percent of the bombs went astray' (quoted, Hammond and Herman, *Degraded Capability*, p. 113). The BBC's defence correspondent, Mark Laity, may not have found love during his coverage of NATO's slaughter, but he did subsequently accept the post of press secretary to the NATO secretary general, George Robertson, who had also moved on from his position as British defence secretary.

## QUESTIONING RACAK

Ex-CBS producer Richard Cohen explained the underlying reality of the media–politics relationship: 'Everyone plays by the rules of the game if they want to stay in the game' (quoted, Danny Schechter, *The More You Watch, the Less You Know*, Seven Stories Press, 1997, p. 39). One of the most important rules of the game is that the media should present the US and British governments as fundamentally benign and well intentioned, so freeing them to wage war out of 'humanitarian' intent. This is a kind of fixed canvas on which world events must be painted. The illusion is maintained by overlooking crimes committed by us and our allies, and by emphasising crimes committed by officially designated 'enemies'.

The last is extremely important – in politics, as in everyday life, our emotional reaction to events largely depends on how we label them: the term 'genocidal massacre' fills us with horror in a way that 'human rights abuses' does not. For example, the *Observer* described as a 'massacre' the alleged killing of Albanian civilians in Racak by Serb armed forces on January 16, 1999:

> History will judge that the defining moment for the international community took place on 16 January this year ... Albanians returning after an attack by Serb security forces discovered the bodies of men they had left behind to look after the houses. The dead of Racak, 45 in all, included elderly men and young boys, most shot at close range, some mutilated after death, eyes gouged out. One man lay decapitated in his courtyard. William Walker, U.S. head of the international monitoring group, called it unequivocally a Serb police 'massacre'. (Peter Beaumont, Justin Brown, John Hooper, Helena Smith and Ed Vulliamy, 'Hi-Tech War and Primitive Slaughter – Slobodan Milosevic Is Fighting on Two Fronts', *Observer*, March 28, 1999)

Over a number of reports, Peter Beaumont used the word 'massacre' repeatedly when describing events at Racak:

> Feriz Brahimi was returning to a village empty except for the dogs. After the massacre, no one wants to live here. Those who come – Brahimi, an Albanian actor and comedian, among them – visit only to make sure that their houses still stand. (Beaumont, 'Kosovo Cowers in the Rubble', Guardian Unlimited, February 28, 1999, <www.guardian.co.uk/Kosovo/Story/0,,208388,00.html>)

Like so many mainstream journalists, Beaumont considered Racak evidence, not just of a massacre, but of actual genocide. Thus the *Observer* team wrote: 'His [Slobodan Milosevic's] troops in Serbia are out of barracks. But in Kosovo they are scouring the fields, villages and towns, pursuing their own version of a Balkan Final Solution' (Beaumont et al., 'Hi-Tech War and Primitive Slaughter'). This was a remarkable statement, given the sheer scale of the claim; the *Observer* was drawing comparisons between Serb actions and one of the most appalling atrocities in all history. But it becomes truly mind-boggling when we consider the *Observer*'s own assessment of the credibility of the evidence on which it was based: 'Without the humanitarian monitors, who left the south Serbian province seven days ago, and journalists, who were expelled last Thursday, it is impossible to verify the dark stories that are emerging' (ibid.). This presents no problem – with Serbia designated an official enemy of the West, journalists were free to present a 'Balkan Final Solution' as fact, in the knowledge that no questions would be asked (talk of a 'US Final Solution in Iraq' would have had different consequences).

In the months leading up to the start of NATO bombing, the alleged 'massacre' at Racak was exceptional, with deaths occurring at an average of one per day. The last NATO report prior to the bombing (January 16–March 22, 1999) cited dozens of incidents, with approximately half initiated by the Kosovo Liberation Army (KLA) and half by Serb security forces. This was horrific enough, but to make a comparison with the Nazis' 'Final Solution' is simply outrageous.

Beaumont et al. quoted William Walker, the head of the OSCE's Kosovo Verification Mission, who denounced the alleged massacre. Walker did indeed say: 'It looks like executions. From what I personally saw, I do not hesitate to describe the event as a massacre – obviously a crime very much against humanity' (quoted, Hammond and Herman, *Degraded Capability*, p. 118). The *Observer* failed to mention that this was the same William Walker who was US ambassador to El Salvador in 1989 under Reagan, at the height of the US-backed bloodbath there. Walker said of the Salvadoran army's murder of six Jesuit priests, their housekeeper and her daughter: 'Management control problems exist in a situation like this' (ibid.). Walker more generally dismissed the vast massacres of unarmed civilians by the Salvadoran government, saying that 'in times like these of great emotion and great anger, things like this happen' (ibid.). Walker's pedigree as an apologist for US crimes during the 1980s surely deserved mention when reporting his views on alleged Serb atrocities in the 1990s.

Although the *Guardian* and other UK media constantly accused the Serbian government of hiding bodies, they did not notice the curious failure to remove bodies at Racak. French reporter Christophe Chatelet, who arrived in the village after the fighting, found the site calm. He spoke to OSCE observers helping some elderly people who told him that nothing momentous had happened. There were no signs of a massacre.

The *Guardian* and the *Observer* also ignored a 2001 report in a German newspaper, *Berliner Zeitung*, on Racak. Deutsche Presse-Agentur gave a summary:

> Finnish forensic experts in a final report on the circumstances of the deaths two years ago of some 40 people in the village of Racak in Kosovo found no evidence of a massacre by Serb security forces, a German newspaper reported

Wednesday. (Deutsche Presse-Agentur, 'Finnish Experts Find No Evidence of Serb Massacre of Albanians', January 17, 2001)

The report was by a panel of Finnish forensic experts, led by Helena Ranta, which was asked by the European Union to investigate the killings in the spring of 1999. The panel was unable to confirm that the victims were villagers from Racak. It was unable to reconstruct events prior to the autopsies of the bodies, reporting that even the exact site of the incident had not been established. There was also no evidence that the bodies had been disfigured after their deaths. The 40 bodies examined were found to show between one and 20 bullet wounds – only in one case were traces of gun smoke found that might point to an execution.

Deutsche Presse-Agentur noted that Belgrade authorities at the time of the 'massacre' insisted the bodies were slain rebels of the KLA, which they said had deliberately set up the scene to make OSCE observers believe there had been a massacre. Ranta described Racak as 'a crime against humanity', but added, 'all killings' are crimes against humanity (quoted, Edward Herman, 'The Milosevic Trial, Part 2: Media and New Humanitarian Normalization of Victor's Justice', *Z Magazine*, April 2002). Recall that this was described as 'the defining moment' in Serb–West relations by Beaumont and his *Observer* colleagues, and many other journalists.

Racak gave the West the pretext it needed for launching an assault on Serbia. BBC correspondent Allan Little quoted Madeleine Albright as saying to national security adviser Sandy Berger, after hearing of the alleged massacre, 'Spring has come early' (Little, 'How NATO Was Sucked into the Kosovo Conflict', *Sunday Telegraph*, February 27, 2000).

Gore Vidal once noted ironically how the US media manage to conjure 'the image of America the beauteous on its hill, envied by all and subject to attacks by terrorists who cannot bear so much sheer goodness to triumph in a world that belongs to their master, the son of morning himself, Satan' (quoted, William Blum, 'Why America?', *Ecologist*, Dec 2001/Jan 2002). The UK media play a similar role, with an added emphasis on how the benign British government forever seeks to restrain its equally benign but somewhat over-zealous American allies.

Suffering caused by Western 'enemies' is forever highlighted, boosted and vilified. Suffering caused by the West and its 'friends' is forever ignored, prettified, justified and forgotten. The effect of this continuous propaganda is that many people find it literally inconceivable that the West could be doing anything very wrong in the world: we would not bomb a nation of starving civilians without very good reason, because we have always been a good people who do good things. We would not have been imposing sanctions on Iraq without good reason, or without ensuring adequate protection for Iraqi civilians, because our leaders are good and decent people. We cannot be standing idly by while global warming threatens an unprecedented, perhaps terminal, holocaust within ten years, because we are good, sane, sensible people.

This conviction is utterly crucial – the public will not tolerate the mass killing of foreign innocents unless they believe an honourable goal is being served. And so the media – especially the 'liberal' media in which people place so much trust – are up to their necks in blood.

We live in a world made up of a rich and powerful few ruling over the poor and suffering many. It is a world dominated by rapacious Western corporations legally obliged to pursue the bottom line, and by allied Third World tyrants armed to the teeth with Western weapons. Yet somehow, always, without fail, the media portrays Western violence as moral, humanitarian and defensive. Editors and journalists do not drop the bombs or pull the triggers, but without their servility to power the public would not be fooled and the slaughter would have to end.

If there is to be a way out of the nightmare of history, it will begin with our waking up to the complicity of the corporate mass media in mass murder.

## PERNICIOUS AND ANTI-JOURNALISTIC – MEDIA LENS AND THE BBC'S ANDREW MARR

The BBC never tires of reminding us of its bona fides. In the autumn of 2001, BBC adverts assured us: 'Honesty, integrity – it's what the BBC stands for.' During the general election that year, the same source declared: 'The BBC is fighting the election on a single issue: The Truth!' No surprise, then, that the BBC requires that reporters undergo some demanding, even gruesome, procedures prior to taking up their positions. The BBC's Andrew Marr, a former editor of the *Independent*, noted: 'When I joined the BBC, my Organs of Opinion were formally removed' (*Independent*, January 13, 2001).

However, during the NATO bombing of Serbia, Marr's Organs of Opinion were very much in place, and inflamed with war fever. As noted in Chapter 4, Marr urged Blair to take 'the Macbeth option' by threatening Milosevic with a ground war (Marr, 'War in the Balkans: The Issues: Do We Give War a Chance?' *Observer*, April 18, 1999).

Kamal Ahmed of the *Observer* noted the obvious: 'Marr ... is close to senior officials in Downing Street and makes no secret of his New Labour credentials. He is well-liked by the prime minister and his official spokesman, Alastair Campbell' ('BBC Braced for Row over New Political Editor', *Observer*, May 14, 2000).

Prior to becoming the BBC's political editor, Marr discussed how 'we' had moved from Cold War stalemate to 1999 hot war with Serbia:

> After the permafrost, the beasts. We are not well-prepared for this. The idea that our people should go and die in large numbers appals us. Killing our enemies appals us too. The war-hardened people of Serbia, far more callous, seemingly readier to die, are like an alien race. So, for that matter, are the KLA. ('War is Hell – but not being Ready to go to War is Undignified and Embarrassing', *Observer*, April 25, 1999)

We present below an exchange between Marr and ourselves, in the wake of these remarkable observations. Our media alert 'New Chairman Confirms the BBC as a Mouthpiece for Establishment Views' (October 3, 2001, <www.medialens.org/alerts>) provoked a response from Marr. This was his response (October 7, 2001) followed by the reply from Media Lens:

Dear David Cromwell

thank you. It is very easy, an old game, to caricature someone's views with brutally selective quotation. I was concerned enough about what you said I had said to go back and look up the article in which you allege I said the Serbs were beasts, etc.

Well, surprise, surprise, I didn't say that – as you must know perfectly well. And the 'like an alien race' comment was in the context of describing the division that has occured between the post-war consciousness of nuclear-protected Western society and others, for whom the old raw excitements and sacrifices of war remain – like the Serbs in Kosovo AND, I said, the KLA. I was attacking a policy of bombing civilians and poisoning water supplies from '15,000 feet', rather than threatening to push out Milosevic with the more dangerous option of ground troops. (As, you fail to note, then happened, leading to the Serb withdrawal and Milosevic's fall, neither of them, I assume events that you welcome.)

But I don't really know why I am bothering to say all this. You must have read the original. You must therefore know what a deliberate and cynical distortion of the original article you have published. I'm afraid I think it is just pernicious and anti-journalistic. I note that you advertise an organisation called Fairness and Accuracy in Reporting so I guess at least you have a sense of humour. But I don't think I will bother with 'medialens' next time, if you don't mind.

Andrew Marr

Reply to Andrew Marr from Media Lens, October 13, 2001:

Dear Andrew Marr,

Thank you for your prompt response to our media alert of October 3. We appreciate you responding to our serious concerns. Our intention is to promote honest and rational debate; not to make personal attacks on you or anyone else.

You say that you did not use the word 'beasts' in describing the Serbian people. Here is the paragraph in full from which we quoted you, as it appears on the Guardian Unlimited website at: <www.guardian.co.uk/Archive/Article/0,4273,3857957,00.html>.

'The Cold War, in short, could also have been called the Cold Peace. It was a time of stability – terrifying stability. When it ended we found ourselves in a new world, a place of reassuring instability, where the prospect of a final, crashing Armageddon seemed much less, but where, nevertheless, local conflicts could ignite more easily. After the permafrost, the beasts. We are not well-prepared for this. The idea that our people should go and die in large numbers appals us. Killing our enemies appals us too. The war-hardened people of Serbia, far more callous, seemingly readier to die, are like an alien race. So, for that matter, are the KLA.'

You wrote 'after the permafrost, the beasts', and then immediately introduced the Serbs whom you described as: 'war-hardened ... far more callous, seemingly readier to die ... like an alien race.' If you were not describing the Serbs as 'beasts', to whom were you referring? Including the KLA as callous beasts only added to your harsh judgement of the Serbs as a people. Such demonisation of groups targeted as 'the enemy' by our government has, sadly, been standard practice in establishment-friendly reporting since WWI and earlier. As an admirer of Orwell's writing, you are doubtless aware of this.

Your ill-posed division of 'post-war consciousness of nuclear-protected western society and others' is obfuscation – a cover for western crimes against humanity. As Arundhati Roy noted recently, such words are but an 'equivocating distinction between civilisation and savagery', with the west, of course, comprising the civilised peoples and 'others' being savages ('The Algebra of Infinite Justice', Arundhati Roy, *Guardian*, September 29, 2001; <www.guardian.co.uk/Archive/Article/0,4273,4266289,00.html.>).

There was no mention in your article of the many victims of 'nuclear-protected western society': the millions killed in Vietnam, Cambodia, Laos or in Central and Latin America, Iraq, Indonesia, East Timor and elsewhere. These victims make a nonsense of any notion of a 'feminised' west and the 'far more callous' beasts.

You say that you were 'attacking a policy of bombing civilians and poisoning water supplies from "15,000 feet", rather than threatening to push out Milosevic with the more dangerous option of ground troops.' Nowhere in your article did you accuse NATO of 'poisoning water supplies from "15,000 feet"' – a truly shocking claim. Instead you lamented 'attacking TV stations and civilian water supplies' and warned of what might happen were the Danube to be poisoned by the effects of war – not the same thing.

You did describe the attacking of civilian targets as 'decadent' – a curious word to describe what were, in fact, war crimes. Presumably you would not describe Milosevic's crimes in Kosovo as 'decadent'. Your article addressed your concerns that NATO victory might not be achieved by air power alone. But what about the welfare of civilians, who would have suffered far more had your advice on launching a ground war been taken?

Your claim that you were primarily concerned with the welfare of civilians is further undermined by your point that, 'NATO could yet win the war and yet fail in its most important, undeclared war aim, which is to stay together and alive as the world's most potent military alliance.' You added: 'whether this happens or not – and on balance I'm more optimistic ...', suggesting that you shared NATO's view that the war's most important – and undeclared – aim was to preserve NATO as 'the world's most potent military alliance'. Any 'humanitarian' intent, then was presumably secondary. In fact, we would argue that it was non-existent, or almost so. [See, for example, Noam Chomsky's *The New Military Humanism: Lessons from Kosovo*, Pluto Press, 1999.]

Finally, we reject your presumption that we did not 'welcome' the withdrawal of Serbs from Kosovo or the fall of Milosevic. However, to present these events as retrospective justification for NATO's war crimes is crass. As Robert Fisk of The Independent concluded in the wake of the bombing: 'NATO's bombing brought a kind of peace to Kosovo – but only after it had given the Serbs the opportunity to massacre or dispossess half the Albanian population of the province, caused billions of dollars in damage to Yugoslavia's infrastructure, killed hundreds of Yugoslav civilians, destabilised Macedonia and gravely damaged relations with China. And the media called this a successful war.' [*Independent*, June 29, 1999].

There are other aspects of your article, and mainstream reporting of the Balkans war, that we do not have space to address fully here: such as the nature of NATO's accept-or-be-bombed proposal, i.e. an ultimatum, to the Serbs in March 1999. Or the relative timing of NATO bombing and refugee flows: the west's leaders told us that the bombing was taken in 'response' to expulsions of Kosovar Albanians and to 'reverse' the flow. But there was scant mention anywhere in the mainstream media that the NATO bombing actually *precipitated* a huge flood of refugees, creating conditions that allowed Serbian atrocities actually to escalate.

The aim of our media alert of October 3 was to show how the media – in particular, the BBC – act as an establishment mouthpiece. Accusing those who opposed NATO bombing of not welcoming the removal of Milosevic is an irrational and lamentable response.

David Edwards and David Cromwell, Media Lens

Andrew Marr did not respond.

# 7
# East Timor – The Practical Limits of Crusading Humanitarianism

## A TOOTHLESS MORAL CRUSADE

On August 30, 1999, despite months of murderous intimidation by militia forces organised and armed by the Indonesian military (TNI), the East Timorese voted overwhelmingly for independence: 78.5 per cent voted in favour and 21.5 per cent voted against. The aftermath was a horrendous bloodbath as militias escalated their attacks on pro-independence supporters. It took until September 9 before Washington, under growing public pressure, finally suspended the Pentagon's formal military ties with the TNI – a step the US government could have taken much earlier. Almost immediately, Jakarta announced that it would allow in an international peacekeeping force.

Indonesian historian John Roosa, an official observer of the referendum, reported:

> Given that the pogrom was so predictable, it was easily preventable ... But in the weeks before the ballot, the Clinton Administration refused to discuss with Australia and other countries the formation of [an international force]. Even after the violence erupted, the Administration dithered for days. ('Fatal Trust in Timor', *New York Times*, September 15, 1999)

As Amnesty International noted:

> If US leverage was ultimately the critical factor in persuading Indonesia to stop the killing and permit peacekeepers, why weren't these steps taken sooner? Every day between the vote and President Clinton's [September] 9th statements meant more corpses, more burned buildings, more refugees. (Quoted, Stephen Shalom, 'Humanitarian Intervention', ZNet Commentary, January 18, 2000)

Remarkably, all of this happened just weeks after the conclusion of the West's 'humanitarian crusade' in Kosovo. With stunning audacity, the press feigned not to notice the hypocrisy. Hugo Young of the *Guardian* explained the sudden silence and inaction of the West's 'moral crusaders' thus: 'British intervention, a la Kosovo, will not happen: too far away, not enough troops. The Blair doctrine of crusading humanitarianism has its practical limits' ('Stop Selling UK Arms to the Cruellest Regimes on Earth', *Guardian*, September 9, 1999).

Discussing the Western failure to react to the atrocity until 70 per cent of all public buildings and private residences in East Timor had been destroyed, and 75 per cent of the population had been herded across the border into militia-controlled camps in West Timor, where hostage taking, killings and sexual assault were a daily occurrence, Matt Frei of the BBC observed sagely: 'This is a moral crusade by the West, like Kosovo ... but a moral crusade without teeth' (*BBC News* at 18:00, BBC1, October 10, 1999).

Mary Robinson, then UN commissioner for human rights, took a different view:

> For a time it seemed the world would turn away altogether from the people of East Timor ... Action, when it came, was painfully slow; thousands paid with their lives for the world's slow response. It was the tide of public anger that stirred world leaders to intervene, however belatedly, on behalf of the East Timorese. ('We Can End This Agony', *Guardian*, October 23, 1999)

Robinson's words came exactly six months after Tony Blair had declared: 'But the principle of non-interference must be qualified in important respects. Acts of genocide can never be a purely internal matter' (Colin Brown, 'War in the Balkans: Blair's Vision of Global Police', *Independent*, April 23, 1999). But on East Timor, Blair had almost nothing to say.

Long after the truth emerged with great clarity to Mary Robinson and most other people, the BBC seemed to find it excruciatingly difficult to admit that our Indonesian allies were behind the massacres in East Timor. As late as October 12, 1999 newscaster Nicholas Witchell described how the Indonesian armed forces 'have failed to protect the people of East Timor' (*BBC News* at 20:50, October 12, 1999). Much as the SS 'failed to protect' the Jews of the Warsaw ghetto.

Frei gave several reasons for the lack of teeth this time around: there was no stomach for bombing or putting troops in harm's way after the attack on Serbia (see Chapter 6), and Western leaders feared that intervention in Timor might cause this huge, fragile country to collapse, heralding an even worse tragedy. Frei made no mention of the fact that the military regime that ran the country was a major Western ally and business partner, or of the fact that Britain had long supported Indonesian terror in East Timor for reasons that had nothing to do with protecting the stability of the invading force. These facts are not, perhaps never can be, reported as news by the BBC: news ceases to be news when it seriously damages establishment interests. Frei's arguments on the reluctance to deploy British troops were virtually of a piece with those of the then British foreign secretary Robin Cook, who initially claimed that Britain did not have sufficient troops to deal with both the Balkans and East Timor.

Not much of this is conscious deception; John Pilger has talked of 'the subliminal pressures applied by organisations like the BBC, whose news is often selected on the basis of a spurious establishment "credibility"' (Introduction to Phillip Knightley, *First Casualty – The War Correspondent as Hero and Myth-Maker from the Crimea to Kosovo*, Prion Books, 2000, p. xiii).

## NO ONE GAVE A DAMN – THE 'BLESSING' OF THE WEST

The emergence of an independent East Timor on May 20, 2002 provided a superb example of how the British 'free press' acts as a propaganda system covering up Western crimes. Many news reports did mention that around 200,000 East Timorese – a third of the population – had been massacred or starved to death following Indonesia's illegal invasion of the territory in 1975. Almost completely missing from the reports, however, were honest descriptions of the massive US/UK support for Indonesia's assault, and the ruthless motives informing it.

Consider the *Guardian*'s John Aglionby, who reviewed 'Landmarks on the bitter path to freedom' in East Timor by observing merely that Suharto had invaded 'with the blessing of the US, Australia and Britain' ('Landmarks on the Bitter Path to Freedom', *Guardian*, May 20, 2002). Compare this version with that of Philip Liechty, CIA desk officer in Jakarta at the time of the invasion:

We sent the Indonesian generals everything that you need to fight a major war against somebody who doesn't have any guns. We sent them rifles, ammunition, mortars, grenades, food, helicopters. You name it; they got it. And they got it direct. Without continued, heavy US logistical military support, the Indonesians might not have been able to pull it off ... No one cared. No one gave a damn. It is something that I will be forever ashamed of. The only justification I ever heard for what we were doing was there was concern that East Timor was on the verge of being accepted as a new member of the United Nations and there was a chance that the country was going to be either leftist or neutralist and not likely to vote [with the United States] at the UN. (Quoted, John Pilger, *Hidden Agendas*, Vintage, 1998, pp. 285–6)

A month after Indonesia invaded, as tens of thousands of people were being massacred, a US State Department official told a major Australian newspaper that 'in terms of the bilateral relations between the U.S. and Indonesia, we are more or less condoning the incursion into East Timor ... The United States wants to keep its relations with Indonesia close and friendly. We regard Indonesia as a friendly, non-aligned nation – a nation we do a lot of business with' (*Australian*, January 22, 1976. Quoted, <www.fair.org>, Action Alert, September 2, 1999).

US Senator Daniel Patrick Moynihan, UN ambassador at the time of the invasion in December 1975, explained his role in preventing the UN from acting to halt Indonesia's aggression:

The United States wished things to turn out as they did and worked to bring this about. The Department of State desired that the United Nations prove utterly ineffective in whatever measures it undertook. This task was given to me, and I carried it forward with no inconsiderable success. (Quoted, Noam Chomsky, *Powers and Prospects*, Pluto Press, 1996, p. 209)

In December 1975, the British ambassador in Jakarta informed the Foreign Office:

it is in Britain's interest that Indonesia should absorb the territory as soon and as unobtrusively as possible, and that if it should come to the crunch and there is a row in the United Nations, we should keep our heads down and avoid taking sides against the Indonesian government. (Quoted, Mark Curtis, *The Ambiguities of Power – British Foreign Policy since 1945*, Zed Books, 1995, pp. 219–20)

There was little chance of the Western public coming to the aid of East Timor, for reasons explained by American journalist Amy Goodman:

In 1979, when the killing was at its worst, there wasn't one mainstream press article in the New York Times and the Washington Post – not one. ABC, NBC and CBS 'Evening News' never mentioned the words East Timor and neither did 'Nightline' or 'MacNeil Lehrer' between 1975, the day of the invasion, except for one comment by Walter Cronkite the day after, saying Indonesia had invaded East Timor – it was a 40 second report – until November 12, 1991. ('Exception to the Rulers, Part II', *Z Magazine*, December 1997)

A study of the *New York Times* Index 1975–79 shows that East Timor received 70 column inches of entries over this period, as compared with 1,175 column inches afforded to contemporaneous atrocities by the West's enemies in Cambodia.

All of this lies hidden behind Aglionby's description of Indonesia invading 'with the blessing' of the US, Australia and Britain. Likewise, the *Independent*'s Richard Lloyd Parry referred to Indonesia's devastating occupation as 'straightforward international thuggery, colluded in by the United States, Britain and Australia' ('Amid Tears, Cheers and Prayers, East Timor is Finally a Free Country', *Independent*, May 20, 2002). Recall that Lloyd Parry was here describing one of the worst genocides of the twentieth century by proportion of population. We can imagine the reaction if Lloyd Parry had described the Holocaust as 'international thuggery'. At the time of the invasion, a lone radio voice in East Timor was picked up sending a desperate call for help: 'The soldiers are killing indiscriminately. Women and children are being shot in the streets. We are all going to be killed. I repeat, we are all going to be killed' (quoted, *Age*, Melbourne, December 8, 1975). This indeed was the boast of Indonesian general Try Sutrisno, who said: 'These ill-bred people have to be shot ... and we will shoot them' (quoted, *Amnesty* magazine, British Section, September/October 1994, p. 5). The line commonly used by the Indonesian military when dealing with East Timorese civilians was, 'we will kill your family to the seventh generation' (quoted, Goodman, 'Exception to the Rulers'). This is 'international thuggery' only if a thug is comparable to a mass murderer.

In *The Times*, reporter Ian Timberlake wrote that 'British and Australian troops led an intervention force that ushered in a United Nations administration [that] began the task of rebuilding East Timor and preparing it for self-government' ('East Timor Rises from Ruins as Newest Nation', *The Times*, May 18, 2002). In fact, the intervention was primarily an Australian initiative following enormous public support for the East Timorese; but it was too little, too late. As Noam Chomsky observed at the time:

> It would have sufficed for the U.S. and its allies to withdraw their active participation [in arming and supporting Indonesia], and to inform the Indonesian military command that the territory [East Timor] must be granted the right of self-determination that has been upheld by the United Nations and the World Court. ('East Timor', October 4, 1999, <www.zmag. org/sustainers/content/1999–10/4chomsky.htm>)

In the *Daily Telegraph*'s account of how 'bloodied' East Timor gained independence, reporter Chris McCall made no reference to the West's complicity in 'the territory's bloody recent history' ('Bloodied East Timor Becomes a Nation', *Daily Telegraph*, May 20, 2002). However, the *Telegraph*'s anonymous report the previous day did note correctly:

> Indonesia's 1975 invasion was carried out with the support of former US president Gerald Ford and then-secretary of state Henry Kissinger – who visited Jakarta on the eve of the attack. Successive US administrations later backed Indonesian dictator Suharto in his bloody crackdown against the rebels. (*Daily Telegraph*, May 19, 2002)

The extent of this 'support' and 'backing' was not explored.

### IMPOVERISHED TERRITORY – THE CALCULATIONS OF REALPOLITIK

So why the silence? What interests were the media protecting?

Successive US administrations, the *New York Times* noted in 1999, 'made the calculation that the United States must put its relationship with Indonesia, a mineral-rich nation of more than 200 million people, ahead of its concern [sic] over the political fate of East Timor, a tiny impoverished territory of 800,000 people that is seeking independence' (Elizabeth Becker and Philip Shenon, 'With Other Goals in Indonesia, US Moves Gently on East Timor', *New York Times*, September 9, 1999). Becker and Shenon forgot to mention the role of the *New York Times* in putting minerals ahead of concern for impoverished people by blanketing the horror in silence.

Western motives for supplying 90 per cent of the weapons used against East Timor are further clarified by a secret cable sent by Richard Woolcott, the Australian ambassador to Jakarta, in August

1975. Woolcott advised that Australia approve the likely invasion because favourable arrangements to gain a share of East Timor's oil 'could be much more readily negotiated with Indonesia ... than with Portugal or an independent East Timor' (quoted, Pilger, *Hidden Agendas*, p. 256). Tipped off by the Indonesian regime that an invasion was imminent, Woolcott secretly cabled the Department of Foreign Affairs, proposing that '[we] leave events to take their course and act in a way which would be designed to minimise the public impact in Australia and show private understanding to Indonesia of their problems' (ibid.). This 'private understanding' assisted in Australia's subsequent carving up of the considerable oil and gas reserves covered by the Timor Gap Treaty, signed with Indonesia in 1989.

Indonesia under Suharto was a significant market for Western arms. By providing 'political stability', Suharto also offered Western business interests the opportunity to benefit from the country's extensive natural resources. A few months before the invasion, a Confederation of British Industry report noted that Indonesia presented 'enormous potential for the foreign investor' and that, according to one press report, the country enjoyed a 'favourable political climate' and the 'encouragement of foreign investment by the country's authorities' (Curtis, *The Ambiguities of Power*, p. 225). RTZ, BP, British Gas and Britoil were some of the companies that took advantage of Indonesia's 'favourable political climate'.

The tendency to overlook horrors committed by the West and its allies is The Golden Rule of media reporting. In the updated introduction to their book *Manufacturing Consent*, Edward Herman and Noam Chomsky analyse the number of times the word 'genocide' has been used in the mainstream media. A Nexis database search showed that between 1998 and 1999 the *Los Angeles Times*, the *New York Times*, the *Washington Post*, *Newsweek* and *Time* used 'genocide' 220 times to describe the actions of Serbia (a Western enemy) in Kosovo. It is estimated that some 3,000 people were killed on all sides in that conflict over that period. Between 1990 and 1999 the same media used the word 33 times to describe the actions of Indonesia (a Western ally) in East Timor. As discussed above, since Indonesia invaded in 1975, some 200,000 East Timorese, or one third of the population, are estimated to have been killed in one of history's worst bloodbaths. Between 1990 and 1999 the word was used 132 times to describe the actions of Iraq (a Western enemy) against Kurds. Between 1990 and 1999 the word was used 14 times to describe the actions of Turkey (a Western ally) against Kurds. Between 1991 and 1999 the word was used in connection with Western sanctions against Iraq 18 times, despite the resignation of senior UN diplomats describing the sanctions as 'genocidal'. Herman and Chomsky summarise:

> The table shows that the five major print media surveyed engage in a similar biased usage, frequently using 'genocide' to describe victimization in the enemy states, but applying the word far less frequently to equally severe victimization carried out by the United States or its allies and clients. We can even read who are U.S. friends and enemies from the media's use of the word. (email from Herman to Media Lens, August 27, 2002)

# 8
# Haiti – The Hidden Logic of Exploitation

In Chapter 4, we cited Thomas Carothers' observation of a 'strong line of continuity' in the US pursuit of self-interest in promoting and downplaying 'democracy'. Writing in the 1980s, Carothers, who served in the Reagan State Department on 'democracy enhancement' projects in Latin America during the 1980s, found that the Reagan and Bush I administrations had reluctantly adopted 'prodemocracy policies as a means of relieving pressure for more radical change' in Latin America, 'but inevitably sought only limited, top-down forms of democratic change that did not risk upsetting the traditional structures of power with which the United States has long been allied'. He described the goals of these 'democracy assistance projects' as being to maintain 'the basic order of ... quite undemocratic societies' and to avoid 'populist-based change' that might upset 'established economic and political orders' and open 'a leftist direction' (quoted, Neil A. Lewis, 'What Can the US Really Do About Haiti?', *New York Times*, December 6, 1987).

The results have been horrific for the poor of Latin America. Consider Haiti as a case in point.

Haiti is the poorest country in the Western hemisphere and the fourth poorest country in the world – 50 per cent of the country's wealth is owned by 1 per cent of the population. Life expectancy hovers around 52 years for women and 48 for men. Unemployment is about 70 per cent. Some 85 per cent of Haitians live on less than $1 US per day (Yifat Susskind, 'Haiti – Insurrection in the Making', February 25, 2004, <www.zmag.org>).

The United States is Haiti's main commercial 'partner' accounting for about 60 per cent of the flows of exports and imports. Along with the manufacture of baseballs, textiles, cheap electronics and toys, Haiti's sugar, bauxite and sisal are all controlled by American corporations. Disney, for example, has used Haitian sweatshops to produce Pocahontas pyjamas, among other items, at the rate of 11 cents per hour. Most Haitians are willing to work for almost nothing. The US Network For Economic Justice reported:

> Whereas corporations receive vast incentives to set up plants in Haiti ... returns to the Haitian economy are minimal, and working and living standards

of Haitian people, whose wages are generally below the minimum of thirty cents an hour, steadily decline ... Decades of public investments and policy manipulation by the World Bank, the IMF, and the US government have deliberately created an environment where the exploitation of workers is hailed as an incentive to invest in Haiti. ('50 Years is Enough: Corporate Welfare in Haiti', <www.50years.org>)

The US, in other words, is *not* a disinterested spectator of events in Haiti.

## CONQUERING PARADISE – THE LOGIC OF EXPLOITATION

When Cristóbal Colón (Columbus) first arrived on Hispaniola – today's Haiti and Dominican Republic – in October 1492, he found something close to an earthly paradise. Of the Taino people he encountered, he said:

They are the best people in the world and above all the gentlest ... All the people show the most singular loving behaviour and they speak pleasantly ... They love their neighbours as themselves, and they have the sweetest talk in the world, and are gentle and always laughing. (Quoted, Kirkpatrick Sale, *The Conquest of Paradise*, Papermac, 1992, pp. 99–100)

But Colón did not allow sentiment to stand in his way. Formal instructions for the second voyage to Hispaniola in May 1493 were significant, historian Kirkpatrick Sale wrote, in that they constituted 'the first statement of the colonial strategies and policies of empire that were eventually to carry Europe to every cranny of the earth'. Colón's plans were almost entirely concerned with 'establishing the means of exploitation and trade, providing no suggestion of any other purpose for settlement or any other function for government' (ibid., p. 127). The rights of the Taino people were not an issue – the concern was to steal their gold.

Las Casas, a Spanish eyewitness, described how the invaders were motivated by 'insatiable greed and ambition', attacking the Tainos 'like ravening wild beasts ... killing, terrorizing, afflicting, torturing, and destroying the native peoples' with 'the strangest and most varied new methods of cruelty, never seen or heard of before' (quoted, Noam Chomsky, *Year 501: The Conquest Continues*, Verso, 1993, p. 198). The intention seems to have been to utterly crush the spirit of the Tainos. Las Casas comments:

As they saw themselves each day perishing by the cruel and inhuman treatment of the Spaniards, crushed to the earth by the horses, cut in pieces by swords, eaten and torn by dogs, many buried alive and suffering all kinds of exquisite tortures ... [they] decided to abandon themselves to their unhappy fate with no further struggles, placing themselves in the hands of their enemies that they might do with them as they liked. (Ibid., pp. 198–9)

Near-identical horrors are documented under the subsequent French rulers of Haiti, who shipped in hundreds of thousands of African slaves to work plantations. From that time to this, the logic of Western exploitation of the Third World has remained fundamentally the same: dreams of a better life must be crushed by violence and grinding poverty so extreme that local people will accept any work at any rate, and abandon all notions of improving their lot.

This is why death squads, tyrants and economic oppression are such a standard feature of the Third World – hope is always being born and is always being killed by local thugs serving Western elites. This is also why weapons consistently flow from the rich West to the world's worst human rights abusers. In the 1980s, the leading academic scholar on human rights in Latin America, Lars Schoultz, found that US aid, including military aid, 'has tended to flow disproportionately to Latin American governments which torture their citizens ... to the hemisphere's relatively egregious violators of fundamental human rights' (quoted, Chomsky, *Year 501*, Verso, 1993, p. 120). Terror was required, Schoultz added, 'to destroy permanently a perceived threat to the existing structure of socioeconomic privilege by eliminating the political participation of the numerical majority' (ibid.).

Between 1849 and 1913, the US Navy entered Haitian waters 24 times to 'protect American lives and property'. The US invasion of 1915 returned slavery to Haiti in all but name and imposed a US-designed constitution giving US corporations free rein. After ruling for 19 years the US withdrew, leaving its wealth in the safe hands of the murderous National Guard it had created. In November 1935, Major General Smedley D. Butler explained the logic of intervention:

I spent thirty-three years and four months in active service as a member of our country's most agile military force – the Marine Corps ... And during that period I spent most of my time being a high-class muscle man for Big Business, for Wall Street, and for the bankers. In short, I was a racketeer for capitalism ...

Thus I helped make Mexico and especially Tampico safe for American oil interests in 1914. I helped make Haiti and Cuba a decent place for the National City boys to collect revenues in ... I helped purify Nicaragua for the international banking house of Brown Brothers in 1909–1912. I brought light to the Dominican Republic for American sugar interests in 1916. I helped make Honduras 'right' for American fruit companies in 1903. In China in 1927 I helped see to it that Standard Oil went its way unmolested. (Quoted, Sidney Lens, *The Forging of the American Empire*, Pluto Press, 2003, pp. 270–1)

In the 1950s, with firm US support, the Duvalier dictatorship took over. Anthropologist Robert Lawless commented that US support was conditional on Haiti accepting an economic programme featuring private investments from the United States that would be drawn to Haiti by such incentives as no customs taxes, a minimum wage kept very low, the suppression of labour unions, and the right of American companies to repatriate their profits: 'Largely because of its cheap labour force, extensive government repression, and denial of even minimal labour rights, Haiti is one of the most attractive countries for both the subcontractors and the maquilas' (quoted, Paul Farmer, *The Uses of Haiti*, Common Courage Press, 1994, p. 114).

This is the *Guardian* editors' version of Haiti's history: 'The US ignored [Haiti's] existence until 1862. Later, beginning in 1915, it occupied Haiti for 19 years and then abruptly left. Years of dictatorship and coups ensued' (Leader, 'From Bad to Worse', *Guardian*, February 14, 2004). Years of dictatorship merely 'ensued' – no mention is made of the dictatorship *during* the US occupation. There is also no hint that the following years of dictatorship were imposed by the US in order to maximise returns on investments.

On the rare occasions when US support for terror is admitted, the motivation – maximised profits – is out of sight. Thus Lyonel Trouillot wrote in the *New York Times* of how 'the United States's automatic backing of the Duvalier dictatorship because it was anti-Communist' resulted in terror ('In Haiti, All the Bridges Are Burned', *New York Times*, February 26, 2004).

## HAITI'S BIG SURPRISE – ARISTIDE

Terror-backed US exploitation continued in an unbroken line until December 1990 when Jean-Bertrand Aristide, a Catholic priest, won national elections with 67.5 per cent of the vote, beating the US-backed candidate, former World Bank official Marc Bazin, into second place with 14.2 per cent. The grass-roots movement that swept Aristide to power took the West completely by surprise. Aristide took office in February 1991 and was briefly the first democratically elected president in Haiti's history before being overthrown by a US-backed military coup on September 30, 1991. The Washington-based Council on Hemispheric Affairs observed after the coup: 'Under Aristide, for the first time in the republic's tortured history, Haiti seemed to be on the verge of tearing free from the fabric of despotism and tyranny which had smothered all previous attempts at democratic expression and self-determination.' His victory 'represented more than a decade of civic engagement and education on his part', in 'a textbook example of participatory, "bottom-up" and democratic political development' (quoted, Chomsky, *Year 501*, p. 209).

Aristide's balancing of the budget and 'trimming of a bloated bureaucracy' led to a 'stunning success' that made White House planners 'extremely uncomfortable'. The view of a US official 'with extensive experience of Haiti' summed up the reality beneath US rhetoric. Aristide – slum priest, grass-roots activist, exponent of Liberation Theology – 'represents everything that CIA, DOD and FBI think they have been trying to protect this country against for the past 50 years', he said (quoted, Paul Quinn-Judge, 'US Reported to Intercept Aristide Calls', *Boston Globe*, September 8, 1994).

Before deciding to run for office, Aristide had observed: 'Of course, the US has its own agenda here', namely: maximising its returns on investments.

> This is normal, capitalist behaviour, and I don't care if the US wants to do it at home ... But it is monstrous to come down here and impose your will on another people ... I cannot accept that Haiti should be whatever the United States wants it to be. (Quoted, Chomsky, *Year 501*, p. 211)

A Haitian businessman told a reporter shortly before the September 1991 coup: 'Everyone who is anyone is against Aristide. Except the people' (quoted, Farmer, *The Uses of Haiti*, p. 178).

Following the fall of Aristide, the Haitian army 'embarked on a systematic and continuing campaign to stamp out the vibrant civil society that has taken root in Haiti since the fall of the Duvalier dictatorship', Americas Watch noted (quoted, Chomsky, *Year 501*, p. 211). At least 1,000 people were killed in the first two weeks of the coup and hundreds more by December. The paramilitary forces were led by former CIA employees Emmanuel Constant and Raoul Cédras. Aristide was forced into exile from 1991 until 1994.

In response to the coup, the Organisation of American States announced an embargo and sanctions. The US immediately declared 800 of its firms 'exempt'. As a result levels of US trade increased by around 50 per cent under the embargo. Noam Chomsky summarises the situation:

> Well, as this was all going on, the Haitian generals in effect were being told [by Washington]: 'Look, murder the leaders of the popular organisations, intimidate the whole population, destroy anyone who looks like they might get in the way after you're gone.' ... And that's exactly what Cédras and those guys did, that's precisely what happened – and of course they were given total amnesty when they finally did agree to step down. (*Understanding Power*, The New Press, 2002, p. 157)

Writing in the *Nation* in October 1994, US journalist Allan Nairn quoted paramilitary leader Emmanuel Constant as saying that he had been contacted by a US military officer, Colonel Patrick Collins, who served as defence attaché at the United States Embassy in the Haitian capital, Port-au-Prince. Constant said Collins pressed him to set up a group to 'balance the Aristide movement' and to do 'intelligence' work against it (U.S. Newswire, 'Haitian Terror Group Promoted and Backed by U.S. Intelligence Says Article in Nation Magazine', October 6, 1994). Constant admitted that, at the time, he was working with CIA operatives in Haiti. Constant and other paramilitary leaders were trained in Ecuador by US Special Forces between 1991 and 1994.

One phone call from Washington would have been enough to stop the generals, Howard French noted in the *New York Times*. But 'Washington's deep-seated ambivalence about a leftward-tilting nationalist' prevented action. 'Despite much blood on the army's hands, United States diplomats consider it a vital counterweight to Father Aristide, whose class-struggle rhetoric ... threatened or antagonized traditional power centres at home and abroad' (French, 'Aristide Seeks More than Moral Support', *New York Times*, September 27, 1992).

In 1994, the US returned Aristide in the company of 20,000 troops after the coup leaders had slaughtered much of the popular movement that had brought him to power. The title of a 1994 article by Douglas Farah in the *International Herald Tribune* summed up the horror: 'Grass Roots of Democracy in Haiti: All but Dead' (May 10, 1994).

The day before US troops landed, the Associated Press reported that American oil companies had been supplying oil directly to the Haitian coup leaders in violation of the embargo with the authorisation of the Clinton and Bush administrations at the highest level. Although the world's media were intensely focused on Haiti at the time, the revelations were met with near-total silence in the US press.

Human Rights Watch described 'disappointing' aspects of the US military intervention:

> The United States, notably, showed little enthusiasm for the prosecution of past abuses. Indeed, it even impeded accountability by removing to the US thousands of documents from military and paramilitary headquarters, allowing notorious abusers to flee Haiti, and giving safe haven to paramilitary leader Emmanuel 'Toto' Constant. ('Recycled Soldiers and Paramilitaries on the March', February 27, 2004)

Kenneth Roth, executive director of Human Rights Watch, wrote about the documents seized by the US in a letter to the *New York Times*:

> The Clinton Administration refuses to return these documents without first removing the names of Americans. The Administration's apparent motive is to avoid embarrassing revelations about the involvement of American intelligence agents with the military regime that ruled Haiti. ('US Must Release Evidence on Haitian Abuses', *New York Times*, April 12, 1997)

Crucially, Aristide's return was permitted only when he accepted both the US military occupation and Washington's harsh neo-liberal agenda. His government was to implement a standard 'structural adjustment' package, with foreign funds devoted primarily to debt repayment and the needs of the business sectors, and with an 'open foreign investment policy'.

The plans for the economy were set out in a document submitted to the Paris Club of international donors at the World Bank in August 1994. The Haiti desk officer of the World Bank, Axel Peuker, described the plan as beneficial to the 'more open, enlightened, business class' and foreign investors. The Haitian Minister in charge of rural development and agrarian reform was not even told about the plan (quoted, Noam Chomsky, 'Democracy Restored', *Z Magazine*, November 1994).

Aristide also agreed to dismiss his prime minister and to replace him with a businessman from the traditional elite who was 'known to be opposed to the populist policies during Aristide's seven months in power' and was 'generally well regarded by the business community' (Michael Norton, 'Deal to Restore its President Leaves Haiti Hopeful, Wary', *Chicago Sun-Times*, July 18, 1993).

## MEDIA SILENCE ON WASHINGTON'S 'DOUBLE GAME'

Now consider the 'free press' version of these events. First, *The Times*:

> Mr Aristide, a former Roman Catholic priest, won Haiti's first free elections in 1990, promising to end the country's relentless cycle of corruption, poverty and demagoguery. Ousted in a coup the following year, he was restored to power with the help of 20,000 US troops in 1994. (Tim Reid, 'Barricades Go Up as City Braces for Attack', *The Times*, February 26, 2004)

There was not a word about the long, documented history of US support for mass murderers attacking Aristide's democratic government and killing his supporters; no mention of the hidden agenda behind Aristide's restoration to power, or of the limits imposed on his range of options by the superpower protecting its business interests.

The *Guardian* wrote:

> To a degree, history repeated itself when the US intervened again in 1994 to restore Mr Aristide. Bill Clinton halted the influx of Haitian boat people that had become politically awkward in Florida. Then he moved on. Although the US has pumped in about $900m in the past decade, consistency and vision have been lacking. (Leader, 'From Bad to Worse', *Guardian*, February 14, 2004)

In reality there has been *great* consistency and vision in exploiting the people of Haiti for Western gain. Ignoring mountains of evidence, the *Guardian* reported: 'The US [was] at one time a staunch ally' of Aristide (Agencies, 'Haitian Rebels Continue Advance on Capital', Guardian Unlimited, February 27, 2004).

In the *Daily Mail*, Ross Benson wrote of the Haitian boat people:

> It was to stem that flow and keep what the former American presidential candidate, Pat Buchanan, colourfully if disgracefully called 'the Zulus off

Miami Beach' that, three years later, 20,000 US Marines invaded and restored Aristide to his white-domed palace that looks as if it might have been built for Saddam Hussein ... ('The Land of Voodoo', *Daily Mail*, February 28, 2004)

There was no mention of Aristide's achievements or of the US determination to destroy them. We note that Buchanan's 'colourful' language was disgraceful enough to merit repetition.

The BBC reported: 'Months later [Aristide] was overthrown in a bloody military coup, but returned to power in 1994 after the new rulers were forced to step down under international pressure and with the help of US troops' ('Country profile: Haiti', February 14, 2004, <http://news.bbc.co.uk>). Again, not a word about the double game being played by the US at the expense of the Haitian people and their democracy. Indeed, in the mainstream reports we saw, we found almost no mention of US commercial interests in Haiti, or of the ruthless US determination to protect them.

## ARISTIDE TOPPLED – THE DISPUTED ELECTIONS

Jean-Bertrand Aristide told the Associated Press that he had again been forced to leave Haiti in 2004, this time by US military forces. Asked if he had left of his own accord, Aristide answered: 'No. I was forced to leave. Agents were telling me that if I don't leave they would start shooting and killing in a matter of time' (Eliott C. McLaughlin, Associated Press, March 1, 2004).

'Haiti, again, is ablaze', Jeffrey Sachs, professor of economics at Columbia University, wrote: 'Almost nobody, however, understands that today's chaos was made in Washington – deliberately, cynically, and steadfastly. History will bear this out' (Sachs, 'Fanning the Flames of Political Chaos in Haiti', *Nation*, February 28, 2004). As Sachs argued, the Bush administration had been pursuing policies likely to topple Aristide since 2001:

I visited President Aristide in Port-au-Prince in early 2001. He impressed me as intelligent and intent on good relations with Haiti's private sector and the US.

Haiti was clearly desperate: the most impoverished country in the Western Hemisphere, with a standard of living comparable to sub-Saharan Africa despite being only a few hours by air from Miami. Life expectancy was 52 years. Children were chronically hungry. (Ibid.)

When he returned to Washington, Sachs spoke to senior officials in the IMF, World Bank, Inter-American Development Bank, and Organisation of American States. He described how he expected to hear that these organisations would be rushing to help Haiti. Not so:

> Instead, I was shocked to learn that they would all be suspending aid, under vague 'instructions' from the US. America, it seemed, was unwilling to release aid to Haiti because of irregularities in the 2000 legislative elections, and was insisting that Aristide make peace with the political opposition before releasing any aid.
>
> The US position was a travesty. Aristide had been elected President in an indisputable landslide [in 1990] ... Nor were the results of the legislative elections in 2000 in doubt: Aristide's party had also won in a landslide. (Ibid.).

Two elections took place in May and November 2000. A range of political parties, including Aristide's Lavalas party, contested elections in May. As a result, Aristide dominated the new parliament, holding 19 of the 27 Senate seats and 72 of the 82 lower house seats. Two hundred international observers assessed the elections as satisfactory. Peter Hallward of King's College London commented in the *Guardian*:

> An exhaustive and convincing report by the International Coalition of Independent Observers concluded that 'fair and peaceful elections were held' in 2000, and by the standard of the presidential elections held in the US that same year they were positively exemplary. ('Why They Had to Crush Aristide', *Guardian*, March 2, 2004)

Why then were the elections criticised as 'flawed' by the Organisation of American States (OAS)?

> It was because, after Aristide's Lavalas party had won 16 out of 17 senate seats, the OAS contested the methodology used to calculate the voting percentages. Curiously, neither the US nor the OAS judged this methodology problematic in the run-up to the elections. (Ibid.)

Methodology was contested in the election of eight senators out of a total of 7,500 posts filled. President Aristide persuaded seven of the eight senators to resign. He also agreed to OAS proposals for new elections. The opposition Democratic Convergence, however, rejected the suggestion, demanding instead that Aristide immediately vacate the presidency. Analyst Yifat Susskind explained: 'Members of Haiti's elite, long hostile to Aristide's progressive economic agenda, saw the controversy as an opportunity to derail his government' ('Haiti', op. cit.). On November 26, 2000, Aristide was nevertheless re-elected president with his Lavalas party winning 90 per cent of the vote.

Haiti's 2000 elections may have been imperfect but, given Haiti's history of appalling dictatorships and violence, they marked a major step forward in democracy. It made no sense, other than to protect its interests, for the US to react so aggressively by cutting off vital aid, just as it made no sense for the West to insist that Haiti should, yet again, submit to military violence in 2004. US Congresswoman Barbara Lee challenged Colin Powell: 'It appears that the US is aiding and abetting the attempt to violently topple the Aristide government. With all due respect, this looks like "regime change" ... Our actions – or inaction – may be making things worse' (quoted, Anthony Fenton, 'Media vs. Reality in Haiti', February 13, 2004, <http://zmag.org>).

Consider *The Times'* version of these events:

> Mr Aristide will doubtless protest that a democratically elected figure such as himself should never be asked to submit to the will of self-appointed rebels. He has a point, but, in his case, it is a limited one. Mr Aristide won a second term in office four years ago in a manner that suggested fraud on a substantial scale. The resentment left by his flawed victory, his increasingly despotic and erratic rule and the wholesale collapse of the local economy inspired the rebellion against him. (Leader, 'Au Revoir Aristide', *The Times*, March 1, 2004)

This is the same *Times* which, in response to Iraq's invasion of Kuwait in 1990, called for 'a worldwide expression of anger at a small nation's sovereignty rudely shattered by brute force' (Leader, 'Iraq's Naked Villainy', *The Times*, August 3, 1990). The cause in Kuwait was 'simple on a world scale', *The Times* wrote grandly, 'the defence of the weak against aggression by the strong' (Leader, 'No Mock Heroics', *The Times*, January 18, 1991). Imagine *The Times* suggesting that the current leaders of Iraq would only have a limited point in refusing to 'submit to the will of self-appointed rebels'. In Iraq, after all, there is no mere suggestion of fraud but the clear fact of a government installed under illegal superpower occupation.

In an article titled, 'The Little Priest Who Became a Bloody Dictator Like the One He Once Despised', the *Independent*'s Andrew Gumbel wrote of Aristide:

> Then in 1994, undaunted, he returned, messianic again, backed by 20,000 US troops and disbanded the Haitian military. He had the goodwill of the world, the overwhelming support of his electorate and plentiful funds from international aid agencies to breathe life into Haiti's moribund economy. ('The Little Priest Who Became a Bloody Dictator Like the One He Once Despised', *Independent*, February 21, 2004)

As we described above, the 'goodwill of the world' was expressed by supporting the massacre of the grass-roots movement that had brought Aristide to power.

Aristide *had* presided over human rights abuses, including corruption and attempts to suppress dissent and intimidate opponents. However, journalist Tom Reeves put the title of Gumbel's article into perspective: 'Whatever Aristide's mistakes and weaknesses have been (and they are many), they pale when compared to the extreme brutality of those who are today implicated in the violence in Gonaives and elsewhere in Haiti' ('The US Double Game in Haiti', February 16, 2004, <www.countercurrents.org/haiti-reeves170204. htm>). In 2003, Reeves asked a group of Haitians in Cap-Haïtien about Aristide's performance. One responded:

> We don't think Aristide is doing a good job, but at least now we can talk, we are free to come and go. The Macoute must not come back ... Yes, there is corruption and police brutality. But to compare our government with dictators is a hypocritical lie! (Reeves, 'Haiti and the US Game', ZNet, March 27, 2003, <www.zmag.org/content/print_article.cfm?itemID=3337&sectionID=2>)

The US lawyer representing the government of Haiti accused the US government of direct involvement in the 2004 military coup against Aristide. Ira Kurzban, the Miami-based attorney who had served as general counsel to the Haitian government since 1991, said that the paramilitaries who overthrew Aristide were backed by Washington: 'I believe that this is a group that is armed by, trained by, and employed by the intelligence services of the United States. This is clearly a military operation, and it's a military coup' (Amy Goodman and Jeremy Scahil, 'Haiti's Lawyer: US Is Arming Anti-

Aristide Paramilitaries, Calls for UN Peacekeepers', February 26, 2004, <www.democracynow.org>). Kurzban added: 'There's enough indications from our point of view, at least from my point of view, that the United States certainly knew what was coming about two weeks before this military operation started. The United States made contingency plans for Guantanamo' (ibid.).

Writing of the rebels in the *Daily Mail*, Ross Benson buried the known facts past and present:

> One of their commanders is Louis Jodel Chamberlain, leader of the army death squads before and after the 1991 coup, who is held to be responsible for the death of 5,000 men, women and children. He is not, to put it mildly, the kind of man that any American administration would wish to deal with. ('The Land of Voodoo', *Daily Mail*, February 28, 2004)

For the *Independent*'s comment editor Adrian Hamilton, the US's worst crime was inaction: 'It is quite wrong to wash our hands of Haiti's future as we are now doing. It doesn't mean instant invasion, but it does mean making clear that we will not accept a military regime without democratic legitimacy' ('Why it Is Wrong to Wash Our Hands of Haiti,' *Independent*, February 26, 2004). Once again we find ourselves asking the question posed by dissident playwright Harold Pinter:

> When they said 'We had to do something', I said: 'Who is this "we" exactly that you're talking about? First of all: Who is the "we"? Under what heading do "we" act, under what law? And also, the notion that this "we" has the right to act,' I said, 'presupposes a moral authority of which this "we" possesses not a jot! It doesn't exist!' (interview with David Edwards, 1999, <www.medialens. org/articles/the_articles/articles_2001/de_Pinter.htm>)

It is a standard response of the liberal press to concoct a false, lesser Western misdemeanour – here, 'washing our hands of Haiti' – and then to rage at that invention. This promotes the liberal media's 'dissident' credentials, without harming, or calling down the wrath of, power.

The BBC reported: 'Haiti's political opposition has rejected a US-backed power-sharing plan aimed at ending the country's crisis' ('Haiti Power-Sharing Plan Rejected', February 25, 2004, <http://news. bbc.co.uk>). Once again, the US is depicted as an 'honest broker', as though Haiti's history were mere fantasy, non-existent. The BBC was happy to report without comment the proposal that a democratically elected government might share power with a gang of killers with a history of gross human rights abuses.

In similar vein, prior to Aristide's departure, ITN's international editor, Bill Neely, talked of George Bush 'losing patience' with the Haitian president – thus depicting Bush as somehow the benevolent father-figure in the wings (*ITV News* at 22:15, ITN, February 28, 2004). Reversing the truth on *BBC News*, Kathy Kay reported: 'Long-term stability in Haiti isn't likely without a long-term American commitment' (*BBC News at Ten*, BBC1, February 29, 2004). Krishnan Guru-Murthy of *Channel 4 News* wrote:

> The democratically elected leader finally gave in to the rebels saying he wanted to avoid bloodshed while the international community stood by and did nothing. Sometimes it seems, it isn't worth waiting for elections. The US had helped Aristide before, restoring him to power years ago, but they were not going to do it again and said his resignation was in the interests of the Haitian people. (Snowmail bulletin, February 29, 2004)

The level of analysis was hardly worthy of a high-school student. The *Guardian* wrote: 'Despite what Mr Aristide says, Haiti has no terrorists, no al-Qaida cells, as in Afghanistan' (leader, 'Failure of Will', *Guardian*, February 28, 2004). This was technically correct – for the media, 'terrorists' are by definition people who use terror and violence to threaten Western interests. People who use terror and violence to *promote* Western interests are therefore not terrorists. The *Guardian* continued:

> Yet what, at this moment of dire need, have the powers done about it? Nothing much is the answer. For all their doctrines and declarations, they have dithered and debated, ducked and dodged, and danced that old, slow diplomatic shuffle. (Ibid.)

No question, then, that 'the powers' might have been doing something other than wringing their hands behind the scenes.

On February 11, 2004, US Congresswoman Maxine Waters issued a press release calling on the Bush administration to condemn the 'so-called opposition' that was 'attempting to instigate a bloodbath in Haiti and then blame the government for the resulting disaster in the belief that the US will aid the so-called protestors against

President Aristide' (quoted, Fenton, 'Media vs. Reality in Haiti').
Waters pointed out:

> Under his leadership, the Haitian government has made major investments
> in agriculture, public transportation and infrastructure ... The government
> [recently] doubled the minimum wage from 36 to 70 gourdes per day, despite
> strong opposition from the business community ... President Aristide has
> also made health care and education national priorities. More schools were
> built in Haiti between 1994 and 2000 than between 1804 and 1994. The
> government expanded school lunch and school bus programs and provides
> a 70% subsidy for schoolbooks and uniforms. (Ibid.)

But, for Ross Benson of the *Daily Mail*, Aristide was the problem with
no redeeming achievements worth mentioning:

> Instead of enacting a programme of social and economic reform 'to give the
> people what is rightfully theirs', Aristide allowed his cronies to plunder the
> national till, as so many have done before in this lush island paradise with
> its turbulent past of bloodshed, greed and endless tyrannies. ('The Land of
> Voodoo')

Some time soon when Western interests are under attack, the media
will once again obediently rise up in outrage as the forces of violence
and terror threaten some distant democracy (real or imagined). But,
in 2004, our journalists and editors were happy to accept that Aristide
'had to go', that he had 'lost the support of his people and of the
international community'.

Forget the democratic process. Forget the landslide victories that
made a mockery of the popularity of Bush and Blair. Forget the tidal
waves of blood that preceded the first, imperfect sign that Haiti
might at last be waking from the nightmare of history – of endless
dictatorships, poverty, military coups, torture and death. None of
that mattered. What mattered to the media was power. What power
says goes.

As the writer Humbert Wolfe observed in 1930:

> You cannot hope to bribe or twist,
> thank God! the British journalist.
> But, seeing what the man will do
> unbribed, there's no occasion to.
> (Cited, Anthony Jay, *The Oxford Dictionary of Political Quotations*, Oxford
> University Press, 2001, p. 387)

# 9
# Idolatry Ink – Reagan, the 'Cheerful Conservative' and 'Chubby Bubba' Clinton

Victors do not investigate their own crimes, so that little is known about them, a principle that brooks few exceptions: the death toll of the US wars in Indochina, for example, is not known within a range of millions. (Noam Chomsky, *Hegemony or Survival – America's Quest for Global Dominance*, Routledge, 2003, p. 20)

## WILL THE REAL PAUL WOLFOWITZ PLEASE STAND UP?

As we have already seen in this book, the media has an almost unlimited capacity for obscuring the sins of the powerful. Consider BBC Washington correspondent Matt Frei's glowing report on US deputy secretary of defence, Paul Wolfowitz, as he was appointed president of the World Bank: 'You have to try and distinguish between the perception of Paul Wolfowitz as he starred in the Michael Moore film *Fahrenheit 9/11*, the famous neo-conservative, and the reality of Paul Wolfowitz, which is actually quite different' (*BBC News at Ten*, BBC1, March 16, 2005). Frei continued:

Well, before he was at the Pentagon, Paul Wolfowitz was many other things. He was a very powerful intellectual. He headed one of the great American universities. He was a very skilful diplomat, ambassador in Indonesia. He was under-secretary of state dealing with the Philippines at the time that that country was moving from dictatorship to democracy. He is someone who believes passionately in the power of democracy and grass-roots development. He knows a lot about developing countries. He knows about their problems. And actually even in the World Bank there are many people who think that if he combines the kind of technocratic ability from the Pentagon with his developing philosophy he could be extremely effective. (Ibid.)

This all sounds pretty admirable. Back in the real world Wolfowitz admirers agree that 'hawk' is too mild a description for the man they call 'Velociraptor'. After all, it was Wolfowitz who commented in the immediate aftermath of the September 11, 2001 attacks: 'It's not just a matter of capturing people and holding them accountable, but removing the sanctuaries, removing the support systems, ending states who sponsor terrorism' (quoted, Julian Borger, 'Washington's Hawk Trains Sights on Iraq', *Guardian*, September 26, 2001). Even Colin Powell, then US secretary of state, expressed contempt for these brutal words: 'I think "ending terrorism" is where I would leave it and let Mr Wolfowitz speak for himself' (ibid.).

Wolfowitz served as Reagan's ambassador to Indonesia, under the rule of Suharto, one of the worst mass murderers of the late twentieth century. Suharto presided over the killing of more than 1 million Indonesians in the bloodbath that began in 1965, and of 200,000 East Timorese, one-third of the entire population, beginning in 1975 (see Chapter 7). Suharto also amassed a family fortune estimated at anything between 15 billion and 35 billion US dollars.

Shortly before Suharto's overthrow in May 1997, Wolfowitz told Congress that

> any balanced judgment of the situation in Indonesia today, including the very important and sensitive issue of human rights, needs to take account of the significant progress that Indonesia has already made and needs to acknowledge that much of this progress has to be credited to the strong and remarkable leadership of president Suharto. (Cited, Noam Chomsky, email to David Edwards, March 18, 2005)

After the October 2002 Bali bombings, Wolfowitz informed a defence forum that 'the reason the terrorists are successful in Indonesia is because the Suharto regime fell and the methods that were used to suppress them are gone' – methods that included mass killings and horrific torture in East Timor, West Papua, and Aceh (ibid.).

Within days of the September 11, 2001 attacks, Wolfowitz began a campaign for military action against Iraq. He paid for former CIA director James Woolsey to travel to Britain to look for evidence of prior Iraqi involvement in terrorism. The US state department and the CIA were reported to be furious at Wolfowitz's role. One US source with close links to intelligence said: 'This is a group of people pursuing their own political agenda to bomb Iraq' (quoted, Julian Borger, 'Hawks Try to Damn Iraq by Hunting for Evidence in UK', *Guardian*, October 13, 2001).

Gerard Baker described this same man in *The Times* as 'a deeply cultured man with a firm and sometimes overly romantic belief in the centrality of human freedom as the defining theme of foreign policy' ('Cold-Eyed Ideologue Who Is a Romantic at Heart', *The Times*, March 18, 2005).

By contrast, consider Matt Frei's judgement of former US treasury secretary Paul O'Neill. O'Neill courageously broke ranks in 2004 to explain how the Bush administration had come to office determined to topple Saddam Hussein, using the September 11 attacks as a pretext (see Chapter 3).

O'Neill's claims were extremely important, confirming much that was known, or suspected, about the Bush–Blair commitment to war. Matt Frei, however, was unimpressed:

> If you remember, Paul O'Neill was sacked mainly because he was incompetent, and he was more infamous for his gaffes than his insights on economic theory. He once famously said that the collapse of the energy giant Enron was an example of the genius of capitalism, and perhaps more accurately that the tax code in America was 9,500 words of complete gibberish. (*Newsnight*, BBC2, January 12, 2004)

One can only guess at why Frei felt it was more important to focus attention on O'Neill's 'gaffes' than on his highly credible revelations exposing the lie that was the Bush–Blair case for war on Iraq.

## REAGAN – 'AN EXTRAORDINARILY SUCCESSFUL PRESIDENCY'

The death of Ronald Reagan on June 5, 2004 provided an even more dramatic case study in apologetics. On the BBC's *Newsnight* programme, presenter Gavin Esler said of Reagan: 'Many people believe that he restored faith in American military action after Vietnam through his willingness to use force, if necessary, in defence of American interests' (*Newsnight*, June 9, 2004). Reagan was, Esler insisted, 'a man who was loved even by his political opponents in this country [America] and abroad'. Esler portrayed Reagan as virtually an enlightened being, quoting Nancy Reagan to the effect that her husband 'had absolutely no ego' (ibid.).

Writing in the *Daily Mail*, Esler took the idea further still, presenting the egoless Reagan as a self-help guru:

> above all, Ronald Wilson Reagan embodied the best of the American spirit – the optimistic belief that problems can and will be solved, that tomorrow

will be better than today, and that our children will be wealthier and happier than we are. ('The Great Communicator', *Daily Mail*, June 7, 2004)

Reagan's politics were 'liberal' Esler noted, adding thoughtfully: 'What Reagan lacked in intellect, he more than made up in good looks and temperament' (ibid.).

It is interesting to recall that in December 2003, the *Guardian* had reported that senior BBC journalists and presenters had been banned from commenting on 'current affairs and contentious issues' in newspaper and magazine columns. Journalists would be able to pen 'non-contentious articles and food, film and music reviews', Jason Deans noted ('BBC Confirms Ban on Columnists', *Guardian*, December 16, 2003). Some columns would be in more difficulty than others, Matt Wells observed two days later. It was felt that Andrew Marr would be allowed to keep his *Daily Telegraph* diary column so long as he stuck to 'cultural matters' (Wells, 'Arts Reporter Rosie Millard Quits BBC for Fleet Street', *Guardian*, December 18, 2003).

The real meaning of the BBC ban becomes clear enough when we consider Esler's comments – highly contentious, indeed deeply offensive, propaganda, but promoting a power-friendly, patriotic view of the world, and therefore labelled 'non-contentious' by the scrupulously unbiased BBC. Eyebrows would perhaps have been raised if some of the facts we describe below had appeared in Esler's *Daily Mail* article.

Esler managed to make passing mention of the Iran–Contra affair in the *Mail*: 'They sold the Iranians U.S. weapons for use against Iraq, and then in a complicated plot channelled the profits to the Rightwing Contra guerrillas in Nicaragua ... The scandal blighted the last two years of an otherwise extraordinarily successful presidency', he noted. Readers might like to keep Esler's judgement of Reagan's 'extraordinarily successful presidency' in mind while reading what follows, while also recalling that Esler is a presenter of the BBC's flagship *Newsnight* programme.

Younger readers would of course have had little or no clue what the reference to 'Rightwing Contra guerrillas' funded by Iran–Contra signified, and almost no one can fully understand the reality for the people who paid the price in Nicaragua. But then it is not important to make sense in the media; it is important only to be able to bandy the jargon of media discourse in a way that suggests in-depth knowledge: Iran–Contra, IMF, G8, the 'roadmap to peace', 'UN resolution 1441', and so on. Media analyst Robert McChesney comments:

We are bombarded with information, although if you look closely, most of it has a similar grammar, a similar focus and similar sources, all revolving around institutions and topics that most viewers admit in survey after survey they don't really understand. (Danny Schechter, *The More You Watch, the Less You Know*, Seven Stories, 1997, p. 43)

'Iran–Contra' – whatever it might mean – was given passing mention throughout the media in the wake of Reagan's death. Thus, 'One of the low-points of the presidency was the Iran–Contra scandal', Peter Hitchens wrote in the *Sunday Express*. Hitchens explained that this involved a 'disastrous attempt to trade arms for hostages with Iran, linked with arms supplies to the right-wing Contra rebels in Nicaragua' ('The Man Who Knocked Down the Berlin Wall', *Sunday Express*, June 6, 2004). Hitchens thus explained precisely nothing.

Other commentators provided glimpses of a larger picture: 'His [Reagan's] hatred of Communism meant he bent over backwards to support anti-communist insurgencies in Central America, Asia and Africa' (Chris Mclaughlin, Political Editor, 'Ronald Reagan 1911–2004', *Sunday Mirror*, June 6, 2004). At least a hint of some larger involvement in Central America was provided – but once again it was impossible to understand what this meant for people in the region. The *Sunday Times* provided a few more clues:

In Central America he [Reagan] proved incapable of curbing Nicaragua's left-wing Sandinista regime, although he had more success in the fight against leftist guerrillas in El Salvador ... His get-tough policy on terrorism and the 'enemies of America' proved little more than rhetoric. (Tony Allen-Mills, 'Reagan, the Cowboy President Who Rallied the Western World', *Sunday Times*, June 6, 2004)

Presumably, then, nothing very nasty happened to the 'enemies of America', untroubled by mere 'rhetoric'. In the *Guardian*, David Aaronovitch promised much with his title, 'The Terrible Legacy of the Reagan Years', before burying the truth in standard apologetics:

What isn't so easy to forgive is the Reagan Doctrine, sometimes known as Third World Rollback. Rollback was the American end of the proxy war fought between the two superpowers for power and influence in the developing world. The basis was childishly simple: my enemy's enemy is my friend ... In Central America the doctrine required supporting the 'contra' rebels in Nicaragua, and backing for the Guatemalan government which – during the Reagan era – may have killed more than 100,000 Mayan Indians. Reagan described the contras as being like America's 'founding fathers' and Guatemala's hard man, Rios Montt, as 'a man of great personal integrity'. ('The Terrible Legacy of the Reagan Years', *Guardian*, June 8, 2004)

In fact, the real motive behind the American slaughter in the Third World – profits, not fear of the Soviet Union – is indicated by patterns of investment. The 1973 coup in Chile that installed the murderous Pinochet regime led to a 558 per cent increase in US economic aid and a 1,079 per cent increase in US and multinational credits (see Milan Rai, *Chomsky's Politics*, Verso, 1995, p. 67 for figures that follow).

The 1964 military coup in Brazil led to a deterioration in human rights while overall US aid and credits increased 110 per cent in the three years following the coup, compared with the three years preceding it.

After the CIA-driven coup in Iran in 1953, total US and multinational aid and credits increased nine-fold. US Iran specialist Eric Hoogland commented on the Shah: 'The more dictatorial his regime became, the closer the US–Iran relationship became' (quoted, Curtis, *The Ambiguities of Power – British Foreign Policy Since 1945*, Zed Books, 1995, p. 95). This of a country that had the 'highest rate of death penalties in the world, no valid system of civilian courts and a history of torture' which was 'beyond belief', in a society in which 'the entire population was subjected to a constant, all-pervasive terror', according to Amnesty International (Martin Ennals, secretary general of Amnesty International, cited in an Amnesty Publication, *Matchbox*, Autumn 1976).

After the US overthrew the government of Guatemala in 1954, total US and multinational aid and credits increased 5,300 per cent. Within two months of the coup, some 8,000 peasants had been murdered in a terror campaign that targeted union organisers and Indian village leaders. The US Embassy lent its assistance, providing lists of 'communists' to be eliminated, imprisoned and tortured. Exiled journalist Julio Godoy, who had worked on the Guatemalan newspaper *La Epoca*, whose offices were blown up by US-backed terrorists, compared conditions in Guatemala with those in Eastern Europe:

While the Moscow-imposed government in Prague would degrade and humiliate reformers, the Washington-made government in Guatemala would kill them. It still does, in a virtual genocide that has taken more than 150,000 victims [in what Amnesty International calls] 'a government programme of political murder'. (Quoted, Noam Chomsky, *What Uncle Sam Really Wants*, Odonian Press, 1993, p. 50)

Finally, a *Guardian* editorial:

What is beyond doubt is that Mr Reagan made America feel good about itself again. He was ... 'the first truly cheerful conservative'. He gave American conservatism a humanity and hope that it never had in the Goldwater or Nixon eras, but which endures today because of him, to the frustration of many more ideological conservatives. Unlike them, Mr Reagan was a congenital optimist, 'hardwired for courtesy', as his former speechwriter Peggy Noonan puts it. (Leader, 'A Rose-Tinted President', *Guardian*, 7 June, 2004)

This is establishment propaganda of the most wretched kind from the UK's 'leading liberal newspaper'.

Let us now consider what this 'first truly cheerful conservative' actually did to Central America.

## KILLING IS NOT ENOUGH

Forget the smiles, the great communicating, the good looks and the talk of fighting Communism – the basic policy goals of US power in Central America are clearly spelled out in US government documents. In 1954, the National Security Council produced a Top Secret Memorandum titled 'US Policy Toward Latin America' (NSC 5432).

The document described how the biggest regional threat to US interests was 'the trend in Latin America toward nationalistic regimes' that responded to 'popular demand for immediate improvement in the low living standards of the masses' and for production geared to domestic needs. This trend was in direct collision with US policy, the report noted, which was committed to 'encouraging a climate conducive to private investment', and had to 'encourage' the Latin American countries 'to base their economies on a system of private enterprise, and, as essential thereto, to create a political and economic climate conducive to private investment of both domestic and foreign capital', including guarantees for the 'opportunity to earn and in the case of foreign capital to repatriate a reasonable return'.

In other words, US policy in Central America had nothing to do with anti-Communism; it had to do with controlling Third World natural and human resources for the benefit of Western corporations at the expense of local peoples. US internal documents have since restated these principles many times.

Reagan's eight years in office (1981–89) produced a vast bloodbath as Washington funnelled money, weapons and supplies to client dictators and right-wing death squads battling independent nationalism across Central America. The death toll over that period was staggering: more than 70,000 political killings in El Salvador, more than 100,000 in Guatemala, and 30,000 killed in the US Contra war waged against Nicaragua. Journalist Allan Nairn describes it as 'One of the most intensive campaigns of mass murder in recent history' (Democracy Now, June 8, 2004). Analyst Chalmers Johnson noted that 'the Reagan years [were] the worst decade for Central America since the Spanish conquest' (quoted, Milan Rai, *War Plan Iraq*, Verso, 2002, p. 29).

Consider the fate of El Salvador. In the 18-month period leading up to elections in El Salvador in March 1982, 26 journalists were murdered. In December 1981, the Salvadoran Communal Union reported that 83 of its members had been murdered by government security forces and death squads. The entire six-person top leadership of the main opposition party, the FDR, was seized by US-backed government security forces in 1980, tortured, murdered and mutilated. More generally, any left-wing political leader or organiser who gained any kind of prominence in El Salvador in the years 1980–83 was liable to be murdered. Between October 1979 and March 1982, killings of ordinary citizens occurred at the average rate of over 800 per month, on conservative estimates.

To put this level of violence in perspective, Edward Herman and Frank Brodhead converted the figures to a country with the population size of the United States. Doing so, they reported, 'allows us to imagine an election in the United States preceded by the murder of a thousand-odd officials of the Democratic Party; 5,000 labour leaders; 1,200 journalists; and a million ordinary citizens. Internal and external refugee numbers in El Salvador would correspond to a US equivalent of over 30 million refugees' (Herman and Brodhead, *Demonstration Elections*, South End Press, 1984, p. 125).

Between 1980 and 1983, Amnesty International 'received regular, often daily, reports identifying El Salvador's regular security and military units as responsible for the torture, "disappearance" and killing of noncombatant civilians from all sectors of society'. Moreover, 'the vast majority of the victims' were 'characterised by their association or alleged association with peasant, labour or religious organisations, with human rights monitoring groups, with the trade union movement, with refugee or relief organisations, or with political parties' (quoted, Curtis, *The Ambiguities of Power*, p.161). This was at a time when the US was directing vast amounts of military aid into the country.

The terror continued throughout the decade. In November 1989, six Jesuit priests, their cook and her daughter, were murdered by the army. That same week, at least 28 other Salvadoran civilians were murdered, including the head of a major union, the leader of the organisation of university women, nine members of an Indian farming cooperative and ten university students.

The Jesuits were murdered by the Atlacatl Battalion, created, trained and equipped by the United States. It was formed in March 1981, when 15 specialists in counter-insurgency were sent to El Salvador from the US Army School of Special Forces. The battalion was consistently engaged in mass killing. A US trainer described its soldiers as 'particularly ferocious ... We've always had a hard time getting them to take prisoners instead of ears' (quoted, Chomsky, *What Uncle Sam Really Wants*, <www.thirdworldtraveler.com/Chomsky/ChomOdon_ElSalvador.html>).

In December 1981, the battalion killed a thousand civilians in a massacre that involved murder, rape and burning. Later, it was involved in the bombing of villages and the murder of hundreds of civilians by shooting, drowning and other horrors. The majority of its victims were women, children and the elderly.

The results of Salvadoran military training were graphically described in the Jesuit journal *America* by Daniel Santiago, a Catholic priest working in El Salvador. Santiago told of a peasant woman who came home one day to find her three children, her mother and her sister sitting around a table, each with their own decapitated head placed carefully on the table in front of the body, the hands arranged on top 'as if each body was stroking its own head'. The killers, from the US-backed Salvadoran National Guard, had struggled to keep the head of an 18-month-old baby in place, so its hands were nailed onto it. A large plastic bowl filled with blood stood in the centre of the table. Noam Chomsky comments:

According to Rev. Santiago, macabre scenes of this kind aren't uncommon. People are not just killed by death squads in El Salvador – they are decapitated and then their heads are placed on pikes and used to dot the landscape. Men are not just disembowelled by the Salvadoran Treasury Police; their severed genitalia are stuffed into their mouths. Salvadoran women are not just raped by the National Guard; their wombs are cut from their bodies and used to cover their faces. It is not enough to kill children; they are dragged over barbed wire until the flesh falls from their bones, while parents are forced to watch. (Ibid.)

Raising a classic 'red scare', secretary of state Alexander Haig asserted in 1982 that he had 'overwhelming and irrefutable' evidence that the guerrillas were controlled from outside El Salvador (quoted, William Blum, *Killing Hope: US Military and CIA Interventions Since World War II*, Common Courage Press, 1995, p. 363). However, a *New York Times* reporter asked former Salvadoran leader Jose Napoleon Duarte why there were guerrillas in the hills. The reason, Duarte said, was:

Fifty years of lies, fifty years of injustice, fifty years of frustration. This is a history of people starving to death, living in misery. For fifty years the same people had all the power, all the money, all the jobs, all the education, all the opportunities. (Ibid., p. 353)

As elsewhere in the Third World, desperate poverty and crude exploitation, not Soviet designs, were at the heart of the conflict, a view confirmed even by the US ambassador to El Salvador, Robert White: 'The revolution situation came about in El Salvador because you had what was one of the most selfish oligarchies the world has ever seen, combined with a corrupt security force ...' (Ibid., pp. 364–5).

This was an example of the 'Communism' that US-backed insurgents were fighting, according to the *Sunday Mirror*. As Piero Gleijeses wrote: 'Just as the Indian was branded a savage beast to justify his exploitation, so those who sought social reform were branded communists to justify their persecution' (*Politics and Culture in Guatemala*, University of Michigan, 1988, p. 392).

The American media watch site Fairness and Accuracy in Reporting (FAIR) reported that a search of major US newspapers turned up the phrase 'death squad' just five times in connection with Reagan in the days following his death – twice in commentaries and twice in letters to the editor. Remarkably, only one news article mentioned death squads as part of Reagan's legacy. The three broadcast networks, CNN and Fox made no mention of death squads at all (Media Advisory: 'Reagan: Media Myth and Reality', June 9, 2004, <www.fair.org>). At time of writing (April 2005), the *Guardian/Observer* website records 180 articles mentioning the words 'Saddam and Halabja' between

1998 and the present; the words 'Reagan and death squads' are mentioned in 15 articles over the same eight-year period.

## NICARAGUA – THE THREAT OF A GOOD EXAMPLE

The Sandinista revolution of 1979 overthrew Nicaragua's brutal, US-backed Somoza dictatorship. Under Somoza, two-thirds of children under five were malnourished; less than one-fifth of under-fives and pregnant women received health care; nine out of ten rural homes had no safe drinking water. The UN estimated that over 60 per cent of the population lived in critical poverty (Diana Melrose, 'The Threat of a Good Example', Oxfam, 1985). In this society the richest 5 per cent of the population accounted for one-third of national income while the poorest half received 15 per cent.

Four years later, in 1983, the World Council of Churches reported that post-revolutionary Nicaragua 'for the first time offers the Nicaraguan people a modicum of justice for all rather than a society offering privilege exclusively to the wealthy ... and the powerful' (quoted, ibid.). In 1985, Oxfam reported:

> The cornerstone of the new development strategy, spelled out by the Sandinista Front some years before taking power, was to give priority to meeting the basic needs of the poor majority ... In Oxfam's experience of working in seventy-six developing countries, Nicaragua was to prove exceptional in the strength of that government commitment. (Ibid.)

This may come as news to many British readers. British historian Mark Curtis examined over 500 articles on Nicaragua in the *Financial Times*, *Times* and *Daily Telegraph* for the years 1981–83. On the subject of the unprecedented Sandinista success in directing resources to the Nicaraguan poor, out of the 500 articles, Curtis found *one* (in *The Times*) that discussed the issue.

In 1981, in support of fierce economic sanctions, the CIA allocated $20 million to building a 500-man force to conduct political and para-military operations against Nicaragua. Joining with Somoza supporters, this 'Contra' force enjoyed zero support within the country. A leaked Defence Department document in July 1983 described how 'support for democratic resistance [the Contras] within Nicaragua does not exist' (quoted, Curtis, *The Ambiguities of Power*, p. 160).

In 1982–84 alone, over 7,000 civilians were killed by the Contras. According to Oxfam, the 'prime targets', were 'individual leaders and community organisers who have worked hardest to improve the lives of the poor' (Melrose, 'The Threat of a Good Example', pp. 27–9).

A 1984 CIA manual designed for the Contras advised: 'It is possible to neutralise carefully selected and planned targets, such as court judges, mesta judges [justices of the peace], police and state officials, etc.' Writer Holly Sklar commented: 'A hit list that starts with court judges and ends with *etcetera* is a mighty broad license for murder' (quoted, William Blum, *Rogue State*, Common Courage Press, 2002, p. 47).

Also in 1984, congressional intelligence committees were informed by the CIA, by present and former Contra leaders, and by other witnesses, that the Contras had 'raped, tortured and killed unarmed civilians, including children' and that 'groups of civilians, including women and children, were burned, dismembered, blinded and beheaded' (*New York Times*, December 27, 1984). In 1985, Americas Watch reported that the Contras 'have attacked civilians indiscriminately; they have tortured and mutilated prisoners; they have murdered those placed *hors de combat* by their wounds; they have taken hostages; and they have committed outrages against personal dignity' (quoted, Curtis, *The Ambiguities of Power*, p. 172). These are the rebels Ronald Reagan described as 'freedom fighters' and as 'the moral equal of our Founding Fathers' (quoted, John Pilger, *Heroes*, Pan, 1989, p. 505).

In January 1984, the British prime minister, Margaret Thatcher, said: 'We support the United States' aim to promote peaceful change, democracy and economic development' in Central America (quoted, Curtis, *The Ambiguities of Power*, p. 162).

In June 1986, the World Court rejected US claims that it was exercising 'collective self-defence' in its policy towards Nicaragua and declared that the US 'by training, arming, equipping, financing and supplying the Contra forces' had acted 'in breach of its obligations under customary international law not to intervene in the affairs of another state' (quoted, Holly Sklar, *Washington's War on Nicaragua*, Between the Lines, 1988, p. 314). Following the judgement of the World Court, the US escalated its terrorist war ordering its forces to go 'after soft targets' and to avoid engaging the Nicaraguan army, according to General John Galvin, commander of US Southern Command. Teachers, health workers, human rights activists – all were targeted for torture and death (quoted, Fred Kaplan, *Boston Globe*, May 20, 1987).

Thomas Carothers, a former Reagan State Department official, observed that the death toll in Nicaragua 'in per capita terms was significantly higher than the number of US persons killed in the US Civil War and all the wars of the twentieth century *combined*.' (quoted, Chomsky, *Hegemony or Survival*, p. 98). Carothers added that the US sought to maintain 'the basic order of ... quite undemocratic societies' and to avoid 'populist-based change' that might upset 'the traditional structures of power with which the United States has long been allied' (quoted, ibid., p. 137).

The real problem was that the Sandinistas were working to lift the yoke of crushing poverty from the poor in one small Central American country. Their success threatened to unleash a wave of hope among poor people across the region at potentially huge cost to Western corporations profiting from despair. This was the reality of Nicaragua's 'threat of a good example'. Mark Curtis explained:

> Rather than the fantasy of preventing the creation of a 'Soviet bridgehead' on the Central American mainland or preventing the USSR from dominating the world ... the principal US goal in the war against Nicaragua was clearly the destruction of this threat of a good example; the war was, therefore, a continuation of traditional US foreign policy priorities. (*The Ambiguities of Power*, p. 165)

This is the full horror of Reagan's policy in Central America – it involved terrorising impoverished people into accepting a status quo that condemned them to lives of profitable misery.

A crucial component of this terror is simple media silence – wealthy Western journalists do not torture and kill, but the torture and killing could not occur without their complicity. It is why high-profile journalists are paid such large sums. Even journalistic souls do not come cheap, and there is much at stake.

The killing silence takes many forms. Thus, as noted, David Aaronovitch described the assault on Nicaragua as part of 'the proxy war fought between the two superpowers for power and influence'. In fact it was about profit and greed. The BBC noted that Reagan was 'Banned by Congress from supporting anti-Communist fighters in Nicaragua' ('Critics Question Reagan legacy', June 9, 2004, <http://news.bbc.co.uk>). Anything can be said as long as it leads the public away from the ferocious truth.

The consequences of Reagan's annihilation of the Sandinistas were catastrophic for Nicaragua – a 35 per cent increase in child deaths from malnutrition, mass starvation on the Atlantic coast, and UN warnings that the next generation would be 'smaller, weaker, and less intelligent' as a result.

## REAGAN'S LEGACY IN CENTRAL AMERICA

In Guatemala some 200,000 people were killed in a 'government programme of political murder' over 36 years from 1954 onwards, according to Amnesty International. The government in question was installed, armed and trained by the United States. The UN Economic Commission for Latin America and the Caribbean reported that the percentage of the Guatemalan population living in extreme poverty increased rapidly from 45 per cent in 1985 to 76 per cent in 1988, in the last half of the Reagan presidency.

Other studies estimated that 20,000 Guatemalans were dying of hunger every year under Reagan's 'extraordinarily successful presidency', that more than 1,000 children died of measles alone in the first four months of 1990, and that 'the majority of Guatemala's four million children receive no protection at all, not even for the most elemental rights' (quoted, Noam Chomsky, 'The Victors', Z Magazine, November 1990; January 1991; and April 1991).

In 1990, the Inter-American Development Bank reported that per capita income had fallen to the level of 1971 in Guatemala, 1961 in El Salvador, and 1960 in Nicaragua. The Pan American Health Organization estimated that of 850,000 children born every year in Central America, 100,000 would die before the age of five and two-thirds of those who survived would suffer from malnutrition, with attendant physical or mental development problems (Cesar Chelala, 'Central America's Health Plight', Christian Science Monitor, March 2 and March 22, 1990). All of this happened on the doorstep of the wealthiest, most powerful nation in history – the nation willing, we are told, to spend billions of dollars and hundreds of lives installing 'democracy' half a world away in Iraq.

Barely hinting at any of this, the Guardian told us that Reagan 'is chiefly remembered now for ... his tax cutting economic policies, his role in bringing about the end of the cold war and his ability to make America feel so good about itself after the turmoil of Vietnam, civil rights and Watergate' (Leader, 'A Rose-Tinted President').

'Reagan's interference in Central America was shameful', the Independent editors noted, without mentioning numbers killed – the slaughter being simply 'the low-point' of Reagan's presidency; one that 'summed up' the 'deficiencies' of his foreign policy (Leader, 'Ronald Reagan's Achievements Should Not Blind Us to the Failings of his Presidency', *Independent*, June 7, 2004). Imagine the *Independent* suggesting that the Holocaust summed up the 'deficiencies' of Nazi foreign policy. As Thomas Carothers suggested (above), in per capita terms the Reagan presidency really was comparable to the Holocaust for the people of Nicaragua.

Rupert Cornwell, the *Independent*'s Washington editor, conceded 'harsh complaints, and grievous mistakes' over US foreign policy in the region. 'But somehow they are beside the point' because 'Mr Reagan is best judged by two different measures.' One measure 'is the difference between the America he inherited in January 1981 and the America he bequeathed to George Bush senior eight years later'. The second measure 'is the change he wrought to US politics, the US economy and to the world' (Cornwell, 'A President whose Optimism Earned Him a Place in History', *Independent*, June 7, 2004). Perhaps these 'different measures' might appear 'beside the point' to survivors of Reagan's atrocities in the region.

The *Observer*'s Paul Harris noted cheerily that Reagan was able to 'skip through the scandals' of his presidency ('How the Gipper Stole into American Hearts', *Observer*, June 6, 2004). In a long obituary, the *Financial Times* noted darkly that Reagan was 'not averse to displaying American muscle'. The FT's Jurek Martin described, without irony, how 'Central America remained a thorn in the president's flesh' ('The Star-Spangled President', *Financial Times*, June 7, 2004).

Year after year, decade after decade, the money pours into journalists' bank accounts – and the cacophony of words pours out, explaining nothing, revealing nothing, hiding everything. Riverbend, a 24-year-old Iraqi female author of the internet blog Baghdad Burning, describes her impressions of American media broadcasts:

> The thing that strikes me most is the fact that the news is so ... clean. It's like hospital food. It's all organized and disinfected. Everything is partitioned and you can feel how it has been doled out carefully with extreme attention to the portions – 2 minutes on women's rights in Afghanistan, 1 minute on training troops in Iraq ... All the reportages are upbeat and somewhat cheerful, and the anchor person manages to look properly concerned and completely uncaring all at once. ('Riverbend Is a Blogger, "Embedded" in the Real Baghdad, Telling It Like It Is, Helping Us See with New Eyes', April 15, 2005, <www.buzzflash.com>)

A June 7, 2004 Snowmail news digest from Jon Snow of *Channel 4 News* observed: 'Ronnie Reagan lies in state. Particular pangs for me I must admit, having been ITN's Washington correspondent in the creamier moments of Ronnie's reign. The great eulogies seem to evade the moments of madness.' We wrote to Snow the same day:

> Hi Jon
>
> Yes, and beyond 'the moments of madness', the eulogies also seem to evade the years of searing, barely believable torture and mass murder in places like Nicaragua, East Timor, and El Salvador. We'll be watching at 7:00, but we won't hold our breath ...
>
> Best wishes
>
> DE and DC

Snow replied instantly:

> you cynics! If you'd been around at the time you'd have seen me exposing his outrages in central america ... you may think i'm a sell ouyt [sic] these days but i can assure u, I have been there ... . (email to Media Lens, June 7, 2004)

We responded:

> Thanks, Jon. We don't think you're a sell-out. But we'd be more reassured if you'd mentioned your future planned, rather than remembered past, exposures of his outrages.
>
> Best
>
> DE and DC

After seeing *Channel 4 News*' shameful hagiography of Reagan by Washington correspondent Jonathan Rugman, we wrote again:

> Thanks, Jon.
>
> That's about as bad as it gets! We wonder if Rugman has ever asked himself why the pervasive culture of lying over the Iran–Contra affair is worthy of

mention while the mass slaughter of innocents it made possible is not. Imagine reviewing the life of some official enemy of the West responsible for mass murder and emphasising: 'He was found to have been involved in deception.' It's remarkable. Actually it's a lethal form of propaganda.

Sincerely

DE and DC

Snow replied:

> people are not as ignorant as you make them out to be ... dont underestimate the viewer!

Cryptic, meaningless responses, cringe-making hagiography, cartoon versions of politics and history – all is unreality, confusion and absurdity. Meanwhile, our victims continue to be trampled underfoot by our psychopathic corporate system.

## CLINTON – THE BITTER IRONIES

'It is a bitter irony of source journalism', historian Walter Karp once noted, 'that the most esteemed journalists are precisely the most servile. For it is by making themselves useful to the powerful that they gain access to the "best" sources' (quoted, Sharon Beder, *Global Spin – the Corporate Assault on Environmentalism*, Green Books, 1997, p. 199). The servility is hidden behind a specious presumption that prime ministers and presidents are to be afforded unlimited respect bordering on reverence. To raise their responsibility for war crimes and mass death would be 'disrespectful', even 'irresponsible'.

On an October 2002 front page of the *Guardian*, chief political correspondent Patrick Wintour responded to a speech by Bill Clinton:

> Bill Clinton yesterday used a mesmerising oration to Labour's conference ... in a subtle and delicately balanced address ... Mr Clinton's 50-minute address captured the imagination of delegates in Blackpool's Winter Gardens. He received a two-and-a-half minute standing ovation ... He had brought a touch of Hollywood to the conference as his friend and Oscar winning actor Kevin Spacey watched proceedings, but observers also described the speech as one of the most impressive and moving in the history of party conferences. ('Clinton Tells Party Blair's the Man to Trust', *Guardian*, October 3, 2002)

A *Guardian* editorial on the same day gushed even more helplessly:

> In an intimate, almost conversational tone, speaking only from notes, Bill
> Clinton delivered the speech of a true political master ... If one were reviewing
> it, five stars would not be enough ... What a speech. What a pro. And what a
> loss to the leadership of America and the world. (Leader, 'What a Pro – Clinton
> Shows What a Loss He Is to the US', *Guardian*, October 3, 2002)

Like Reagan, the man hailed by the *Guardian* as 'a loss to the
leadership of America and the world' is responsible for truly awesome
crimes against humanity. In June 1993, Clinton bombed Baghdad in
retaliation for an unproven Iraqi plot to assassinate former president
George Bush. Eight Iraqi civilians, including the Iraqi artist Layla al-
Attar, were killed in the raid, and twelve were wounded.

Unknown numbers were killed in Clinton's 1998 bombing of
Afghanistan and the Sudan. In his cruise missile attack on the
Sudanese Al-Shifa factory, half the pharmaceutical production
capacity for the country was destroyed. The German ambassador
to Sudan reported: 'It is difficult to assess how many people in this
poor African country died as a consequence of the destruction ... but
several tens of thousands seems a reasonable guess' (quoted, Noam
Chomsky, *9–11*, Seven Stories Press, 2001).

Clinton gave ceaseless military support empowering Turkey and
Colombia's lethal wars of internal repression. In 1994, 80 per cent
of Turkey's arsenal was American, including M-60 tanks, F-16 fighter
bombers, Cobra gunships, and Blackhawk helicopters, all of which
were used against the Kurds. Recorded horrors in 1993 and 1994
include the destruction of some 3,500 villages, use of napalm, the
throwing of people from helicopters, civilians bound with electric
cables and burned alive, and so on.

The tightening of the embargo on Cuba under the Toricelli-Helms
bill, signed into law under Clinton, also had devastating effects.
According to a 1997 report of the American Association of World
Health, the food sale ban 'contributed to serious nutritional deficits,
particularly among pregnant women, leading to an increase in low
birth-weight babies. In addition, food shortages were linked to a devastating outbreak of neuropathy numbering in the tens of thousands.
By one estimate, daily caloric intake dropped 33 percent between
1989 and 1993' (quoted, Edward Herman, 'Clinton Is the World's
Leading Active War Criminal', *Z Magazine*, December 1999).

In the journal *Foreign Affairs*, John and Karl Mueller claimed that Clinton's 'sanctions of mass destruction' had caused 'the deaths of more people in Iraq than have been slain by all so-called weapons of mass destruction [nuclear and chemical] throughout all history' (*Foreign Affairs*, May/June 1999. See Chapter 2 for details).

On June 7, 2000 Amnesty International claimed that, during Clinton's bombing of Serbia in 1999, NATO had committed serious violations of the laws of war that resulted in the unlawful killings of civilians (see Chapter 6).

In 1998–99 Clinton and his administration knew of Indonesian plans to wreak havoc in East Timor in the event of a defeat following the August 1999 referendum, but took no action to avert the slaughter (see Chapter 7). Just weeks after the 'moral crusade' in Kosovo, Clinton, like Blair, had fallen suddenly silent – there were no five-star speeches to save the people of East Timor, indeed no speeches at all.

Referring to Bill Clinton's autobiography, *My Life*, in June 2004, the *Guardian*'s editor Alan Rusbridger and leading *Guardian* commentator Jonathan Freedland (rumoured to be next in line for the editorship) proudly announced they had been granted 'an exclusive interview', being 'the only British newspaper granted access to the book' ('Mandela Helped Me Survive Monicagate, Arafat Could not Make the Leap to Peace – and for Days John Major Wouldn't Take My Calls', *Guardian*, June 21, 2004).

In a long interview that fully bore out Karp's observation on source journalism, Rusbridger and Freedland described Clinton as 'the man who was hailed, even by his enemies, as the most gifted politician of the post-war era'. Recall Gavin Esler's equally fatuous assertion that Reagan was, 'a man who was loved even by his political opponents in this country [America] and abroad' (*Newsnight*, BBC2, June 9, 2004).

The focus of the *Guardian* article was on Clinton the globe-trotting celebrity. The former president 'still lives on CST – Clinton Standard Time', Rusbridger and Freedland gushed: 'Aides pop in and out of the anonymous hotel conference room to explain that "The president is running about half an hour late"'. Political rivals initially teased Clinton as 'a chubby "Bubba", a good ol' boy from the south with a taste for junk food and a waistline to match', and so on.

In the midst of this fawning focus on celebrity and lifestyle, Rusbridger and Freedland devoted 616 words to Clinton's policies on Iraq – the overwhelming political crisis of our time – and 1,252 words to the Monica Lewinsky affair. No mention was made of Clinton's responsibility for the deaths of more than 1 million Iraqi civilians, including 500,000 children under five, as a result of sanctions. The article had separate sections 'On standing up to his stepfather', 'On being a fat child', and 'On the influence of his grandmother'. But in this 5,347-word article, the word 'sanctions' was not mentioned.

Who would guess from this kind of coverage that, as John Pilger noted, 'in a league table of death and destruction, Clinton beats Bush hands down'? ('Bush or Kerry? Look Closely and the Danger Is the Same', *New Statesman*, March 4, 2004).

When Media Lens asked Jonathan Freedland, co-author of the article, why he had ignored Clinton's responsibility for mass death, he replied: 'As a journalist, I'm sure you understand that there is never room for everything you would like to include' (email to David Cromwell, June 21, 2004).

Media Lens also challenged Sam Ingleby of the *Independent*, who wrote a 2,000-word article on Clinton without mentioning sanctions on Iraq ('Bill's Presidential Tips: Be Wussy and Macho', *Independent*, June 22, 2004). Ingleby also managed to avoid mentioning the word 'sanctions' in his article. Ingleby responded: 'My brief was to cover the two interviews Clinton did with Time and CBS and concentrate on personality over policy – given that so much had already been written about the latter over the weekend' (email to David Cromwell, June 22, 2004). Needless to say, the *Independent*'s coverage over the previous weekend had *also* neglected to cover Clinton's devastating policies on Iraq.

Likewise, the *Daily Telegraph*'s Stephen Robinson responded to a challenge from Media Lens about his article titled 'Clinton's Excuses No Longer Matter' (June 23, 2004). Robinson wrote: 'Well, the short answer to your question is that in a 1,050 word review of a 950-page book, something has to give. I'm afraid I didn't mention Rwanda either, where the numbers were even worse' (email to David Cromwell, June 23, 2004).

We replied to Robinson:

Your concession that you didn't mention Rwanda either, 'where the numbers were even worse', hardly does you credit. Instead, around 20% of your piece is devoted to Clinton's relationship with Monica Lewinsky. Meanwhile, Clinton's culpability for the deaths of over a million Iraqis, not to mention his delayed response to the tragedy of Rwanda (actually, his deep apathy and downright obstruction to international action – see Mark Curtis's 'Web of Deceit', Vintage, 2003), passes underneath your journalistic radar. (David Cromwell, email to Stephen Robinson, June 23, 2004)

We received no further response.

## DIMBLEBY DUMBS DOWN

The day after the *Guardian*'s 'exclusive interview', Clinton spoke 'frankly', if not exclusively, to the BBC's David Dimbleby. 'The way I kept score in my Presidency', Clinton said, 'was, Did more people have jobs or not? ... What was our record in the world? Did we advance peace and prosperity and security or not?' (*The Clinton Interview, A Panorama Special*, June 22, 2004, <http://news.bbc.co.uk). Dimbleby said not a word in response to the man who presided over 'infanticide masquerading as policy' in Iraq, according to 70 members of the US Congress (quoted, John Lancaster and Colum Lynch, 'U.S. Looks at Easing Sanctions on Iraq; Pressure Mounts for Increasing Humanitarian Aid', *Washington Post*, February 25, 2000).

To his credit, Clinton berated Dimbleby for focusing excessively on the wretched Lewinsky affair – Dimbleby spent 25 per cent of the interview on the issue, mentioning 'oral sex' three times. Clinton suggested that the focus should be on serious humanitarian issues, such as whether, as president, he had 'brought a million people home from Kosovo'. Later in the interview, Dimbleby affirmed that Clinton had indeed been 'prepared to use bombing raids to save Kosovo'. In fact, as discussed in Chapter 6, the mass exodus of people from Kosovo began *after* Clinton and Blair began bombing on March 24, 1999. But in accordance with the 'bitter irony' of source journalism, Dimbleby made no mention of the fact.

In discussing Iraq, Clinton described how, in December 1998, 'Saddam kicked the inspectors out to try to force us to lift the sanctions'. Dimbleby again failed to challenge the claim. (See Chapter 3 for details.)

Dimbleby did ask Clinton about Rwanda. Clinton explained his failure to stop the genocide: 'Partly it was the preoccupation with Haiti at the time, where there was a lot of mass slaughter going on, and we were trying to get in there.' Dimbleby, again, might have pointed out that the killers were US-trained and financed, slaughtering a democratic mass movement on US orders (see Chapter 8 for details). Dimbleby said nothing.

The truth is no less obvious, and no less true, for being banished by the mass media: elite politicians are protected by elite journalists. Elite journalists, in turn, are protected by a psychopathic corporate media system locked into a status quo serving greed – profit over people, profit over truth.

This is the obscene reality of *Guardian* columnist Martin Kettle's 'strident and confrontational press becoming yet more strident and confrontational', and of what former *New Statesman* political editor John Lloyd would have us believe is a constant journalistic 'aggression' and 'suspicion' towards politicians (Kettle, 'Who Am I to Tell You What to Think About Politics?', *Guardian*, June 22, 2004; Lloyd, 'Who Really Runs the Country?', *Guardian*, June 21, 2004).

The truth is hardly in doubt when culture secretary Tessa Jowell can declare at a media awards ceremony: 'Talented, courageous teams of reporters, producers and technical staff have brought us the news that we need to know ... 2001 showed the task gets no easier, the expectations get higher, yet the standards still rise' (*The British Academy Television Awards*, ITV, April 22, 2002).

# 10
# Climate Change –
# The Ultimate Media Betrayal

If the year past is anything to go by, there will be many more than two million deaths from climate change-related disasters worldwide in the next ten years, and the damages to property will be worth hundreds of billions of pounds. (Global Commons Institute, letter to the *Guardian*, March 14, 2000.)[*]

## UNINHABITABLE PLANET?

The evidence has been mounting inexorably, year on year. The Intergovernmental Panel on Climate Change (IPCC), the United Nations body set up in 1988 to study the climate, has stated that a 60–80 per cent reduction in greenhouse gas emissions is required to stabilise global temperatures at existing (high) levels. Nobel Laureate Henry Kendall, chairman of the Union of Concerned Scientists, is clear: 'Let there be no doubt about the conclusions of the scientific community that the threat of global warming is very real and action is needed immediately. It is a grave error to believe that we can continue to procrastinate' (Paul Brown, 'Clinton Told to Act on Global Warming', *Guardian*, October 1, 1997).

In June 1999, the Red Cross reported that natural disasters uprooted more people in 1998 than all the wars and conflicts combined. Climate change, it warned, was about to precipitate a series of 'super-disasters' (CNN, 'Report Predicts Decade of Super-Disasters', June 24, 1999; <www.cnn.com/NATURE/9906/24/disaster.enn/>).

[*] The London-based Global Commons Institute, led by Aubrey Meyer, has proposed a climate framework known as 'contraction and convergence' to reduce global carbon emissions sufficiently to avert climate catastrophe. Eye-catching computer graphics available at the GCI website (www.gci.org.uk) illustrate past emissions and future allocation of emissions by country (or region), achieving per capita equity by 2030, for example. This is the convergence part of C&C. After 2030, carbon emissions drop off to reach safe levels by 2100. This is the contraction part. C&C attracts international support from many quarters including governments, industry and grass-roots groups.

In 2002, the US National Academy of Sciences warned of a very sudden global climate disaster, perhaps within ten years. Reviewing the academy's report, the then British environment minister, Michael Meacher, wrote: 'We do not have much time and we do not have any serious option. If we do not act quickly to minimise runaway feedback effects we run the risk of making this planet, our home, uninhabitable' (quoted, Nicholas Watt, 'US Rejection of Kyoto Climate Plan "Risks Uninhabitable Earth"', *Guardian*, May 16, 2002).

In late March 2005, *New Scientist* reported on a climate science meeting in Exeter, England, held the previous month. Called Stabilisation 2005, the international meeting was convened by the British government to coincide with its 2005 presidency of the G8 group of rich nations. The meeting warned that 'the risks are more serious than previously thought'. Chief among the threats raised were several 'tipping points' that could trigger irreversible global changes, such as melting of the Greenland ice sheet, which would raise sea levels by 7 metres and could shut down ocean currents. It was 'scary stuff', *New Scientist* noted, 'because we appear to be much closer to those tipping points than previously supposed – only a decade or so away, in some cases' ('The Edge of the Abyss', *New Scientist*, March 26, 2005).

Human-induced climate change has been killing people for decades. Climatologists estimate that global warming has led to the deaths of 150,000 people since 1970. (Meteorological Office, 'Avoiding Dangerous Climate Change', 1–3 February 2005, Table 2a. In 'Impacts on human systems due to temperature rise, precipitation change and increases in extreme events', p. 1). By 2050, as temperatures rise, scientists warn that 3 billion people will be under 'water stress', with tens of millions likely dying as a result.

While the media do report the latest disasters and dramatic warnings, there are few serious attempts to explore the identity and motives of corporate opponents to action on climate change, or to draw attention to the true significance of their folly. The refusal to respond to the threat is presented almost as a natural human phenomenon, or is loosely blamed on 'America' or 'China'. But in fact the opponents of action are easily identifiable.

## THE HIGH COST OF BUYING TIME

The sum total of the world's meaningful response to the threat of climate disaster is the pitiful Kyoto climate treaty. Proposing just a

5.2 per cent cut in emissions, as opposed to the minimum 60 per cent required, the Kyoto treaty is described by Dr Mike Hulme of East Anglia University as 'trivial in terms of stabilising the climate' (Quoted, David Edwards, 'Climate Wars', October 2000, <www.medialens.org>).

It is not trivial to big business, however. John Grasser, vice-president of the US National Mining Association and member of the Global Climate Coalition (GCC) had this to say at the 1997 Kyoto convention:

> We think we have raised enough questions among the American public to prevent any numbers, targets or timetables to achieve reductions in gas emissions being agreed here ... What we are doing, and we think successfully, is buying time for our industries by holding up these talks. (Quoted, Paul Brown, 'Temperature Rises at Global Warming Talks', *Guardian*, December 5, 1997)

Similarly, the US National Association of Manufacturers (NAM), representing much of US industry, was candid enough in its letter to George W. Bush in May 2001:

> Dear Mr. President:
>
> On behalf of 14,000 member companies of the National Association of Manufacturers (NAM) – and the 18 million people who make things in America – thank you for your opposition to the Kyoto Protocol on the grounds that it exempts 80 percent of the world and will cause serious harm to the United States. (Michael E. Baroody, NAM executive vice-president, Letter to the President Concerning the Kyoto Protocol, May 16, 2001, <www.nam.org>)

The NAM website added further: 'The NAM strongly opposes the [Kyoto] accord ... President Bush also opposes Kyoto and is now pursuing a more reasonable approach to climate change' (<www.nam.org>, July 19, 2001).

That other great voice of US business, the US Chamber of Commerce, declared in a letter to the US President: 'Global warming is an important issue that must be addressed – but the Kyoto Protocol is a flawed treaty that is not in the U.S. interest' (<www.uschamber.org> July 19, 2001). The US Chamber's website noted that it was the world's largest business federation representing more than 'three million businesses and organisations of every size, sector and region'.

Readers will do well to find even whispered references to this extraordinary depth of business opposition to action on climate change in what is, after all, a corporate press. The fact and significance of the NAM's opposition have never been explored by the *Guardian* or the *Independent*, for example, even though NAM members include corporations with operations in the UK, such as Intel, ExxonMobil and General Motors.

We need only recall the Cold War era and imagine how the media would react were organisations inside society found to be working to undermine attempts to prevent an 'evil empire' slaughtering tens of thousands, or perhaps tens of millions, of people around the world. Instead, because the corporate media are elements of the same system, are indeed owned by members of the US Chamber and the NAM, the reaction is very different. Journalist Ross Gelbspan has noted how news stories about global warming evoke an 'eerie silence' (*The Heat is On: The Climate Crisis, The Cover-up, The Prescription*, Perseus Books, 1998, p. 172). This, indeed, is the mother of all silences, because the fossil fuel economy is the mother of all vested interests.

## GLOBAL CLIMATE CATASTROPHE – MUSTN'T GRUMBLE!

In the aftermath of 9/11, the media reported endlessly on the likely identities and motives of those responsible, on the options open to Western leaders, and on the urgent need for decisive action. On September 12, 2001, for example, an impassioned *Guardian* editorial wrote of 'the heartfelt conviction that Britain and the British people … will do all in their power to assist the American government in finding those who are responsible. The United States, its government, and its people did not deserve this. For this day of carnage and tears there can be no justification or excuse' (Leader, 'The Sum of All Our Fears', *Guardian*, September 12, 2001).

Compare and contrast the media response to the many days of carnage and tears wrought by the record-breaking heatwave in August 2003, likely as a result of climate change: 13,600 additional deaths in France; 1,500 heat-related deaths in India; 1,316 deaths in Portugal in two weeks; 500–1,000 deaths in the Netherlands; 900 additional deaths in Britain; 569 deaths in China. In Italy and Spain, death rates rose by 20 per cent in some areas.

Professor John Schellnhuber, head of the UK's Tyndall Centre for Climate Change Research said: 'What we are seeing is absolutely unusual. We know that global warming is proceeding apace, but most of us were thinking that in 20–30 years time we would be seeing hot spells [like this]. But it's happening now' (John Vidal, 'Global Warming May Be Speeding Up, Fears Scientist', *Guardian*, August 6, 2003).

As this tragedy spread around the world, the *Independent* had this to say on Britain hitting the 100°F mark for the first time: 'Inevitably, it was late and we almost despaired of its arriving. Finally, though, the wish produced the fact ... We can boast that ours was the generation that first experienced subtropical Britain' (Leader, 'Under Pressure', *Independent*, August 11, 2003). In an equally surreal editorial, headed 'Mustn't Grumble', the *Guardian* declared:

> At last the hot nights, strumming crickets and warm sea which we usually pay so much to visit for a fortnight's package holiday are here on our doorstep. Rejoice, as Lady Thatcher once instructed us, rejoice. But er ... judging by the comatose and in some quarters almost hostile reaction to the heatwave, Britain has a long way to go before centuries of phlegm and caution are discarded for the fervour and excitement of permanently warmer climes. (Leader, 'Mustn't Grumble ... Summer Heats Up to More than 311K', *Guardian*, August 11, 2003)

No matter that thousands had died already, or that the London-based Global Commons Institute had predicted more than 2 million deaths from climate change-related disasters worldwide over the next ten years (Global Commons Institute, letter to the *Guardian*, 14 March, 2000. Full text of letter available at <www.gci.org.uk/signon/signon.html#Guardian>). Quite simply climate change had not been labelled a 'serious and current threat' by the vested interests with the power to make things real for journalists.

## PUT A 'HOG' IN IT – LIBERAL MEDIA GREENWASH

In January 2004, it was announced that over the next 50 years, global warming could commit a quarter of land animals and plants to extinction. According to a four-year research project by scientists from eight countries, published in the prestigious journal *Nature*, by 2050 one million species will be doomed to die out. The findings were described as 'terrifying' by the paper's lead author, Chris Thomas, professor of conservation biology at Leeds University, who said:

> When scientists set about research they hope to come up with definite results, but what we found we wish we had not. It was far, far worse than we thought, and what we have discovered may even be an underestimate. (Quoted, Paul Brown, 'An Unnatural Disaster', *Guardian*, January 8, 2004)

The predicted disaster is based on a mid-range forecast of possible outcomes. The worst case suggests as many as 58 per cent of species could become extinct; the best case suggests 9 per cent, still catastrophically high.

The *Guardian* and *Independent* both devoted editorials to the *Nature* paper. The *Independent*'s editors warned of the coming mass death: 'it is not an asteroid that will have caused this, of course: it is us. The Sixth Great Extinction will be an entirely human achievement' (Leader, 'The Sixth Great Extinction Is Avoidable – If We Act Now', *Independent*, January 8, 2004). It is 'us', apparently; although most of us, the public, are excluded from meaningful politics, debate and action by state–corporate interests. The *Independent* concluded: 'There is still time to take action against climate change, and some world leaders, notably Tony Blair, are committed to doing so'; but the continuing reluctance of George Bush to take the threat seriously invited disaster. In fact the environmental record of Blair's government has been lambasted even by the normally conservative Royal Society. In June 2005, its president, Lord May of Oxford, who had been the government's chief scientific adviser from 1995 to 2000, derided Blair's green policies as 'gutless' and said the government needed to do 'a hell of a lot more' (Michael McCarthy, 'UK's Top Scientist Delivers Stinging Attack on Government's Environmental Record', *Independent*, June 10, 2005).

The *Guardian* wrote of 'a fresh wake-up call about the dangers of global warming' (Leader, 'The Death of Species', *Guardian*, January 8, 2004). In terms of a possible response, the editors cited Professor Thomas who had suggested 'an immediate and progressive' switch to technologies that produce little or no greenhouse gases, combined with active removal of carbon dioxide from the atmosphere. 'The usual response to the problem is to blame governments', the *Guardian* continued: 'They certainly carry a great deal of the responsibility ...' (ibid.). The United States was then criticised for abandoning the Kyoto Protocol to limit greenhouse gases. Britain was praised for being 'more or less on target' with regards to Kyoto, with its performance assisted 'fortuitously by the unrelated decline of its polluting coal-mining industry' (ibid.). No mention was made of the fact that Kyoto is itself a trivial response to climate change (see below). Finally, the *Guardian*'s editors noted:

> Although governments undoubtedly have a leading role to play, there are plenty of things that individuals can do that could make a dramatic difference ... having a shower rather than a bath, putting a 'hog' in the lavatory cistern, recycling household rubbish, disposing of household chemicals carefully, encouraging wildlife in the garden and composting vegetable cuttings. (Ibid.)

Governments and individuals aside, there is of course one other group that might be deemed worthy of mention: transnational corporations. In 1991, in his book *US Petroleum Strategies in the Decade of the Environment*, Bob Williams, a consultant to the oil and gas industry, described the industry's number one priority: 'to put the environmental lobby out of business ... There is no greater imperative ... If the petroleum industry is to survive, it must render the environmental lobby superfluous, an anachronism' (quoted, Andrew Rowell, *Green Backlash – Global Subversion of the Environment Movement*, Routledge, 1996, p. 71). Ron Arnold, also an industry consultant, told a meeting of the Ontario Forest Industries Association: 'You must turn the public against environmentalists or you will lose your environmental battle' (quoted, *Sharon Beder, Global Spin – The Corporate Assault on Environmentalism*, Green Books, 1997, p. 22).

The business response to such exhortations was overwhelming, as Kirkpatrick Sale observed:

> Right wing businessmen like Richard Mellon Scaife and Joseph Coors, and conservative treasuries like the Mobil and Olin foundations, poured money into ad campaigns, lawsuits, elections, and books and articles protesting 'big government' and 'strangulation by regulation', blaming environmentalists for all the nation's ills from the energy crisis to the sexual revolution. (*The Green Revolution*, Hill & Wang, 1993, p. 49)

Frank Mankiewicz, a senior executive at transnational public relations firm Hill and Knowlton, predicted accurately:

I think the companies will have to give in only at insignificant levels. Because the companies are too strong, they're the establishment. The environmentalists are going to have to be like the mob in the square in Romania before they prevail. (Quoted, Beder, *Global Spin*, p. 22)

With much of life on earth threatened by mass death, literally not one word of this business offensive appeared in the *Guardian* or the *Independent* leaders, where climate change continues to be presented as a kind of wildlife issue existing outside the realities of psychopathic corporate greed, propaganda and control.

Of course, the corporate media occasionally laments the destruction of our world in editorials, but it is not in the business of doing anything about it. In fact, literally the reverse is true. The same edition of the *Guardian* that featured the 'terrifying' report of global species loss, also carried adverts for Lexus cars, Toyota cars, Audi cars, BMW cars, American Airlines, Dixons computer equipment, Office World, HSBC, Magnet, and so on: adverts promoting endlessly rising mass consumption on which all the quality press depend for 75 per cent of their revenue. 'Doing something' should mean taking on exactly these corporate interests; exactly these materialist versions of life, liberty and happiness. 'Doing something', in fact, means taking on corporate interests like the *Guardian* newspaper.

## NEITHER DO I, TOO! – THE FOSSIL-FUELLED *GUARDIAN*

On January 8, 2004 we published a Rapid Response Media Alert, 'Climate Catastrophe – the Ultimate Media Betrayal' (<www.medialens.org>). This focussed on media coverage of the 'terrifying' new scientific findings on climate change and impending species loss. We suggested people send the following questions to the editors and environment editors of the *Guardian* and *Independent*:

Why, in reporting the catastrophic effects of global warming, do you make no mention of the global corporate efforts to obstruct even trivial action on climate change and to destroy the environment movement? Why are these political and economic factors bringing mass death to our planet unworthy even of mention by you and your newspaper?

An indignant Paul Brown, environment correspondent of the *Guardian*, responded: 'I have frequently been abused for having a one track mind and never doing anything but attacking corporations for their failure to act on climate change, particularly Exxon. Perhaps you should read the paper. Paul Brown' (email to Media Lens readers, January 8, 2004).

This brusque email fits a standard pattern of journalistic responses to polite and rational challenge. Brown implied that no reasonable reader of the *Guardian* could possibly agree with the dozens of emailers who questioned the paper's silence on corporate obstructionism on climate change, its spectacularly hypocritical dependence on, and promotion of, fossil fuel advertising, and its utter failure to expose the role of the corporate mass media in demolishing the environment. All of these points were answered, according to Brown, by the fact that he had been criticised in the past for 'never doing anything but attacking corporations for their failure to act on climate change'. This recalled the classic Laurel and Hardy dialogue:

> Mrs Hardy: And how is Mrs Laurel?
> Stanley: Oh, fine thank you.
> Mrs Hardy: I'd love to meet her some time.
> Stanley: Neither do I, too. (Laurel and Hardy, *Chickens Come Home*, 1931)

Journalists often find it impossible to believe dissident critics have actually seen their papers or broadcasts. Thus *Observer* editor Roger Alton:

> What a lot of balls ... do you read the paper old friend? (Forwarded to Media Lens, February 14, 2003)

And again:

> Do you read the paper or are you just recycling garbage from Medialens? (Alton, forwarded to Media Lens February 14, 2003)

Thus *Guardian* editor Alan Rusbridger:

> As a matter of interest, do you ever read the Guardian? (Forwarded to Media Lens, October 22, 2002)

And again:

If you read the Guardian regularly – as opposed to sites offering critiques of the paper – you'd know we'd done more than any other British title on climate change. (Rusbridger, forwarded to Media Lens, October 16, 2003)

The *Independent*'s Andrew Buncombe:

I can only presume that you have not 'actually' read the independent and are happy to be guided by medialens' editors quoting paragraphs out of context to get your view of what the paper has been writing about. (Forwarded to Media Lens, August 21, 2003)

The *Observer*'s Ben Summerskill in response to a media alert:

I work on the policy area here so was a tiny bit surprised. I just don't think medialens has even studied the Observer – all the evidence is not – so am astounded that they assume to lecture other people about what's in it. (Forwarded August 20, 2003)

From the *Observer*'s Peter Beaumont:

Finally, an appeal to all medialens readers. Before you launch into bombarding people with letters please go back to what people have actually written. (Forwarded, May 5, 2002)

And David Mannion, ITV's news editor in chief, put us right:

You are clearly not watching closely enough. (Mannion to Media Lens, May 7, 2003)

On January 11, 2004, Paul Brown wrote directly to the Media Lens editors:

Thanks for you [sic] reply. Having been chided for the terse nature of my response by about 30 people I have replied in some detail to about another 10 but generally given up now (my email is clogged so the chances of doing any work would be nil if I replied to anything or is that the idea, to stop environmental journalists working). But we are basically on the same side. I do not think it generally makes the slightest difference to whether people advertise with us whether we attack them or not and often it has the opposite effect. They advertise more.

As I think I said before very often people feel powerless to do anything so for a change we suggested things they might do. Generally speaking we have sympathetically reported boycotting Exxon/Esso, Shell and other corporations, attacked 4 by 4s etc than any other group, to the point where our balance as reporters has been questioned by our own editors not by outsiders.

I think George Bush and his supporters are the most dangerous and nasty people on the planet. I can think of a place in Cuba where they should be placed for the next 20 years ago, but if I am to be effective as a journalist I have to protect myself to sticking to basic journalistic rules about balance. Would you prefer that we got fired and replaced by someone less inclined to attack big business. I do not object to engaging in debate, but this is Sunday, and I cannot work all the time. Paul Brown

In responding to Brown (January 20, 2004) we pointed out that the *Guardian* had consistently misrepresented business obstructionism on climate change as involving only a few fundamentalist fossil fuel companies, notably Exxon/Esso. The truth is that business opposition is widespread throughout virtually *all* sectors of industry and commerce (the insurance sector, arguably, being an obvious exception). This is something Brown explained in his own book, *Global Warming*:

Despite the fact that few have heard of the pressure groups created by the oil and coal interests to fight their corner there can be no doubt that they represent the most powerful industries in the world: coal, oil, and automobiles. In this case they also have the message politicians most want to hear – do nothing at all; continue with business as usual; any action to combat climate change will damage established interests, and millions of workers. To back up their campaigns they have unlimited resources which they have used to good effect since before Rio [Earth Summit], realising what a threat the Climate Change Convention was to their interests. Fearful that politicians might take decisions which will damage their profits by cutting consumption of fossil fuels they have been paying teams of lobbyists to work on their behalf.

At every meeting anywhere in the world where climate change is to be discussed the oil industry is there ... Their brief is simply to slow down the business of doing something about climate change as much as possible. (*Global Warming – Can Civilisation Survive?*, Blandford, 1996, p. 176)

These points sit uncomfortably with Brown's mention of how he had been accused of 'never doing anything but attacking corporations for their failure to act on climate change' in the *Guardian*. As he himself recognised, the real issue is not corporate inaction at all – it is fierce corporate *action* to oppose measures to tackle climate change. We were asking why, with the world facing catastrophe, the *Guardian* had made no reference to these crucial issues in its recent reports and leaders on impending climate catastrophe.

Brown wrote: 'I have to protect myself to sticking to basic journalistic rules about balance. Would you prefer that we got fired and replaced by someone less inclined to attack big business.'

It is remarkable that by refraining from systematically examining one of the most important issues of our time – the perhaps terminal consequences of corporate domination – Brown implied he believed he was 'sticking to basic journalistic rules about balance'. This mirrors US media critic Edward Herman's warning that journalistic notions of 'balance' and 'professionalism' actually mask a deep-seated compromise with authority (Herman, *The Myth of the Liberal Media*, Peter Lang Publishing, 1999).

Why would the *Guardian* be likely to fire Brown for criticising big business too much rather than too little? And why would it be likely to replace him with someone less, rather than more, critical of business? These comments suggest that Brown knows only too well that he is pushing at the limits of a corporate media system, that he knows his efforts are not welcomed but tolerated, at best. And yet we are speaking of 'the country's leading liberal newspaper'.

Brown's willingness to push the limits in this way is to be applauded. But our point is that these limits *do* exist and their existence is a serious problem for all of us and should be openly discussed. This problem blows a wide hole in the idea that the 'liberal' press is free, fair and independent. The fact is that the *Guardian* is a major commercial enterprise deeply dependent on other businesses and entrenched in the corporate system. There are very real limits to what it is willing to say about the system of which it is a part.

Naturally, then, we have never seen an article discussing the bottom line and other corporate pressures to which Brown, John Vidal and all other journalists are subjected in the media – nothing about how, as journalists, they have to 'protect' themselves. It is simply understood that some issues – particularly issues that expose the fundamental pro-business bias of the corporate media – are not fit subjects for discussion. Above all, as with every other corporation, journalists are not to criticise the product in front of customers – even though the 'product' is supposed to be the unvarnished truth!

We asked Brown if it did not concern him that he could not tread on powerful toes without the risk of being fired? Did he and his colleagues not feel compelled to blow the whistle on all of this – to go public on the pressures that compromise honest, full and accurate reporting in his own newspaper?

Finally, Brown argued, 'I do not think it generally makes the slightest difference to whether people advertise with us whether we attack them or not ... ' This is not a remotely credible view. In fact, the press is dependent on advertising revenue for around 75 per cent of its income. Unsurprisingly, then, negative criticism of major advertisers is all but unknown in these 'serious' newspapers. Obviously, such criticism would risk damaging the success of the advert, alienating the advertiser, and so losing advertising revenue to competitors. If Brown subjected the *Guardian*'s major fossil fuel advertisers to the kind of criticism they deserve, the *Guardian* would cease to exist as a commercial entity.

In an interview with Ralph Nader, author and broadcaster David Barsamian asked: 'Wouldn't it be irrational for them [the media] to even discuss corporate power, since their underwriting and sponsors come from very large corporations?' Nader's reply: 'Very irrational ... [There are] a few instances almost every year where there's some sort of criticism of auto dealers, and the auto dealers just pull their ads openly from radio and TV stations' (Barsamian, 'An Interview with Ralph Nader', *Z Magazine*, February 1995). Fairness and Accuracy in Reporting noted that in a 2000 poll of 287 US reporters, editors and news executives, about one-third of respondents said that news that would 'hurt the financial interests' of the media organisation or an advertiser went unreported. Forty-one per cent said they themselves had avoided stories, or softened their tone, to benefit their media company's interests.

Brown told us that the *Guardian* was 'snowed under' in January 2004 with complaints from readers criticising the *Guardian* for carrying full-page adverts for American Airlines '2 for 1 flights' the day after describing the 'terrifying' prospects for climate catastrophe. As we will see below, not one of these complaints appeared on the *Guardian*'s letters page.

Brown's colleague, environment editor John Vidal, made a telling observation about media limits in a review of George Monbiot's book *Captive State*, published in 2000. Vidal wrote that 'the intellectual and political establishment – and I include the mainstream media of which I am part' are loath to tackle 'the politicians, the local authorities, the corporations, and the many individuals and institutions' whom Monbiot names and shames in his book (*Ecologist*, December 2000/ January 2001). Isn't it outrageous that journalists never investigate and report on *why* the media, including the *Guardian*, is loath to tackle such power? The idea that it is normal and reasonable for the media never to engage in serious self-examination and self-criticism is one of the great Flat Earth ideas of our time.

Why, for example, have the *Guardian's* environment pages been steadily downgraded and marginalised from their prominent position in the mid 1980s? This during a period when environmental crises have worsened dramatically and environmentalists have been largely vindicated. Is it true, as we have been told by a *Guardian* insider, that the paper's science section was prioritised because it was seen as a means of attracting corporate careers advertising?

## DEAD PLANET'S SOCIETY –
## THE MYSTERY OF THE *GUARDIAN*'S POST BOX

We put all of the above points to Brown. He responded on January 20, 2004:

Dear Media Lens, Glad to know you have looked at the book [*Global Warming* by Paul Brown]. A lot of those companies have since resigned from the Climate Change Coalition, but you can see from David Gow's piece on the city pages today the leopard has not really change his spots. There are a lot of issues here, but frankly I do not think that the adversising point is a good one. Years ago we had a long battle with Ford which refused to advertise for (I think) 10 years because of a piece we carried attacking them. Since then companies have written to the editor asking various journalists to be removed, I know I have been one of them, and the Guardian has simply ignored them. I am not aware of any example of companies in the last five years pulling ads because they have been attacked, and internally I have never known a journalist pulling his/her punches because of advertising, still less being asked to do so by the management. That does not mean we are not heavily reliant on ads, we are.

There are lots of journalists here, like people everywhere else, who either try not to think about the impact climate will soon have on their lives and their children, or have genuinely not got the message. There are others who argue that we need a mix of stories to keep the readership happy, reflecting their interests. As I think I said before we need to be commercially viable to survive.

Keep reading the paper and you will [sic] a lot about this – especially the regrettable 2 for 1 offer. I was as appalled by that as you were and have made my feelings clear, Paul Brown

Brown reported being 'snowed under' by emails. He told one reader his 'email count had gone up to 20 an hour of similar letters attacking [sic] both me and the paper' (forwarded to Media Lens, January 21, 2004). A large number of these letters were copied to both the editor and the letters page. Many focused specifically on the conflict of interest between honest reporting and dependence on big business advertising. For example:

Dear Mr Brown,

Where am I to go for serious coverage and debate on the big issues of climate change and global warming? Would the front page headline DEAD PLANET not sell a few papers? Or are the airline, automotive and energy industries such big players that their muscle skews your angle on this topic? As a dissatisfied consumer of your product could you do me the favour of clearing up once and for all what it is exactly that you produce: is it a platform for advertisers or a medium for serious, free-thinking analysis of the facts?

Does it not irk you that while you scribble by beeswax candle light and resolve to take fewer baths, the transnational corporations pollute and plunder like never before?

Regards

[Name withheld] (Forwarded to Media Lens, January 11, 2004)

The media consistently claim to be open to all ideas and voices. So how did the *Guardian* respond to arguments challenging its independence and honesty as an integral part of the corporate system? Letters in response to the *Guardian*'s climate reporting were published on Friday, January 9, but not one mentioned the concerns described above that had poured into the paper's inboxes on January 8. None of these letters appeared on Saturday, January 10, or on Monday, January 12.

On the afternoon of January 12 – four days after the original article on climate change had appeared – we emailed the *Guardian*'s readers' editor, Ian Mayes. We outlined the substance of our media alert dated January 8 (<www.medialens.org/alerts/04/040108_Climate_Betrayal. HTM>), and asked about the letters:

> Why was not one of these letters published on the letters page? We noticed that in following days the Guardian editors did find space for adverts for Citroen cars, Chrysler cars, Fiat cars, Toyota cars, flybmi.com, the easyJet sale – 'every *one* must go' – and another full-page advert for '2 for 1 flights'.

We received no response, but the next morning (January 13) the following letter appeared on the *Guardian*'s letters page:

> Headline on Thursday: 'Global warming to kill off 1m species'; Friday: 'Top Scientist attacks US over global warming'; Saturday: '2 for 1 offer on flights to the US.' Joined-up thinking?

It is supposed to be a given that the letters page honestly reflects a newspaper's post bag. But this short letter, a wretched sop to the paper's critics that appeared five days after the original article, did not remotely reflect either the volume or critical content of the emails sent. Did the *Guardian* simply censor these letters for fear that they might damage its credibility and/or the performance of the American Airlines '2 for 1' flights offer?

An alternative explanation might be that the *Guardian* felt that these letters were mere robotic responses to an 'extreme pressure group', and so did not qualify as authentic correspondence to the letters page. There are three problems with this argument: first, a substantial number of letters forwarded to us were sent before and/or independently of our media alert. Second, many of the emails copied to us were extremely cogent, containing important information and arguments that we had not made in our alert. Third, the *Guardian* clearly *did* feel that the large number of complaints merited, not just a response, but a very substantial response in the form of an article by the readers' editor, Ian Mayes: 'Flying in the Face of the Facts – The Readers' Editor on Promotion, Pollution and the Guardian's Environment Policies', on January 24, 2004.

A very simple question arises: why did this flood of letters merit a column of this kind but zero representation on the letters page?

## THE GUARDIAN'S READERS' EDITOR
## SERVES UP A LIBERAL HERRING

Ian Mayes' January 24 article focused on the *Guardian*'s 'green credentials', on the fact that its journalists had spent £520,000 on flights in 2002, on the prospect of the paper planting trees to compensate for these flights, and on the possibility of inviting readers to pay more for flights to cover the cost of compensatory tree planting.

This was a bizarre response to a large number of emails making some very straightforward points about conflicts of interest at the *Guardian*. Indeed, this was a classic example of what we call a 'liberal herring' – the device whereby the liberal media focus intensely on non-threatening, trivial issues while avoiding far more important, damaging issues. The *Guardian*'s response was particularly disturbing to us because it was a perfect example, in microcosm, of how corporate cynics sought to neutralise the green movement throughout the 1980s and 1990s. Then, as now, sincere public concern was channelled into futile cul de sacs and false 'hopes', with corporate power thereby freed to continue pursuing maximum profits regardless of the cost to people and planet.

In a telling passage, Mayes wrote:

> To return to the promotional offer of two transatlantic flights for the price of one. The environment editor, and the environment and agriculture correspondent of the *Guardian* were among those who saw it as, to put it very mildly, completely in conflict with the *Guardian*'s editorial policies on global warming. They could perfectly understand its conveying an impression of hypocrisy on the paper's part.

But: 'No one I have spoken to in the Guardian believes the curtailment of such offers, let alone airline advertising, is a serious option' (ibid.). Again, some letters did deal with the issue of hypocrisy. But the central issue was the undiscussed contradiction of a profit-driven corporate press reporting on disasters rooted precisely in corporate greed.

In response to Mayes' article, ignoring letters sent by us and others, the *Guardian* published a letter (January 26) from the CEO of Future Forests insisting there are 'simple steps that we can all take to actively address the climate change and environmental impacts caused in our day-to-day lives'. Planting forests is indeed a simple step. One might think, though, that an even more obvious response for an honest newspaper would be to offer a semblance of balance by publishing serious views challenging corporate ownership and control of the media – if only on the letters page. In response to Mayes' article, and the letter from Future Forests, we sent a third letter. This, too, was not published.

## WHAT IS OUR PROBLEM?

Some readers might wonder at our motivation in continually bothering the press in this way. Are we just grumpy malcontents with chips on our shoulders?

Recall the scientific predictions that, by 2050, 25 per cent of our world's species will be doomed to extinction – warnings that quickly vanished from the media radar screen. An honest appraisal of the causes of, and solutions to, climate change is deeply threatening to the powerful interests that dominate politics and media. And so the media is happy to let the most appalling threat of our time drift quietly into the shadows. We recall Joel Bakan's warnings from Chapter 1:

> The people who run corporations are, for the most part, good people, moral people. They are mothers and fathers, lovers and friends, and upstanding citizens in their communities, and they often have good and sometimes even idealistic intentions ... [But] they must always put their corporation's best interests first and not act out of concern for anyone or anything else (unless the expression of such concern can somehow be justified as advancing the corporation's own interests). (*The Corporation*, Constable, 2004, p. 50)

Our motivation, very simply, is that we believe that our lives, the lives of our children, indeed of much animal and plant life on this planet, are in grave danger. We believe, further, that the means of mobilising popular support for action to prevent this catastrophe – the mass media – is fatally compromised by its very structure, nature and goals.

This is no joke; it is not some kind of power-baiting game played out for fun. The drastic limit on rational free speech in response to potentially terminal problems has to be exposed, challenged and changed, or there may well be no future for any of us.

# 11
# Disciplined Media –
# Professional Conformity to Power

## HOW DO YOU SHOOT BABIES?

Facing execution for his role in the murder of more than 1 million people, many of them children, Auschwitz commandant, Rudolf Hoess, reflected on his life and works: 'Today, I deeply regret that I did not spend more time with my family' (*Auschwitz, The Nazis and the Final Solution*, BBC2, February 15, 2005). Hoess, of course, lies at the extreme end of the spectrum, but his inability to recognise the extraordinary horror of what he had done is by no means exceptional. Mike Wallace of *CBS News* interviewed a participant in the American massacre of Vietnamese women and children at My Lai.

Q: You're married?
A: Right.
Q: Children?
A: Two.
Q: How old?
A: The boy is two and a half, and the little girl is a year and a half.
Q: Obviously, the question comes to my mind ... the father of two little kids like that ... how can he shoot babies?
A: I didn't have the little girl. I just had the little boy at the time.
Q: Uh-huh ... How do you shoot babies?
A: I don't know. It's just one of these things. (Quoted, Stanley Milgram, *Obedience to Authority*, Pinter & Martin, 1974, p. 202)

One of the delusions promoted by our society is the idea that great destructiveness is most often rooted in great cruelty and hatred. In reality, evil is not merely banal, it is often free of any sense of *being* evil – there may be no sense of moral responsibility for suffering at all.

We are all familiar with the words that typically accompany the shrug of the shoulders when someone is asked: 'How could you do it?' Time and again during the war on Iraq we have heard obviously well-meaning US and British military personnel insisting that they were just doing their jobs. A typical response is: 'I'm just doing what I'm paid to do.' Repeated often enough, these responses can even come to seem reasonable. But consider, by contrast, these comments made by US soldier Camilo Mejia who refused to return to his unit in Iraq after taking leave in October 2003:

> People would ask me about my war experiences and answering them took me back to all the horrors – the firefights, the ambushes, the time I saw a young Iraqi dragged by his shoulders through a pool of his own blood or an innocent man was decapitated by our machine gun fire. The time I saw a soldier broken down inside because he killed a child, or an old man on his knees, crying with his arms raised to the sky, perhaps asking God why we had taken the lifeless body of his son. I thought of the suffering of a people whose country was in ruins and who were further humiliated by the raids, patrols and curfews of an occupying army.
>
> And I realized that none of the reasons we were told about why we were in Iraq turned out to be true ... I realized that I was part of a war that I believed was immoral and criminal, a war of aggression, a war of imperial domination. I realized that acting upon my principles became incompatible with my role in the military, and I decided that I could not return to Iraq. ('Regaining My Humanity', <www.codepink4peace.org/National_Actions_Camilo.shtml>)

Normally, the implicit assumption is that signing a contract and being paid to do a job absolves us of all further moral responsibility. We have signed an agreement to do as we are told – an ostensibly innocuous act. If the people with whom we made this agreement then choose to send us to incinerate and dismember civilians, that is *their* moral responsibility, not ours.

The psychologist Stanley Milgram noted that this is a classic evasion used by people unwilling to accept responsibility for their own actions:

> The key to the behaviour of subjects [willing to torture and kill on command] lies not in pent-up anger or aggression but in the nature of their relationship to authority. They have given themselves to the authority; they see themselves as instruments for the execution of his wishes; once so defined, they are unable to break free. (*Obedience to Authority*, p. 185)

Other studies, on the psychology of torturers, have come to similar conclusions. Lindsey Williams, a clinical psychologist, notes: ' ... apart from traits of authoritarianism and obedience, and ideological sympathy for the government, there is little evidence that torturers are markedly different from their peers – at least, until the point where they are recruited and trained as torturers' (*Amnesty*, May/June 1995, p. 10). The *fundamentally* immoral act, then – the disaster that clears the way to vast horrors in the complete absence of a sense of responsibility – is the simple one of accepting that we are obliged to 'do as we are told'.

But in our society exactly this self-surrender is promoted and affirmed by the fact that it is demanded of us by every corporation that 'employs' us (like a tool), requiring us to sign our agreement to strict terms and conditions, and by the fact that huge costs are imposed on those of us unwilling to be 'team players'. We are trained to see this as 'just the way the world is' – something to be accepted rather than thought about. But as Noam Chomsky observes, the consequences can be horrendous:

> When you look at a corporation, just like when you look at a slave owner, you want to distinguish between the institution and the individual. So slavery, for example, or other forms of tyranny, are inherently monstrous. But the individuals participating in them may be the nicest guys you can imagine – benevolent, friendly, nice to their children, even nice to their slaves, caring about other people. I mean as individuals they may be anything. In their institutional role, they're monsters, because the institution's monstrous. And the same is true here. (Mark Achbar, Jennifer Abbott and Joel Bakan, *The Corporation*, <www.thecorporation.tv/>)

## THE 'GUSHING' PHENOMENON

Like military personnel, journalists also sign themselves over to authority. Executives are obliged by corporate law to maximise profits for shareholders – corporate journalists are not exempt from the need to prioritise the company's welfare (in an unforgiving political and economic environment) in everything they say and do. Thus, individuals may come and go but, year after year, in an all but unvarying pattern, news reports end up demonising official enemies, prettifying our government's crimes, and overlooking the corporate greed that informs so much politics. Like military personnel, reporters view what happens next as someone else's moral responsibility.

In January 2003, Media Lens wrote to BBC news presenter Fiona Bruce asking her why she had described the build-up of troops in

Kuwait as being 'to deal with the continuing threat posed by Iraq'. Bruce replied simply: 'I'll forward your point to the news editor – thank you' (*BBC News* at 18:00, BBC1, January 7, 2003; Bruce, email to Media Lens, January 7, 2003).

But if we refuse to accept responsibility for the very words that come out of our mouths, have we not lost our humanity? The result, all too often, is that other people lose their lives.

In February 2005, ITN's John Irvine reported on 'the hermit state' of North Korea where people celebrated the birth of the country's leader in a 'display of people in perfect unison – cynics might call it "Come Dancing, or else!"' (*ITV News* at 22:30, ITN, February 16, 2005). The North Korean people, it seems, had been 'treated to hours of gushing television' in honour of the leader. 'When it comes to propaganda', Irvine concluded, 'this is a broadcaster beyond comparison.'

There are ugly ironies here. The first, of course, is that British TV viewers are also familiar with the 'gushing' phenomenon. When Baghdad fell to US tanks on April 9, 2003, British journalists gushed uncontrollably (see Chapter 4). John Irvine, himself, declared: 'A war of three weeks has brought an end to decades of Iraqi misery' (*ITV Evening News*, ITN, April 9, 2003). This, at the height of an illegal invasion based on a set of outrageous lies in which literally tens of thousands of Iraqis were being killed. British journalists also gushed over the June 2004 'transfer of sovereignty' in Iraq and over Iraq's 'first democratic elections for 50 years' in January 2005, just as they had gushed over the 'humanitarian intervention' to end the Serbian 'genocide' in Kosovo in 1999.

The deeper irony is that Irvine's comments on North Korea were made from the heart of the West's own propaganda system – a system that also consistently demonises 'rogue states'. In April 1950, a US National Security Council Directive stated: The citizens of the United States 'stand in their deepest peril', being threatened with the 'destruction not only of this Republic but of civilisation itself' by 'international Communism' (quoted, Mark Curtis, *The Ambiguities of Power – British Foreign Policy since 1945*, Zed Books, 1995, p. 43). The threat was a fraud. Privately, former under-secretary of state and future deputy secretary of defence Robert Lovett pointed out (March 1950): 'If we can sell every useless article known to man in large quantities, we should be able to sell our very fine story [regarding the communist 'threat'] in larger quantities' (ibid., p.44).

In May 1985, Ronald Reagan declared a 'national emergency' to deal with the 'unusual and extraordinary threat to the national security and foreign policy of the United States' posed by 'the policies and actions of the Government of Nicaragua' (World Court Digest, <www.virtual-institute.de/en/wcd/wcd.cfm?107090400100.cfm>).

In September 2002, Tony Blair declared in his foreword to 'the British dossier assessing weapons of mass destruction in Iraq':

> It is unprecedented for the Government to publish this kind of document. But in light of the debate about Iraq and Weapons of Mass Destruction (WMD), I wanted to share with the British public the reasons why I believe this issue to be a current and serious threat to the UK national interest. ('Full Text of Tony Blair's Foreword to the Dossier on Iraq', Guardian, September 24, 2002)

John Morrison, an adviser to the parliamentary intelligence and security committee and a former deputy chief of defence intelligence, told the BBC: 'When I heard him using those words, I could almost hear the collective raspberry going up around Whitehall' (quoted, Richard Norton-Taylor, 'Official Sacked Over TV Remarks on Iraq', Guardian, July 26, 2004). Morrison was sacked for his honesty. A year later, Blair was up for re-election, while his 'retired' spinmeister Alastair Campbell appeared on the quiz show *Who Wants To Be A Millionaire?* Campbell has also been quietly 'welcomed back' into the New Labour fold.

In a companion piece to John Irvine's report on North Korea, Ian Williams of *Channel 4 News* reported on celebrations marking the fall of Saigon to Vietnamese forces in 1975. The tone was of unrelenting mockery: 'Stern-faced communist leaders looked on under slogans proclaiming freedom and independence.' Veterans also participated: 'it must have been a challenge to remain upright under the weight of all those medals' (*Channel 4 News* at 18:30, April 30, 2005). The report continued in the same vein:

> Well there aren't many regimes left that can still mount a spectacle like this and keep a straight face about it. Still, the emphasis of today's speeches was as much about economic change, reform, as it was about liberation.

Recall that Williams was here commenting on a cataclysmic slaughter that had consumed the lives of fully 3–4 million Vietnamese, a war fought to rid the country of an authentically despotic, mass-murdering South Vietnamese regime imposed by American power. The tone was light-hearted but callous: impoverished farmers suffering the ravages of bird flu 'perhaps thought it wiser to bring along a few plastic animals' Williams quipped of one sorry-looking part of the parade. A model aircraft on a float 'looked suspiciously like a model produced by the "imperialist" Americans'.

Over on the BBC, a documentary on the fall of Saigon lamented: 'A twenty-year attempt to build a nation had failed' (*55 days – The Fall of Saigon*, BBC2, May 6, 2005).

On BBC's *Newsnight*, Tim Wheeler observed that Libya is a rogue state which 'made mischief for the West for so long', so how could it become 'such a good boy'? (*Newsnight*, BBC2, December 22, 2003). Also on *Newsnight*, Amman correspondent Jon Leyne challenged the Syrian minister for ex-pat affairs, Buthaina Shaba'n:

> Minister, the President spoke of the need to improve the economy and tackle corruption. Is the President prepared to challenge the wealth and power of those handful of people – known to everyone in this room – who earn so much of Syria's riches? (*Newsnight*, BBC2, June 6, 2005)

Journalists take it for granted that officially designated 'rogue states' should be targeted for fierce criticism and arrogant contempt. It is inconceivable that any BBC journalist would ask a comparable question in a comparable British or US press conference. Imagine Leyne referring a Bush spokesperson to US political corruption, asking: 'Is the president prepared to challenge the wealth and power of those handful of giant corporations – known to everyone in this room – which earn so much of America's riches?'

The companion to media demonisation of the 'bad guys' is the hagiolatry of Western leaders and apologetics for their crimes. Thus Simon Tisdall wrote in the *Guardian*: 'Groundbreaking elections in Afghanistan, Ukraine, Palestine and Iraq, extolled in President Bush's "dawn of freedom" inaugural address, have encouraged western hopes that democratic values are gaining universal acceptance' ('Bush's Democratic Bandwagon Hits a Roadblock in Harare', *Guardian*, February 16, 2005).

On the BBC's main news, Clive Myrie described America as 'the champion of democracy', referring to 'a roll call of newly-minted democracies' (*BBC News* at 13:00, BBC1, February 23, 2005). On *Newsnight*, Paul Wood observed, with scrupulous BBC neutrality, of the illegal invasion of Iraq: 'it is a benign occupation, or ostensibly a benign occupation' (*Newsnight*, BBC2, December 16, 2003).

We need to be clear that the commandant of Auschwitz did not for one moment see himself as evil or destructive. Nor did the troopers at My Lai. And nor, of course, do our well-heeled, well-educated, Oxbridge journalists. They may have tempers and egos – they are surely not mass murderers.

But journalists who reflexively reinforce an authorised, Manichean view of the world – a world made up of 'humanitarian interventionists' ('Us') and 'Monster States' ('Them') – *are* vital cogs in the machinery of industrial killing.

## TRAINED FOR TIMIDITY

In the first ten chapters of this book, and in some 1,800 pages of media alerts since 2001, we have shown how media performance overwhelmingly promotes the views and interests of established power. It might seem curious that we have also consistently argued that this happens in the absence of any conspiracy, with minimal self-censorship, and with even less outright lying.

In his excellent book *Disciplined Minds*, American physicist and writer Jeff Schmidt indicates how it is that professionals, journalists very much included, can come to promote the agenda of the powerful with almost no awareness of the role they are playing. Schmidt, formerly an editor at *Physics Today* magazine for 19 years, points out that professionals are trusted to run organisations in the interests of their employers. Clearly employers cannot be on hand to supervise every decision, and so professionals have to be trained to 'ensure that each and every detail of their work favours the right interests – or skewers the disfavoured ones' in the absence of overt control. Thus, the whole process of selection, training, and even qualification, Schmidt argues, has evolved so that professionals internalise the basic understanding that they should 'subordinate their own beliefs to an assigned ideology' and not 'question the politics built into their work'. Schmidt continues:

> The qualifying attitude, I find, is an uncritical, subordinate one, which allows professionals to take their ideological lead from their employers and appropriately fine-tune the outlook that they bring to their work. The resulting professional is an obedient thinker, an intellectual property whom employers can trust to experiment, theorise, innovate and create safely within the confines of an assigned ideology. The political and intellectual timidity of today's most highly educated employees is no accident. (*Disciplined Minds*

*– A Critical Look at Salaried Professionals and the Soul-Battering System that Shapes Their Lives*, Rowman & Littlefield Publishers, 2000, p. 16, <http://disciplinedminds.com>)

This is a brilliant description of how mainstream journalists operate – they do indeed create, innovate and theorise, but within the ideological 'box' delimited by the requirements and goals of established power.

The psychologist Erich Fromm explained that, not just professionals, but *all* modern individuals are socialised to perceive themselves as morally empty vessels willing to accept whatever is demanded of them. Fromm wrote: 'The "adjusted" person ... is one who has made himself into a commodity, with nothing stable or definite except his need to please and his readiness to change roles' (*Psychoanalysis and Religion*, Yale University Press, 1978, p. 75). This helps explain the remarkable extent to which journalists appear oblivious to the moral consequences of their words and actions. They perceive themselves merely as commodities to be bought and sold for employment. Their job is to please, not to question, their employers.

Schmidt describes the required journalistic attitude perfectly as 'adjusted curiosity'. Thus, despite being a socially approved form of mass insanity, it is simply understood by journalists that it is not their business to 'question the politics built into their work' by the fact that their broadsheets depend for 75 per cent of their revenues on advertisers, by the fact that wealthy business moguls and giant parent companies with fingers in any number of corporate pies have the power to hire and fire journalists reporting on corporate activity, and so on.

Journalists may even attempt to rationalise their failure to challenge systemic media corruption (as opposed to isolated 'bad apples') on the grounds that their particular media entity is somehow free of the compromising pressures that dominate all of society. Even if we were to take this seriously, it hardly explains their silence on the media system as a whole that clearly *is* compromised by such pressures.

Similarly, liberal journalists are able to convince themselves that echoing the words and claims of politicians without comment constitutes 'objective' journalism. Thus Ed Pilkington, foreign editor of the *Guardian*, told Media Lens, 'We are not in the business of editorialising our news reports' (email to Media Lens, November 15, 2002). To give only the establishment view of the world must be 'objective', after all, because the journalist has thereby refrained from giving his or her own personal view! The point being, as Schmidt writes, that 'refraining from questioning doesn't *look* like a political act, and so professionals give the appearance of being politically neutral in their work' (*Disciplined Minds*, p. 35).

But, of course, not questioning *is* a political act. In fact nothing could have been *less* neutral in 2002 and 2003 than echoing yet another Downing Street deception on Iraq without comment, thereby bringing closer a cynical war and the mass death of many thousands of innocent people – it could not be clearer that this 'neutral' act is morally monstrous. It doesn't matter that all the media professionals in the world refuse to recognise the myth of 'objective' echoing of power – the real world of cause and effect, of lies and manipulated public support, of moral responsibility for death nevertheless *does* exist.

The result of this widespread subordination to 'standards of professionalism' – that is, to power – is a culture in which critical thought and honest questioning have come to be feared, and in fact hated, as unprofessional, dangerous and wrong. We at Media Lens meet fear all the time in our dealings with journalists – they are afraid of appearing irrational by denying obvious facts, but they are afraid of revealing truths that might cost them their columns, their credibility, their jobs. They are also, even more significantly, afraid of the implications of what we and our readers have to say for their sense of who they are. Bertrand Russell explained this with great force in an essay published in 1916:

> Men fear thought more than they fear anything else on earth – more than ruin, more even than death … It is fear that holds men back – fear lest their cherished beliefs should prove delusions, fear lest the institutions by which they live should prove harmful, fear lest they themselves should prove less worthy of respect than they have supposed themselves to be. (Bertrand Russell, from *Principles of Social Reconstruction*, 1916. Quoted Erich Fromm, *On Disobedience and Other Essays*, Routledge & Kegan Paul, 1984, pp. 34–5)

Nothing is more fearsome to liberal journalists than the possibility that they might not be the noble defenders of justice and truth they have always imagined themselves to be, and on which image they have built a lucrative, prestigious career. The problem, as John Pilger often reminds us, is that liberals 'want it both ways'. They want to be respected and rewarded by a hideously corrupt media system with the power to demonise or embrace them, but they also want to be seen as defenders of the powerless and suffering who are so often the victims of that very same media system and its state–corporate allies. One option is to simply ignore the obvious role of the media system in human misery, but that is absurd.

This is why so many liberals accuse Media Lens and its readers of 'personal attacks'. And yet we have made no personal attacks against any journalists – we are interested in challenging ideas, not in attacking individuals, for whom we feel no animosity whatever. But in truth our arguments *do* have personal implications for how journalists see themselves.

Schmidt cites a comment by Noam Chomsky on the reception he generally receives from liberals at Harvard University as opposed to conservatives at the Massachusetts Institute of Technology (MIT):

> By conventional measures, the Harvard faculty is much more liberal, in fact left-liberal. MIT faculty are very conservative often, even reactionary. I get along fine with the MIT faculty, even when we disagree about everything (which is the usual case). If I show up at the Harvard faculty club, you can feel the chill settle; it's as if Satan himself had entered the room. (Chomsky, quoted, Schmidt, *Disciplined Minds*, p. 14)

Readers may recall the tale of the little girl who, playing by a deep well, drops her golden ball into the well, whereupon it is rescued and offered to her by an ugly frog. American comparative mythologist Joseph Campbell described the significance of this repulsive character, which appears in different forms in fairy tales and folk tales throughout human culture and history:

> The disgusting and rejected frog or dragon of the fairy tale brings up the sun ball in its mouth; for the frog, the serpent, the rejected one, is the representative of that unconscious deep ... wherein are hoarded all of the rejected, unadmitted, unrecognised, unknown, or undeveloped factors, laws, and elements of existence ... The herald or announcer of the adventure, therefore, is often dark, loathly, or terrifying, judged evil by the world; yet if one could follow, the way would be opened through the walls of day into the dark where the jewels glow. (*The Hero with a Thousand Faces*, Princeton University Press, 1949, pp. 52–3)

Chomsky is just such a frog! And Media Lens, too, we hope!

## HELL, THE SYSTEM WORKS JUST FINE!

The late Gary Webb was a typical example of the kind of journalist who at one time would have dismissed Media Lens out of hand. Webb was an investigative reporter for nineteen years, focusing on government and private sector corruption, winning more than 30 awards for his journalism. He was one of six reporters at the San Jose *Mercury News* to win a 1990 Pulitzer Prize for a series of stories on California's 1989 earthquake. In 1994, he was awarded the H.L. Mencken Award by the Free Press Association, and in 1997 he received a Media Hero's Award. Webb described his experience of mainstream journalism:

> In seventeen years of doing this, nothing bad had happened to me. I was never fired or threatened with dismissal if I kept looking under rocks. I didn't get any death threats that worried me. I was winning awards, getting raises, lecturing college classes, appearing on TV shows, and judging journalism contests. So how could I possibly agree with people like Noam Chomsky and Ben Bagdikian, who were claiming the system didn't work, that it was steered by powerful special interests and corporations, and existed to protect the power elite? Hell, the system worked just fine, as I could tell. It *encouraged* enterprise. It *rewarded* muckraking. ('The Mighty Wurlitzer Plays On', in Kristina Borjesson (ed.), *Into the Buzzsaw – Leading Journalists Expose the Myth of a Free Press*, Prometheus, 2002, p. 296)

Alas, then, as Joseph Heller wrote, 'Something Happened':

> And then I wrote some stories that made me realise how sadly misplaced my bliss had been. The reason I'd enjoyed such smooth sailing for so long hadn't been, as I'd assumed, because I was careful and diligent and good at my job. It turned out to have nothing to do with it. The truth was that, in all those years, I hadn't written anything important enough to suppress. (pp. 296–7)

In 1996, Webb wrote a series of stories entitled *Dark Alliances*. The series reported how a US-backed terrorist army, the Nicaraguan Contras, had financed their activities by selling crack cocaine in the ghettos of Los Angeles to the city's biggest crack dealer. The series documented direct contact between drug traffickers bringing drugs into Los Angeles and two Nicaraguan CIA agents who were administering the Contras in Central America. Moreover, it revealed how elements of the US government knew about this drug ring's activities at the time and did little, if anything, to stop it. The evidence included sworn testimony from one of the drug traffickers – a government informant – that a CIA agent specifically instructed them to raise money for the Contras in California.

The country's three biggest newspapers – the *Washington Post*, the *New York Times* and the *Los Angeles Times* – focusing on Webb rather than on his story, all declared the story 'flawed', empty, and not worth pursuing. Webb commented: 'Never before had the three biggest papers devoted such energy to kicking the hell out of a story by another newspaper' (ibid., p. 306).

Webb's editors began to get nervous; 5,000 reprints of the series were burned, disclaimers were added to follow-up stories making it clear that the paper was not accusing the CIA of direct knowledge of what was going on, 'even though the facts strongly suggested CIA complicity', Webb noted. Despite a lack of evidence or arguments, the story was quickly labelled 'irresponsible' by the media. Ultimately, the *Mercury News* backed away from the material, apologising for 'shortcomings' in a story that had been 'oversimplified' and contained 'egregious errors'. Webb quit the *Mercury News* soon thereafter.

As additional information subsequently came to light, Webb recognised that he had indeed been in error:

The CIA's knowledge and involvement had been far greater than I'd ever imagined. The drug ring was even bigger than I had portrayed. The involvement between the CIA agents running the Contras and drug traffickers was closer than I had written. (Ibid., p. 307)

Despite the press condemnation, Webb wrote, the facts became more damning, not less – but they were never seriously explored. Instead the story was permanently tarred as 'discredited'.

So why did the press turn on the story and on Webb himself?

Primarily because the series presented dangerous ideas. It suggested that crimes of state had been committed. If the story was true, it meant the federal government bore some responsibility, however indirect, for the flood of crack that coursed through black neighbourhoods in the 1980s ... The scary thing about this collusion between the press and the powerful is that it works so well. In this case, the government's denials and promises to pursue the truth didn't work. The public didn't accept them, for obvious reasons, and the clamour for an independent investigation continued to grow. But after the government's supposed watchdogs weighed in, public opinion became

divided and confused, the movement to force congressional hearings lost
steam ... (Ibid., pp. 308–9)

Once enough people came to believe that the story had been
exaggerated or distorted, it could be quietly buried and forgotten.

In the above account, Webb provided an important aid to
understanding how 'dangerous ideas' and 'dangerous' journalists
are filtered from the mainstream media – a very heavy 'stick' awaits
all who seriously step out of line by exposing issues that are perceived
as threatening by a wide range of establishment interests. What is so
important about Webb's account is that he worked courageously and
honestly as a journalist for 17 years without the slightest knowledge
of the existence of this 'stick'. This suggests to us that journalists are
indeed sincere in their belief that they are free and independent. As
Webb himself wrote: 'I had a grand total of one story spiked during
my entire reporting career ... I wrote my stories the way I wanted to
write them, without anyone looking over my shoulder or steering
me in a certain direction' (ibid., p. 296).

This is the account we hear time and again from journalists,
who often think we are 'completely over the top' and 'extreme'
in our views. Indeed, because we are trying to draw attention to
comparatively 'hidden' phenomena – such as the 'stick' that hit Webb
– phenomena that are often invisible to them, journalists assume
we must be driven by some kind of mania: perhaps a deep hatred
of journalists, or an addiction to criticising people. In an interview,
Channel 4 newsreader Jon Snow told us:

> Journalists are lazy, they live in a goldfish bowl, they're not interested in
> breaking out and breaking this stuff [controversial stories] themselves. And
> it isn't because they've got the advertisers breathing down their necks – they
> couldn't give a shit about the advertisers – it's because it's easier to do other
> things, where they're spoon-fed ... I can tell you if somebody rings me up
> from Pepsi-Cola – and I must say I don't think I've ever been rung by any
> corporation, would that I was! – I'd give them short shrift! (interview with
> David Edwards, January 9, 2001, <www.medialens.org/articles_2001/de_
> Jon_Snow_interview.htm>)

We believe this complacent view would radically change if, as Webb
writes, Snow were to report anything 'important enough to suppress'.
Gary Webb was found dead in December 2004 having apparently
committed suicide.

## MAKING A DIFFERENCE – WHY WE *CAN* INFLUENCE THE MEDIA

As Jeff Schmidt makes very clear, professionals, including media professionals, are *not* liars. They are people who have been selected and trained to subordinate their capacity for critical thought to a professional 'standard'. They do this with minimal awareness in the understanding that it is 'just how things are done'.

If media employees were cynical liars, truth would be irrelevant – challenging emails and letters would simply be deleted and binned. But because media professionals, while deeply deluded, do see themselves as basically honest, their sense of self-identity means they cannot simply reject rational, restrained and accurate challenges out of hand. They cannot maintain their idea of themselves as reasonable people without taking account of reasonable views. This provides small but significant leverage for those of us hoping to change and improve the system. Let us consider a couple of examples to indicate the significance of this reality for progressive social change.

On October 12, 2002, one of our readers, Darren Smith, wrote to John Humphrys, senior presenter of BBC Radio's *Today* programme, following the latter's interview with the foreign secretary, Jack Straw, that same day. Smith critiqued Straw's comments:

1) 'Saddam Hussein was able to ... expel the inspectors.' – This is an outright lie – a deliberate mutilation of the truth. I focus on this in further detail below.

2) 'brutal attacks have been launched by the Iraqi regime on Iran ... on Saddam Hussein's own people ... and then ... Kuwait'. This is a half truth. Most of Saddam Hussein's worst atrocities took place while receiving support from Western states, including the US and UK.

3) 'the inspectors were able to get in and to do their work'. Another half truth. The work of UNSCOM inspectors was undermined by infiltration of agents who were spying on Iraq.

In response to Mr. Straw's opening statement, which includes the barrage of distortions listed above, I listened in astonishment to your agreement. You told listeners: 'Well much of that may be true, surely is true, certainly when you talk about Saddam's record and nobody would argue with any of that' (John Humphrys, *Today* – BBC Radio 4, October 12, 2002) ...

I certainly – together with many others – would argue with *all of that*. I'll stick just to Mr. Straw's most blatant distortion – the lie that 'Saddam Hussein was able to ... expel the inspectors.' This surely is not true. UNSCOM evacuated Iraq on 16 December 1998 after being warned by US officials of the risk to their safety posed by an imminent air attack by US/UK bombers and cruise missiles – Operation Desert Fox ... (email forwarded to Media Lens, October 15, 2002)

Humphrys responded:

> What you fail to appreciate is that Today interviewers don't have enough time to challenge every assertion made in every interview. Of course it's true that the inspectors were pulled out as opposed to thrown out – but, as Straw has said in previous interviews with me (which you apparently chose not to hear) the argument was that Sadam made it impossible for them to say [sic]. But I'm wasting my time dealing with your points. You have decided (bizarrely) that I'm in favour of a war with Iraq and there's nothing I can to persuade you otherwise. It is possible to agree that Saddam is a monster (which is what I was agreeing with) and STILL oppose war. Can't you understand that? Don't bother replying. John Humphrys (email to Smith, October 16, 2002)

Despite appearances, these irate words did *not* signify that Humphrys had simply rejected the challenge – indeed the very venom of the response indicated that Smith had hit the mark. Two weeks later, on October 30, John Humphrys again interviewed Jack Straw on Iraq. This is what happened:

> Straw: ... they did throw out the weapons inspectors ...
> Humphrys: Well they didn't actually throw them out. You keep getting into trouble when you say that, as you know, and I keep getting into trouble for letting you say it. The fact is they weren't thrown out, they did withdraw. Their lives were made difficult while they were there, and so they withdrew, which isn't quite the same. (*Today* programme, BBC Radio 4, October 30, 2002)

One individual writing a couple of passionate but rational and factually accurate letters, had helped to neutralise one attempt by Britain's Foreign Secretary to promote a war by deceiving and manipulating a national radio audience. Anyone who thinks writing letters and other forms of dissent make no difference should reflect on this example.

Media Lens has been subjecting the BBC to consistent criticism for its atrocious reporting on Afghanistan, Iraq and other issues. After a particularly dire *Panorama* documentary on Iraq (*Saddam: A Warning from History*, BBC1, November 3, 2002), our readers sent a large number of emails in response to our media alert complaining of the factual errors and omissions in the programme. A month later a much more accurate *Panorama* programme appeared: *Iraq: The Case Against War* (BBC1, December 8, 2002).

Although the programme makers assembled a curious array of dissenting anti-war voices and omitted many important facts and arguments, it was a welcome improvement. We asked a contact of ours at the BBC – acting world service regional editor, Bill Hayton – if he thought Media Lens' criticism played a part in the programme being aired. This was Hayton's response:

> Yes I think the criticism probably did play a part. One (optimistic) explanation would be that it gives programme makers a bit of resolve to overcome any objections and the (cynical) explanation is that it lets other parts of the news machine off the hook. They must have been preparing the programme since at least early November since the sequence with the general was filmed on Remembrance Sunday. But there are clearly people within the organisation who want to make decent programmes, the question is how to make their job easier! (Hayton to David Edwards, December 11, 2002)

Although corporations, including media corporations, are totalitarian structures of power, we do not live in a totalitarian society. Control is maintained, not by violence, but by deception, self-deception, and by a mass willingness to subordinate our own thoughts and feelings to notions of 'professionalism' and 'objectivity'. There is much evil and violence in the world but the people who make it possible are not for the most part evil or violent.

Psychologist Stanley Milgram reported that the most fundamental lesson of his study on obedience in modern society was, 'ordinary people, simply doing their jobs, and without any particular hostility on their part, can become agents in a terrible, destructive process' (*Obedience to Authority*, p. 24).

Milgram's second key lesson was that when even a small number of individuals rebel, refuse to obey; when they claim their human right to speak out in the name of their own perceptions, their own thoughts, their own truly felt compassion for the suffering of others, it has an inordinately powerful impact on the world around them. Greedy and destructive power based on thoughtless obedience is supremely vulnerable to compassionate rebellion.

# 12
# Towards a Compassionate Media

Newspapers in Britain are first and foremost businesses. They do not exist to report news, to act as watchdogs for the public, to be a check on the doings of government, to defend the ordinary citizens against abuses of power, to unearth scandals or to do any of the other fine and noble things that are sometimes claimed for the press. They exist to make money, just as any other business does. To the extent that they discharge any of their public functions, they do so in order to succeed as businesses. (Colin Sparks, quoted in Richard Keeble, *Ethics for Journalists*, Routledge, 2001, p. 2)

## WEST IS BEST –
## HOW MEDIA COMPASSION RADIATES 'OUTWARDS'

Readers will have noticed that journalists reporting from Washington generally look like the officials they are covering: male reporters look, dress and sound like elite male politicians; female reporters look, dress and sound like elite female politicians, replete with power-dressing and lashings of made-over gloss.

Journalists' appearance can hardly be deemed neutral. Imagine, after all, dressing to the nines in this way, standing in front of Congress, and declaring that Western leaders are stooges of big business that do little else but lie and dissemble in order to fool the public into accepting a charade of 'democracy', imposing policies designed to deliver profits to an elite few. Imagine looking, dressing and sounding exactly as elites do, only to pour scorn on all they stand for.

The impression given is of deferential emissaries who, immaculately and respectfully turned out, have been granted the rare privilege of ascending to the summit of power and returning with their vital pronouncements. This is reinforced by what is actually said – the emphasis is forever on what 'Washington thinks', on what 'White House insiders' hope, fear and plan.

The subliminal message is that our rulers are superior, transcendent, benign. They are to be afforded respect, even awe, as the loftiest stratum of a proudly meritocratic political system. We are trained to feel small and humbly attentive at the feet of power. One would never guess from these reports that we, the people, are the ostensible leaders, with politicians merely selected, by us, as *our* representatives.

It follows that the awe-inspiring, benevolent political system suggested by these reports must be motivated by lofty values. And if this benign system emerges out of, and rules over, society, then that society must also be fundamentally benign, civilised and moral.

Indeed, many journalists seem to hold to a kind of moral Darwinism, appearing to equate the West's powerful, high-tech sophistication with moral sophistication. They take it for granted that we are intellectually, culturally and morally superior to the 'less developed' societies of the impoverished South. White, well-heeled Oxbridge journalists are forever being filmed moving, like missionaries, among our stricken brown-skinned brethren. In her article, 'The West Really is the Best', Polly Toynbee wrote:

> In our political and social culture we have a democratic way of life which we know, without any doubt at all, is far better than any other in the history of humanity. Even if we don't like to admit it, we are all missionaries and believers that our own way is the best when it comes to the things that really matter ... ('The West Really Is the Best', *Observer*, March 5, 2000)

In the *New York Times*, Michael Wines warned in 1999 that despite America's 'victory over Communism and inhumanity' in Kosovo, problems remained. Americans often perceived their morals as universal, Wines wrote, but in fact there was 'a yawning gap between the West and much of the world on the value of a single human life' (FAIR, Action Alert, June 17, 1999).

It is only right, then, that we should illuminate the path for the burka-wearing peoples of the world – away from their 'medieval religions' and towards 'democracy' – with laser-guided bombs. Of course it is not appropriate for just anyone to launch wars against a country outside of international law. But we are not just anyone – we are modernity, reason, science. We are the West.

American admiral Gene Larocque spoke in 1985 of his war against the Japanese from 1941 to 1945:

> We'd thought they were little brown men and we were the great big white men. They were of a lesser species. The Germans were well known as tremendous fighters and builders, whereas the Japanese would be a pushover. We used nuclear weapons on these little brown men. We talked about using them in Vietnam. We talked about using our military force to get our oil in

the Middle East from a sort of dark-skinned people. I never hear about us using the military to get our oil from Canada. We still think we're a great super-race. (Quoted, Howard Zinn and Anthony Arnove, *Voices of a People's History of the United States*, Seven Stories Press, 2004, p. 373)

Because we believe we are fundamentally superior, our lives matter more. We are vibrant, modern individuals; they are weary, impoverished groups. When we are killed by terrorists, we die as individuals with names, families, histories. When they die under our guns, they die as anonymous masses.

Journalists occasionally try to rationalise this by suggesting that we care more about Western lives because we more closely identify with people who live as we do. Thus, a *New Statesman* editorial argued:

Compassion radiates outwards: the closer people are to us, the more keenly we feel it when tragedy befalls them ... It is, therefore, wholly understandable that British emotions are touched when more than 5,000 people die at the hands of terrorists in New York and Washington: that people are more deeply troubled than they are by countless deaths in Colombia, Iraq, Afghanistan or the Congo. Most of us cannot imagine life in a poor African village or a Latin American shanty town, but New Yorkers lead lives much like ours, commuting from suburb to office, speaking the same language, nurturing the same aspirations. (Leader, 'It's not the Wild West, Mr President', *New Statesman*, September 24, 2001)

The stark, ugly reality is that many of us *truly* believe we are superior to, more important than, the people of Colombia, Iraq, Afghanistan and the Congo.

## SO WHAT WOULD YOU DO?
## THE *GUARDIAN* EDITOR BOWLS A GOOGLY

People often ask us if we really believe our efforts can result in a less brutal, more compassionate, media system. Do we seriously think that editors and journalists will radically change their performance as a result of receiving emails from the public? Doesn't the propaganda model predict that the framing conditions of state–corporate capitalism will inevitably filter out rogue editors and journalists? Won't any 'converts' simply be replaced? In which case, isn't it hopeless? Why bother at all?

On February 4, 2004, *Guardian* editor Alan Rusbridger emailed us the following challenge:

Dear David,

You make an interesting critique of the general position regarding the funding of newspapers – and you draw the implication you choose to draw. That's an interesting debate, if hardly a new one. I'd be interested to know what alternative business model you propose for newspapers which would sustain a large, knowledgeable and experienced staff of writers and editors, here and abroad, in print as well as on the web. Do you prefer no advertising lest journalists are corrupted or influenced in the way you imagine? If so, what cover price do you propose? Or, in the absence of advertising, what other source of revenue would you prefer?

These are all interesting debates, and I wish you well. I can only answer as to my experience. alan. (email to David Cromwell, February 6, 2004)

These are interesting questions. The first point to make in response is that we are not obliged to respond to the question of alternatives at all. It is quite reasonable to draw attention to an important problem without offering a solution – the highlighting of important issues for discussion is itself an important and legitimate activity.

To our knowledge, Media Lens is the first serious attempt to provide a regular, radical response to mainstream propaganda in the UK. Criticising actual or potential employers means career-death for journalists, as it does in any industry, and so the well-intentioned have by and large attempted to do what they can from inside the media, stepping cautiously around important media toes.

This is not an unreasonable strategy, particularly prior to the internet revolution when dissident outreach was extremely limited. Nevertheless, dozens of skilled media dissidents have long worked at the margins of the mainstream in the United States, while Britain has managed to produce a tiny handful and, otherwise, a complacent, stifling silence.

This complacency may in part be explained by the co-option of dissent by more honest media to the left of the British spectrum – the *Guardian*, *Observer*, *Independent* and *Independent on Sunday* – than can be found in the United States. The existence of this more liberal component may, in turn, be explained by the fact that pre-Blair Britain had a version of left parliamentary opposition to state–corporate power. Now that our political system has 'converged' in the way of

US politics (dominated by two pro-business parties), our media may also be converging towards a similarly closed and intolerant, US-style media system. The recent high-profile dismissals of journalists and politicians challenging power – the BBC's Andrew Gilligan, Gavyn Davies and Greg Dyke, the *Daily Mirror*'s Piers Morgan, and former Labour (now Respect party) MP George Galloway – against the loss of zero pro-war journalists and politicians may be evidence of this.

The point is that the appearance of dissident journalists in the UK 'liberal' press – rare indeed in the US media (Paul Krugman of the *New York Times* is a conspicuous example) – has had an impact on liberal perception that is far greater than their impact on wider public opinion and politics.

Dissident appearances in the mainstream act as a kind of liberal vaccine inoculating against the idea that the media is subject to tight restrictions and control. Thus, many people see papers like the *Guardian* and *Independent* as genuinely enlightened and honest (just as many people see the BBC as benevolent 'Auntie Beeb'). As a result, the atrocious performance of these media in failing to challenge even the most banal government deceptions goes unnoticed. The public may heap blame on governments, but the pivotal role of the media is ignored.

As a 'corporate free press' clearly represents a major contradiction in terms, an attempt to explore these issues is vital, and is justified quite regardless of whether someone making the attempt has solutions to offer. We can imagine someone interrupting a Town Hall meeting to report that the local school is on fire and that children are being burned alive. Such a person would presumably not be chastised for failing, also, to come up with an idea on how best to extinguish the fire. To suggest, as Rusbridger in effect intended, that such a (perceived) failure is a further reason to ignore such warnings, is a cynical diversion.

So we *could* argue that people should decide for themselves what to do about the problems we are highlighting, that we are simply doing what almost nobody else is doing in saying: 'There is a *major* problem with the corporate media.' We could reasonably argue that, although we don't.

### THE NETIZENS ARE COMING!

We do much more than talk about practical solutions – Media Lens is *itself* a practical solution. The promotion of public participation in media criticism is vital work. As discussed in the previous chapter, writing to the media is a powerful part of the solution we are proposing. Journalists, particularly liberal journalists, commonly see themselves as 'the good guys' exposing the depredations of power. Moreover, they see themselves as admired, respected, even loved – broadcast journalists often clearly view themselves as celebrities. This makes them highly sensitive to even the mildest 'left' criticism denting their 'good guy' status.

Challenges of this kind confront their notion of who they are, puncturing their complacency and wounding their egos, so that they are rarely able to resist responding. These responses, in turn, often provide valuable insights into a closed world of privilege largely protected from honest criticism. Important results can include heightened public awareness of media realities and even an improvement in journalistic performance. The media depends on self-delusions normally protected from criticism – rational challenge therefore often leaves journalists unable to justify (even to themselves) obviously erroneous arguments and emphases.

The role of the alternative media in challenging these delusions has never been more important than it is today. For the first time, non-corporate reporters and commentators are able to rapidly reach a mass audience at minimal cost.

In an article in the *New York Times*, Howard French reported of South Korea:

> For years, people will be debating what made this country go from conservative to liberal, from gerontocracy to youth culture and from staunchly pro-American to a deeply ambivalent ally – all seemingly overnight ... But for many observers, the most important agent of change has been the Internet. ('Online Newspaper Shakes up Korean Politics', *New York Times*, March 6, 2003)

South Korea has fast, broadband connections in 70 per cent of households. A Western diplomat in Seoul said: 'This is the most online country in the world. The younger generation get all their information from the web. Some don't even bother with TVs. They just download the programmes' (Jonathan Watts, 'World's First Internet President Logs On: Web Already Shaping Policy of New South Korean Leader', *Guardian*, February 24, 2003).

As elections approached in South Korea in 2002, more and more people began to get their information and political analysis from

Internet news services instead of from the country's conservative newspapers. The most influential Internet service, OhmyNews, registered 20 million page views per day around election time in December 2002. In March 2003, the service still averaged around 14 million visits daily, in a country of 40 million people. OhmyNews was started by Oh Yeon Ho, 41, who said:

> My goal was to say farewell to 20th-century Korean journalism, with the concept that every citizen is a reporter ... The professional news culture has eroded our journalism, and I have always wanted to revitalize it. Since I had no money, I decided to use the Internet, which has made this guerrilla strategy possible. (Ibid.)

Relying almost solely on ordinary readers, OhmyNews helped generate a national movement that resulted in the election of Roh Moo Hyun, a reformist lawyer, in December 2002. Before OhmyNews got involved, the new president had been a relative unknown. After his election, he granted OhmyNews the first interview he gave to any Korean news organisation. 'Netizens won', Oh says of the election. 'Traditional media lost' (Mark L. Clifford and Moon Ihlwan, 'Korea: the politics of peril', *Business Week*, February 24, 2003).

This is a remarkable story of genuine importance to anyone interested in challenging state–corporate control of society. The success of libertarian, Internet-based sites in South Korea suggests that Internet media relying mostly on contributions from ordinary readers represent a potent democratising force.

Writing at the Internet site First Draft, journalist Tim Porter notes that photographs revealing both US military caskets and torture inside Abu Ghraib prison in 2004 were based on digital photographs made, not by journalists, but by participants in both stories. Porter comments: 'Imagine how quickly the slaughter of innocents at My Lai would have become known had it been captured by a palm-sized digital camera (or phone) instead of reported by letter' (Porter, 'Digital Proof', *Human Source*, May 6, 2004, <www.timporter.com>). American media analyst, Edward Herman, commented to us:

> My own view is that the media response is heavily dominated by the need to focus on an unwanted topic, their hands forced by outsiders who obtained and began circulating the photos. The photos are inherently sensational, and so wildly contrary to the self-portrayals of the Bushies as liberators,

that they would be hard to keep under the rug. (email to David Edwards, May 13, 2004)

Digital and internet-based technologies mean that participants in any event are now potentially irrefutable witnesses to what really happened. Backed up by a multitude of websites and bloggers around the world, these 'citizen reporters' represent a very real challenge to the compromised intermediaries of corporate journalism. The rapid appearance of photographs of the Abu Ghraib tortures on the streets of Baghdad after they were published on the net doubtless had a major impact on the insurgency.

It seems likely that the unprecedented, global anti-war protests of 2003 were similarly driven by information flooding across the Internet. And while the mainstream media have mostly sent back propaganda from Iraq, Arabic journalists and Western bloggers have emailed a steady flow of horrific images and honest reportage fuelling deep concern across the Arab world and beyond. Jo Wilding's brave and compassionate reporting (www.wildfirejo.org.uk), and Dahr Jamail's dispatches <http://dahrjamailiraq.com> are two inspirational examples. We appear to be living through an era when, for the first time, ordinary 'citizen reporters' are becoming able to impose a news agenda on the mainstream.

The 'problem' for our argument, we are told, is that the structural realities of the corporate media remain to restrict journalistic freedom and to punish and marginalise dissent. Some readers, feeling sympathy for the plight of journalists we have criticised, have responded: 'Well, what on earth are they supposed to do?'

We should be clear that, beyond marginal improvements, the main rationale for challenging journalists is to generate the kind of debates that illustrate to media *audiences* just how constrained and narrow the existing media system is – our hope is not at all that editors and journalists will respond by somehow revolutionising the system from within by, for example, refusing to carry fossil fuel advertising. That has never been our expectation.

Instead, we have written many times of how we hope that increased public awareness of the limits of political and media freedom will generate truly democratic, alternative media with the power to impose a news agenda on the mainstream, or to replace it as a source of news. The above examples of Internet-led news stories are exactly what we have in mind.

Ideally, beyond even this, powerful alternative media should aspire to inform and motivate large popular movements, including new, libertarian political parties, which might then be in a position to reform media structures to restrict the influence of corporate interests.

But if the question intended by Rusbridger, above, is, 'What can newspapers and journalists do within the system as it actually is now?' – the answer is that, like everyone else, they can do the best they can within tight limits while supporting efforts at radical change through alternative media and movements. Beyond that their options are indeed extremely limited.

And that really is a key message. Our aim is to point out to readers just how powerless even the best-intentioned journalists are in the face of the psychopathic, bottom-line priorities of the corporate media. We are trying to raise awareness of the fact that change is precisely in the *public*'s hands – journalists just cannot do that much. To expect democratic and libertarian 'gifts from above', even from liberal newspapers like the *Guardian* and *Independent*, is naive – progress has only ever been achieved as a result of energetic popular demands for change.

## TOWARDS A COMPASSIONATE MASS MEDIA

In considering the development of honest media, we begin from the premise that truth telling should be motivated by compassion for suffering rather than greed for wealth, status and privilege.

We assume that motivation has a dramatic impact on the capacity for honesty and rationality. It seems clear to us that the presence of a self-serving, greedy motivation tends to distort reason, filtering facts and ideas that obstruct selfish goals. On the other hand, an authentic desire to relieve the suffering of others provides a powerful incentive for rationally identifying the real causes of problems and real solutions in response to them.

Motivation is important because human beings are supremely prone to self-deception. In his book *Vital Lies – Simple Truths*, psychologist Daniel Goleman writes:

> The defences – our bastions against painful information – operate in a shadow world of consciousness, beyond the fringes of awareness. Most often we are oblivious to their operation and remain the unknowing recipient of the version of reality they admit into our ken. The craft of teasing out and

capturing defences in vivo is a tricky endeavour. (*Vital Lies – Simple Truths: The Psychology of Self-Deception*, Bloomsbury, 1997, p. 123)

This capacity for self-deception – for lying without consciously realising we are lying – is a crucial component of the propaganda system afflicting modern democracies.

When we refer to a compassionate motivation, we do not mean someone who merely holds to intellectual concepts of 'equality', 'justice', and 'human rights'; nor do we mean someone primarily motivated by anger at existing inequalities and oppression. We do not even mean someone who has great sympathy for the suffering of others. Instead, we are referring to a motivation rooted in the conviction that the welfare of others is of equal importance to our own, that the welfare of innumerable others is of greater importance than our own, and that compassionate concern contributes to the welfare of both the recipient and generator of compassion (see Chapter 13).

People who have some sense that concern for the well-being of others is also the best strategy for achieving their own well-being are more likely to be able to resist the seductions of wealth, power and status that corrupt and distort so much journalistic output.

Alas, both dissident and mainstream journalism stand mouth agape before such bizarre mentions of kindness, compassion, love and concern for others. Is this really an accidental or natural feature of journalism, or is it a function of power? The American comparative mythologist Joseph Campbell noted of the twentieth century: 'The main awakening of the human spirit is in compassion and the main function of propaganda is to suppress compassion, knock it out. Well, it's in public journalism all the time now, too' (quoted, Cousineau (ed.), *The Hero's Journey*, Harper & Row, 1990, p. 220). Is it any surprise, then, that propaganda has 'knocked out' compassion in the mainstream media? Exploitative power has a vested interest in smearing concern for others as 'naive', 'sentimental' and 'weak' because it benefits from the promotion of greed, hatred and ignorance.

As Noam Chomsky has observed, the corporate goal 'is to ensure that the human beings who [it is] interacting with, you and me, also become inhuman. You have to drive out of people's heads natural sentiments like care about others, or sympathy, or solidarity ... The ideal is to have individuals who are totally disassociated from one another, who don't care about anyone else ... whose conception of themselves, their sense of value, is "Just how many created wants can I satisfy?"' (quoted, Joel Bakan, *The Corporation*, Constable, 2004, pp. 134–5).

A system that needs us to seek isolated satisfaction in selfish desires, to consent to the destruction of official enemies on command, to disregard the impact of our corporate activities on the environment and the Third World, can clearly have no truck with compassion. What Joel Bakan describes as the 'psychopathic' corporate system selects journalists with the right values and promotes servility and brutality in those so selected. BBC correspondent Stephen Sackur provides an insight:

> But there's a flip-side to this extraordinary job. I've seen it in myself. A tendency toward vanity, self-absorption and callousness. Picture for a moment the scene on the morning of the 11 September 2001. I was on assignment in Nicaragua, far from my base in Washington DC. I watched the attacks on the Twin Towers and the Pentagon on a flickering TV. And then I called my wife back home. She was tearful and distraught. Our kids had been rushed out of school in an emergency drill. It felt, she said, like war had broken out.
>
> 'God this is awful,' I said with feeling. 'I know,' she replied, 'there may be thousands dead'.
>
> 'I don't mean that', I snapped. 'I'm talking about me. I'm missing the biggest story of my life.'
>
> Every so often my wife reminds me of that shameful sentiment. But she doesn't need to. I haven't forgotten it. ('Hanging up the Microphone', April 16, 2005, <http://news.bbc.co.uk/1/hi/programmes/from_our_own_correspondent/4448051.stm>)

Sackur's honesty is admirable, but he clearly views this callousness as a shameful aberration. In reality, as we discussed in Chapter 11, it is a required feature of the professional corporate mindset. The focus has to be on getting the job done – whatever it takes – and the job has to be to ensure the success of the media organisation. In this fundamentally inhuman context, thoughts of compassion are unprofessional, unrealistic, even a kind of betrayal. Uncompromising toughness, on the other hand, is worn like a badge of professional honour (which perhaps, in part, explains Sackur's willingness to confess his 'shameful sentiment').

Cooperative efforts to relieve suffering – no matter how successful or inspiring they might have been in the past – must be presented as futile gestures by greed-based media promoting passivity and elite control. The fact that a tiny number of American students forced the fate of East Timor onto the international agenda is not allowed to exist.

Though, in 2003, week after week, millions of people around the world marched against a war that had not yet even started, the public must forever be declared 'selfish', 'indifferent' and hopelessly 'apathetic'. The first BBC *Newsnight* programme after the greatest protest march in British history (February 15, 2003) saw political correspondent David Grossman asking: 'The people have spoken, or have they? What about the millions who didn't march? Was going to the DIY store or watching the football on Saturday a demonstration of support for the government?' (*Newsnight*, BBC2, February 17, 2003).

Macho aggression is a favoured response to public questioning. In response to an online challenge, *Observer* foreign editor Peter Beaumont told one poster: 'piss off' and 'get a life' (*Observer* online debate, June 12, 2003). David Mannion, former editor of ITN News, once sent this email swaggering through our inbox: 'If you misrepresent us I'll have you on toast' (email to Media Lens, May 7, 2003). Journalist John Sweeney told us: 'I don't agree with torturing children. Get stuffed' (email to Media Lens, June 24, 2002). This is so commonly assumed to be what journalism is all about: tough, macho, cynical, aggressive (it is de rigueur to appear stern and unsmiling in photographs, and even to wear severe, oblong-shaped black glasses – there is a discernible 'media style') – that many dissidents also have come to believe it. Indeed, mainstream and dissident journalism are often joined at the hip when it comes to aggression – anger and vitriol are often well to the fore, while compassion and kindness seem to have nothing to do with anything. The predominance of aggression over compassion in the mainstream is a function of power and corruption, not truth. Dissidents should reject this naive 'realism' out of hand.

## HONEST, COMPASSIONATE, NON-CORPORATE

The issue for us, then, is: what kind of media system would be most likely to promote compassionate/rational journalism while allowing such journalism to reach a mass audience?

Clearly, a media corporation legally obliged to maximise returns for shareholders – a corporation run by owners and managers precisely employed to achieve that end – is the last place we would expect a compassionate motivation to thrive. If there is a clash between the need to address important problems of human and animal suffering, and the risk of damaging the interests of owners, parent companies, shareholders, advertisers and government news sources, then managers are obliged to subordinate compassionate impulses to profit.

Green activists, in particular, are fond of reminding us of the humanity of journalists, pointing out that they, too, have children, mothers, and so on. They tell us that individual journalists 'really do care'. This might almost be described as an Anthropomorphic Analysis of media performance.

Bottom-line pressures flow throughout all media corporations. An honest, compassionate press, then, would have to be a not-for-profit, non-corporate press. Ideally, the organisation as a whole would be independent of advertisers – it is clearly absurd for a newspaper like the *Guardian* to be dependent for 75 per cent of its revenue on advertising. What could more clearly compromise the honesty of media reporting?

The media should be primarily dependent on individual subscribers providing for minimum overheads; perhaps funding from large corporate organisations should be disallowed. This is obviously a problem for large print media as printing and distribution costs are high, necessitating reliance on wealthy owners and parent companies, again firmly tying the media into the corporate system. Thus, mere restrictions on advertising would have a minimal effect in liberating media from the other pressures mentioned in Herman and Chomsky's propaganda model: ownership, flak, dependence on state–corporate news sources and so on.

Would it be possible for a corporate media entity to reform itself to a significant extent? Could it refuse, for example, to carry fossil fuel advertising? This goes against the whole 'reason for being' of a corporation – the maximisation of profits. A step of this kind would alienate owners, parent companies, advertisers generally. It would also generate corporate flak both from corporations, and from the left and right wings of the dominant Business Party: Labour/Tories, Democrats/Republicans.

The paper and its editors would doubtless be labelled 'eco-fundamentalists', 'left fanatics', 'Marxist–Leninists', while advertising would haemorrhage to rivals, so raising the dissident paper's cover price while allowing rivals to lower cover prices and entice customers with special offers. Other businesses would likely attack the rogue paper by withdrawing advertising, and so on. The paper would be put at a disadvantage and perhaps out of business. There are plenty of precedents to this effect.

It is conceivable that limits could be placed on advertising for serious news media, or that media could be state-funded in the way of charities. We asked Edward Herman, co-author with Noam Chomsky of the classic work *Manufacturing Consent – The Political Economy of the Mass Media,* for his views:

> BBC and other public service corporations in the media field obviously constitute a different model, but not a 'business' model [BM]. They are all in decline and moving toward the BM, but the result is a more or less corrupt media, with great variations (and the Guardian is surely in the high rungs in BM quality). But if the BM is essentially problematic, we have to keep criticizing it and showing its deep flaws, and pressing it to do better. But obviously we have to try hard to bring forth a non-business model of quality. That is tough given the competitive power of the BM media.
>
> We must support all the new non-BM media in print, broadcast, and Internet as best we can in the hopes that they will find a route to mass audiences. With a real political democracy we could hope for a resuscitation of public broadcasting, and even a mode of government support of independent media with the government's hands strictly off. Getting that real democracy in place is pretty tough, especially with the BM dominating the flow of information to the public. (email to Media Lens, February 16, 2004)

Such changes are far off – depending, as they do, on the creation of powerful popular political movements and parties. Our energies are at present best spent, we believe, in joining, forming, funding and supporting real democratic media initiatives *now* through Internet websites and blogs.

## THE MEDIA IS NOT JUST ANOTHER ISSUE

It is important to bear in mind that reforming the media is not comparable to, say, reforming workers' rights in a standard corporate business. The stakes are much higher in the media. The façade of modern democracy depends on the idea that we are *already* living in a free and open society – the media are a central plank of this 'necessary illusion'. The maintenance of the deception is vital if elites are to continue manipulating the public to fight wars and to wreck the environment for profit. Turning the illusion of media freedom into a reality carries unimaginable costs for elite interests.

The issue is indeed so threatening that, as discussed in Chapter 1, it is never discussed by even society's most liberal media. How much less likely is the media to seriously address actual proposals for reform based on a propaganda model analysis?

Therefore, in our view, significant reform of the corporate media will only be possible in the event of massive, progressive change in the political and general culture of this country, and perhaps globally, perhaps evolving out of Internet-based dissent. Enormous and sophisticated democratic activism is required to generate political movements capable of legislating to institute and protect non-corporate mass media from market pressures and flak.

The Catch-22 problem has always been that the mass media have the power to promote or suppress such widespread cultural changes. In other words, we cannot change the mass media until we change the culture, which cannot change until we change the mass media. The point being that the Internet *does* constitute a revolutionary change in the mass media – the power of non-corporate journalism has increased by orders of magnitude in the last ten or fifteen years.

It is easy to forget just how enormous the change has been. Ten years ago, for example, our own access to dissident material was via radical books ordered from AK Press in Edinburgh (often taking weeks or months), from Books For A Change on Charing Cross Road, from *Z Magazine* sent every month or two from the United States, from the monthly *Ecologist*, from John Pilger's articles in the *New Statesman*, and from one or two other tiny magazines. We read Edward Herman or Noam Chomsky's take on current events many weeks after they had happened, or perhaps a year later in books.

Now, our inboxes are flooded on a daily basis with instant responses by dozens of brilliant mainstream and dissident journalists all over the world. Informed and articulate posters provide instant commentary on our message board generating vibrant debates and floods of emails to mainstream journalists. This, frankly, is bad news for state–corporate propagandists seeking to influence the public mind.

Given this astonishing change, it is remarkable that far more serious effort and funding have not gone into building alternative media to challenge the mainstream – the opportunity is quite clearly there and has not yet been wholly grasped. A rational and compassionate mass media promoting human and animal welfare over profits, truth over 'necessary illusions', is unquestionably within our grasps. But the emphasis is on *our* grasp – it is up to us and no one else. *We* can create a compassionate media. To make it happen we need to do three things.

The first is to *do* nothing. We need to reflect deeply on the benefits of working to remove others' suffering – not just for them but for ourselves, also – and on the utter catastrophe of unrestrained selfishness.

Second, we need to decide that a compassionate media is worth working for, that it is worth sacrificing effort, money and time for. We need to focus clearly on the untold benefits of increased mass media challenges to greed, anger, hatred, violence and ignorance. We need to focus on the increased honesty and rationality of journalism motivated by concern for others rather than by concern for wealth and status.

Finally, having reflected on the clear benefits of compassion, and of a compassionate media, we must act.

# 13
## Full Human Dissent

### THE REALITY FILTERS

In this book, we have shown how facts, ideas and voices in our culture are filtered by a propaganda system promoting the goals of a fundamentally psychopathic corporate system.

This is not achieved through any kind of conspiracy, but through the operation of market forces allied with 'man's capacity of not observing what he does not want to observe', such that 'he may be sincere in denying a knowledge which he would have, if he wanted only to have it', in the words of Erich Fromm (*Beyond the Chains of Illusion*, Abacus, 1989, p. 94).

But how far do the effects of this system of filtering extend into our ideas about ourselves and the world? Consider, for example, the effects of the same filtering process on the literature we read. Noam Chomsky argues that George Orwell's *Animal Farm* and *1984* are as highly regarded as they are, not because they provide brilliant insights into modern systems of political control, but because they were satirical attacks against the ultimate 'rogue state', the Soviet Union. Chomsky comments:

> Fame, fortune, and respect await those who reveal the crimes of official enemies; those who undertake the vastly more important task of raising a mirror to their own societies can expect quite different treatment. George Orwell is famous for *Animal Farm* and *1984*, which focus on the official enemy. Had he addressed the more interesting and significant question of thought control in relatively free and democratic societies, it would not have been appreciated, and instead of wide acclaim, he would have faced silent dismissal or obloquy. (*Deterring Democracy*, Hill & Wang, 1992, p. 372)

Plato is an 'untouchable' of modern culture, historian Howard Zinn argues, because he advocated blind obedience to government, and thus has long been popular with governments and educational systems working to instil appropriate attitudes in the young. In the *Crito*, for example, Plato has Socrates refuse to escape from prison on the following grounds, here paraphrased by Zinn:

'No, I must obey the law. True, Athens has committed an injustice against me by ordering me to die for speaking my mind. But if I complained about this injustice, Athens could rightly say: "We brought you into this world, we raised you, we educated you, we gave you and every other citizen a share of all the good things we could"'. Socrates accepts this, saying: 'By not leaving Athens, I agreed to obey its laws. And so I will go to my death'. (*Failure to Quit*, Common Courage Press, 1993, p. 154)

Fromm described how, not just literature, politics and the mass media, but our deepest personal, ethical and spiritual beliefs are subject to the influence of what he called 'social filters', which work to promote the status quo. Because corporate capitalist society depends on a workforce engaged in machine-like production and relentless consumption, Fromm argued, it ceaselessly promotes the idea that these are the inevitable and proper aspirations of humankind. Thus, mainstream society constantly seeks to persuade us that economic 'success' through high status consumption and production, and the de-repression of blocked sexual impulses (said to be at the root of all neurosis) are paths to happiness rooted in human nature. These claims, Fromm believed, are entirely fraudulent: 'Both the "economic" man and the "sexual" man are convenient fabrications whose alleged nature – isolated, social, greedy and competitive – makes Capitalism appear as the system which corresponds perfectly to human nature, and places it beyond the reach of criticism' (Fromm, *The Sane Society*, Rinehart and Winston, 1955, p. 77).

Fromm even explained how his own profession of psychotherapy had been selected and promoted to support the status quo:

The aim of therapy is often that of helping the person to be better adjusted to existing circumstances, to 'reality' as it is frequently called; mental health is often considered to be nothing but this adjustment ... [Thus] the psychologists, using the 'right' words from Socrates to Freud, become the priests of industrial society, helping to fulfil its aims by helping the individual to become the perfectly adjusted organisation man. (*Beyond the Chains of Illusion*, pp. 131–2)

Fromm's theory of 'social filters' predicted that his own theory would be unlikely to pass through the filters, but would instead be marginalised and ignored by the mainstream. So did the theory successfully predict its own fate? In his biography of Fromm, Daniel Burston notes, intriguingly:

> American psychiatrists of the orthodox Freudian persuasion simply ignored Fromm, as the paucity of references and lack of a single substantive analysis in the orthodox American psychoanalytic literature demonstrate ... Indeed, the grotesque distortions by Fromm's critics and would-be expositors attest to the validity of Fromm's theory of social filters. (*The Legacy of Erich Fromm*, Harvard University Press, 1991, p. 185)

Evidence for Fromm's theory of social filtering is all around us. Historian Elizabeth Fones-Wolf reports that the growth in American workers' expectations and power during the 1940s and 1950s was a major factor in shaping elite policy, leading to a fierce business backlash intended to mould US public opinion. The response was immense in scale, involving all the leading business organisations, including the Chamber of Commerce, the Committee for Economic Development, the National Association of Manufacturers, and industry-specific bodies:

> Manufacturers orchestrated multimillion dollar public relations campaigns that relied on newspapers, magazines, radio, and later television, to re-educate the public in the principles and benefits of the American economic system ... employers sought to undermine unionism and address shop-floor conflict by building a separate company identity or company consciousness among their employees. This involved convincing workers to identify their social, economic, and political well-being with that of their specific employer and more broadly with the free enterprise system. (Fones-Wolf, *Selling Free Enterprise – The Business Assault on Labour and Liberalism, 1945–60*, University of Illinois Press, 1994, p. 6)

In 1950, the National Association of Manufacturers (NAM) distributed almost four and a half million pamphlets to students. By 1954, over three and a half million students watched sixty thousand showings of NAM films. That year school superintendents estimated the investment in free corporate material at $50 million, about half the amount public schools spent on standard textbooks annually. Endless articles and books promoted fears of a Soviet conspiracy plotting to weaken Western defences to the point where a surprise attack could be launched. Between 1948 and 1954, Hollywood made more than 40 anti-Communist films with titles like *I Married a Communist* and *I*

*Was a Communist for the FBI.* Large-circulation magazines were titled, *How Communists Get That Way* and *Communists Are After Your Child.* Capitalists were after children, too, promoting comic strip heroes like Captain America, who declared: 'Beware, commies, spies, traitors, and foreign agents! Captain America, with all loyal, free men behind him, is looking for you' (quoted, Howard Zinn, *A People's History of the United States*, Harper Colophon, 1990, p. 428).

Around this time, US librarians refused to stock Frank L. Baum's *Wizard of Oz* series of books because Baum wrote of how, in his imagined society, 'there were no poor people … because there was no such thing as money, and all property of every sort belonged to the Ruler. The people were her children and she cared for them. Each person was given freely by his neighbours whatever he required for his use, which is as much as anyone may reasonably desire' (quoted, Gore Vidal, *United States*, Random House, 1993, p. 1103). Though not exactly Communism, Gore Vidal notes, it was close enough to offend the powers that be:

> Essentially our educators are Puritans who want to uphold the Puritan work ethic. This is done by bringing up American children in such a way that they will take their place in society as diligent workers and unprotesting consumers. Any sort of literature that encourages a child to contemplate alternative worlds might incite him, later in life, to make changes in the iron Puritan order that has brought us, along with missiles and atomic submarines, the assembly line at Detroit where workers are systematically dehumanised. (Ibid., p. 1097)

Our ideas about the world are manipulated in any number of ways: North Koreans are targeted as the 'bad guys' in James Bond movies, while video games encourage children to track down and kill Saddam Hussein.

Children are, of course, remorselessly targeted by big business advertising campaigns with little protest, and plenty of support, from the media. The chief executive of Prism Communications puts the years of innocence in their proper perspective: 'They aren't children so much as what I like to call "evolving consumers"' (quoted, Sharon Beder, *Global Spin – The Corporate Assault on Environmentalism*, Green Books, 1997, p. 163).

Marketers focus on the Nag Factor in exploiting children as a means of reaching their parents' wallets and purses. Lucy Hughes, director of strategy and insight for Initiative Marketing, explains:

we will try to get the kids to nag them [their parents] with importance to show them the value or benefit this product has to them, why it's important to the child. And in the right circumstances the parents will be receptive to it. (Hughes, quoted, Joel Bakan, *The Corporation*, Constable, 2004, p. 120)

Harvard Medical expert Dr Susan Linn comments:

The average American child sees 30,000 commercials a year on television alone ... Comparing the marketing of yesteryear to the marketing of today is like comparing a BB gun to a smart bomb. The advertising that children are exposed to today is honed by psychologists. It's enhanced by media technology that nobody ever thought was possible. And also it is everywhere. They can't escape it. It finds them in every nook and cranny of their life. (Ibid., p. 123)

One result is the epidemics of obesity, diabetes and other illnesses associated with over-consumption. Speaking on behalf of a group of Australian doctors, Verity Newnham writes:

The aggressive marketing of fast food and confectionary to children does influence their dietary choices early in life, and it puts them at greater risk of becoming obese or overweight later in life ... Children can be extremely vulnerable to television advertising promoting fast food. (Ibid., p. 124)

While most of us find this appalling, marketers view it as 'opportunity in devastation' (ibid., p. 124).

### LIFE, LIBERTY AND HAPPINESS – THE CORPORATE VERSIONS

The corporate manipulation of culture is by now so widespread that it is often accepted as natural – to the extent that the young have even been persuaded to wear corporate logos as symbols of rebellious 'cool'! Retailing analyst Victor Lebow explains:

Our enormously productive economy ... demands that we make consumption our way of life, that we convert the buying and use of goods into rituals, that we seek spiritual satisfaction, our ego satisfaction, in consumption. We need things, consumed, burned up, worn out, replaced, and discarded at an ever increasing rate. (Quoted, Beder, *Global Spin*, p. 161)

We need to be permanently focused on ourselves, permanently dissatisfied, and permanently seeking – but, crucially, never finding – satisfaction through consumption.

The natural result of this promotion of profitable dissatisfaction – 'If you only looked/dressed/lived/married/drove/shopped/holidayed like this you would be happy' – is deep dissatisfaction with our lives. In February 2005, the *Guardian* reported:

> The vast majority of teenage girls in Britain suffer depression and self-doubt, blaming excessive pressure to look good and succeed in school, according to a poll commissioned by the magazine *Bliss*. Nine out of 10 say they have felt depressed, 42% feel low regularly, and 6% think 'life is not worth living'. They reported feeling pressurised on all fronts: at home, at school and in their social lives. (Lucy Ward, 'Doubt and Depression Burden Teenage Girls', *Guardian*, February 24, 2005)

Unsurprisingly, given the 'opportunity in devastation' sought by the fashion and dieting industries, appearance provides the heaviest burden for young girls – 94 per cent reported that there was 'too much pressure to look good (ibid.). A 2004 study by the Institute of Psychiatry, King's College London and the University of Manchester found that emotional problems were increasing, and were experienced by 20 per cent of 15-year-old girls, part of a sharp overall decline in the mental health of teenagers in the past 25 years.

In 2002, the *Observer* reported that around two-thirds of Britons aged between 15 and 35 feel depressed or unhappy at any one time. Young people with the highest living standards since records began were deeply miserable during the 'best years of their lives' (Ben Summerskill, 'Young, Free, Single and Totally Fed Up', *Observer*, May 19, 2002.

Accounting for these epidemic levels of depression in modern society, psychologist Oliver James, author of *Britain on the Couch*, says of the depressed:

> They were led to believe that anything was possible. In reality, in the vast majority of cases, they still end up working very hard to make somebody else rich. And the advertisements which encouraged them to believe consumption was the root of all happiness have been strongly instrumental in creating discontent with their bodies and personalities ... They were soaked in the values of the winner–loser culture and brought up to believe that the pursuit of status and wealth was the root [sic] to fulfilment. This has turned out to

be manifestly not true. (Quoted, Ben Summerskill, 'Shopping Can Make You Depressed', *Observer*, May 6, 2001)

Psychologist Tim Kasser comments: 'Advertisements appear to be detrimental to people's well-being. Just as the government taxes companies that spurt noxious chemicals from their smokestacks, perhaps we should assess a tax on advertisers who spew materialistic messages' (*The High Price of Materialism*, MIT Press, 2002, p. 110).

A crucial reason for modern levels of unhappiness, malaise and depression, then, is found in the impact of a filtering system distorting even our most fundamental ideas about ourselves and the world around us.

## ENLIGHTENED SELF-INTEREST – THE CURIOUS QUALITIES OF KINDNESS

Corporate interests need us to pursue a version of human happiness that serves profits but not people. The results include individual depression, global environmental collapse, and wars for control of natural resources. Thus, much modern suffering is inherent neither to ourselves as individuals, nor to the human condition, but is often rooted in a dominant political-economic system which subordinates human and environmental well-being to profit. The result is that we tend to be exposed to ideas about ourselves and society that satisfy the needs of mass consumer culture, but not our needs as human beings.

The promotion of cynical selfishness, egotism and indifference to others is so pervasive that they seem almost inevitable – we are trained to talk nicely of idealism and hope, but also to be 'practical', recognising the 'harsh reality' as seen in 'the cold light of day'. It never occurs to us that selfishness and egotism might *not* in fact be credible paths to happiness, but might instead come at an appalling cost – to the environment and Third World, but also to us as individuals. To gain a true understanding of these costs, we believe, is to gain the motivation to rebel.

Given everything that has been said so far, it seems clear that if we are to find more humanly productive answers, we will by definition need to investigate areas of human thought that are marginalised, ignored, or deemed 'absurd' by mainstream culture, just as brilliant dissident political thought is marginalised and dismissed as 'angry', 'anti-American' and 'blinkered'.

There are by now good reasons for believing that traditional cultures have often achieved levels of psychological and social well-being far beyond our own. When the linguist Helena Norberg-Hodge began living amongst the villagers of Ladakh in Northern India, for example, she was bewildered by the simple fact that everyone smiled so much:

> At first I couldn't believe that the Ladakhis could be as happy as they appeared. It took me a long time to accept that the smiles I saw were real. Then, in my second year there, while at a wedding, I sat back and observed the guests enjoying themselves. Suddenly I heard myself saying, 'Aha, they really are that happy'. Only then did I recognise that I had been walking around with cultural blinders on, convinced that the Ladakhis could not be as happy as they seemed. Hidden behind the jokes and laughter had to be the same frustration, jealousy, and inadequacy as in my own society. In fact, without knowing it, I had been assuming that there were no significant cultural differences in the human potential for happiness. (Norberg-Hodge, *Ancient Futures*, Sierra Club Books, 1991, p. 84)

According to Norberg-Hodge, the Ladakhis' well-being is rooted in their belief system, which is characterised by kindness and compassion, and a marked absence of hatred and egotism:

> they seem to be totally lacking in what we would call pride. This doesn't mean a lack of self-respect. On the contrary, their self-respect is so deep-rooted as to be unquestioned ... I have never met people who seem so healthy emotionally, so secure, as the Ladkahis. (Ibid., pp. 84–5)

Ladakhi presumptions about happiness are very different from, in fact in some respects diametrically opposed to, Western ideas. A clue to the nature of the difference is indicated by the fifth-century Indian contemplative Buddhaghosa, whose compassionate philosophy also lies at the heart of Ladakhi culture. Buddhaghosa claimed that human happiness actually consists, not in vigorously striving to satisfy our personal desires, but in strengthening our concern for *others*. This could be achieved, he argued, by systematically and repeatedly generating compassion in response to real or imagined suffering:

> 'On seeing a wretched man, unlucky, unfortunate, in every way a fit object for compassion, unsightly, reduced to utter misery with hands and feet cut off, sitting in the shelter for the helpless with a pot placed before him, moaning

... compassion should be felt for him in this way: 'This being has indeed been reduced to misery; if only he could be freed from his suffering!' (Buddhaghosa, *Visuddhimagga*, Buddhist Publication Society, 1991, p. 307)

The nineteenth century meditation master Patrul Rinpoche suggests a comparable approach:

Think of someone in immense torment – a person cast into the deepest dungeon awaiting execution, or an animal standing before the butcher about to be slaughtered. Feel love towards that being as if it were your own mother or child. (*The Words of My Perfect Teacher*, Sage Publications, 1994, p. 201)

It is recommended that we repeatedly imagine, not merely that this unfortunate person or animal has been released from suffering, but that we ourselves have released them.

These recommendations are based on the idea that by repeatedly reflecting on suffering, and on ourselves acting to help, we will strengthen our sensitivity to the reality and importance of the suffering of others. By so doing, we will find that our habitual self-concern is attenuated and replaced by an increased capacity for love and compassion. This, in turn, it is argued, has the effect of strengthening conditions of mind that are conducive to genuine happiness – generosity, patience, empathy, equanimity and affection – while weakening conditions of mind that are conducive to unhappiness – greed, hatred, self-obsession, jealousy and dissatisfaction.

It might be argued that compassion merely serves to increase suffering by increasing our own sadness at the unhappiness of others. According to Geshe Yeshe Thubtop, who has been cultivating compassion through intensive meditation for 23 years, this is not the case:

When you first witness a child who is suffering, your immediate experience is one of sadness. But then this emotion is displaced by the yearning, 'How can I help? Does the child need food? Shelter? What can be done to alleviate the child's suffering?' This is when true compassion arises, and when it is present, the previous sadness vanishes. (Quoted, Alan Wallace, *Genuine Happiness*, Wiley, 2005, p. 132)

Compassion, then, is *not* mere sympathy for suffering. It is not the sentimental, sorrowful indulgence of much Western presumption. Rather, it is a clear-headed, forceful and determined (even fierce!) urge to *relieve* suffering. Indeed, from this perspective, we can see that our best writers – Chomsky, Zinn and Pilger, for example – are also our most compassionate writers. And these are hardly individuals known for wallowing in pity for the plight of the world.

Crucially, increased compassion is not recommended as some kind of stoic self-sacrifice. Richard Davidson, director of the Laboratory for Affective Neuroscience at the University of Wisconsin, has studied brain activity found in a European-born Buddhist monk, Öser, who spent three decades in the Himalayas meditating on compassion using methods of the kind described above.

Davidson's research had previously found that people who show high levels of brain activity in the left prefrontal cortex of the brain simultaneously report positive, happy states of mind, such as zeal, enthusiasm, joy, vigour and mental buoyancy. On the other hand, Davidson found that high levels of activity in a parallel site on the opposite side of the brain – in the right prefrontal areas – correlate with reports of distressing emotions such as sadness, anxiety and worry. People suffering from clinical depression and extreme anxiety, for example, have the highest levels of activation in these right prefrontal areas.

Öser was asked to meditate intensively on compassion and then to relax after 60 seconds while being monitored by a magnetic imaging machine. In his book *Destructive Emotions*, psychologist Daniel Goleman describes the results:

> While Öser was generating a state of compassion during meditation, he showed a remarkable leftward shift in this parameter of prefrontal function, one that was extraordinarily unlikely to occur by chance alone. In short, Öser's brain shift during compassion seemed to reflect an *extremely* pleasant mood. The very act of concern for others' well-being, it seems, creates a greater state of well-being within oneself. (*Destructive Emotions – And How We Can Overcome Them*, Bloomsbury, 2003, p. 12)

In another experiment, Davidson monitored the baseline state of left prefrontal cortex activity indicating normal everyday mood in 175 American individuals. Subsequently, Davidson also monitored the baseline state of a '*geshe*', an abbot, from one of the leading Buddhist monasteries in India. Although the *geshe* was a monk-practitioner who did meditate, he had not spent long periods of time meditating intensively in the way of Öser. Nevertheless, the results were remarkable. Davidson reports:

Something very interesting and exciting emerged from this. We recorded the brain activity of the *geshe* and were able to compare his brain activity to the other individuals who participated in experiments in my laboratory over the last couple of years ... The *geshe* had the most extreme positive value out of the entire hundred and seventy-five that we had ever tested at that point. (Ibid., p. 339)

Davidson describes the *geshe* as 'an outlier' on the graph – his reading was 'three standard deviations to the left', far beyond the rest of the normal distribution, also known as the 'bell curve', for positive emotion.

In a 30-year study, researchers at Cornell University were able to conclude that regardless of number of children, marital status, occupation, education, or social class, women who engaged in volunteer work to help other people at least once a week lived longer. Likewise, in a survey of thousands of volunteers across the United States, Allan Luks discovered that people who helped other people consistently reported better health than peers in their age group. Many also said that their health markedly improved when they began volunteer work. Other studies have repeatedly shown that compassion and affection for others have a measurable impact on human immune system efficiency.

Reviewing a vast array of research studies across the world, American psychologist Tim Kasser of Knox College reports:

Existing scientific research on the value of materialism yields clear and consistent findings. People who are highly focused on materialistic values have lower personal well-being and psychological health than those who believe that materialistic pursuits are relatively unimportant. These relationships have been documented in samples of people ranging from the wealthy to the poor, from teenagers to the elderly, and from Australians to South Koreans. (*The High Price of Materialism*, p. 22)

Kasser adds:

Almost everyone believes that getting what you want makes you feel good about yourself and your life. Common wisdom, as well as many psychological theories, says that if we reach our goals, our self-esteem and satisfaction with life should consequently rise ...

However 'people who are wildly successful in their attempts to attain money and status often remain unfulfilled once they have reached their goal' (ibid., p. 43).

Martin Seligman, professor of psychology at Pennsylvania University, has reported further findings:

> In the laboratory, children and adults who are made happy display more empathy and are willing to donate more money to others in need. When we are happy, we are less self-focused, we like others more, and we want to share our good fortune even with strangers. When we are down, though, we become distrustful, turn inward, and focus defensively on our own needs. Looking out for number one is more characteristic of sadness than of well-being. (*Authentic Happiness*, Nicholas Brealey, 2002, p. 43)

## TOWARDS FULL HUMAN DISSENT

These studies raise the possibility that there may well be approaches to achieving individual and social well-being – long understood and practised in many traditional cultures – that have been filtered out of our culture along with so many other ideas that conflict with corporate goals. These approaches could prove vital in generating resistance to unrestrained greed and violence, and in working towards a more rational and compassionate society.

In the past, we have ourselves held jobs in large multinational corporations. Like most people our goals were to do varied and interesting work, to achieve status and 'success' through promotion and, above all perhaps, to achieve a high standard of living. In short, our lives were centred around fundamentally selfish aims with little or no thought, and even less action, for the plight and suffering of others.

Our experience of self-centred work was of almost unrelieved boredom and stress – the work turned out to be of no intrinsic interest at all, but was simply a means to the end of material acquisition. It seems to us that when life is oriented around money and status, it becomes a depressing dead end, a kind of emotional wasteland. The contrast to our experience of the unpaid human rights and environmental work we have done since – for example, as part of this Media Lens project – could not be more dramatic.

The ultimate root of many contemporary problems is surely that many of us care a great deal about ourselves, our friends and family, but very little about those living beyond this close circle of loved ones. This often lies at the heart of our passive complicity, unthinking obedience, and enthusiastic participation in state–corporate destructiveness.

In turn, this self-centred concern is rooted in the deeply entrenched conviction that personal happiness is best achieved by applying maximum effort to securing the needs of ourselves and our immediate families, such that we have little inclination to attend to the needs of others deemed simply irrelevant – people who often pay an appalling price for our actions.

We often rightly focus on the logic and function of state–corporate systems, but we need to remember that states and corporations are in the end mere abstractions – they are made up of, and run by, real people.

As noted above, compassion and concern for others are central to the best dissident thought. But explicit focus on the importance of such concern as an antidote to individual misery, and to the many problems rooted in unrestrained greed, is almost nowhere to be found in contemporary radical thought, just as it is rarely found in mainstream thought.

Is it possible that the dissident critique of the propaganda system is itself a victim of one aspect of that propaganda – the aspect that dismisses compassion – or, at least, the idea that it can be systematically cultivated and increased – as belonging to the realm of mere 'religion' and 'primitive' Third World belief systems?

Is factual analysis of foreign policy, party politics and media propaganda really enough? Is it, for example, a sufficient response to the claim that happiness in this fleeting, fraught life can only realistically be achieved by working all out for 'Number One' – for hedonism, consumption, status and pleasure? Would anything we have written in this book make one jot of difference to someone passionately convinced of this belief? And if this really were the best bet for happiness, could anyone really begrudge such indifference? When the mainstream propaganda system is waging an all-out war to win our hearts, is it enough for dissidents to restrict the struggle to our heads?

Does unrestrained hedonism really make us happy, or does it destroy our happiness even as it destroys the world around us? Is compassion just a pious ideal, or could it be something much more? Could it be an authentic path to personal and global well-being?

The result of the failure to ask these questions is a humanly cold, arid, disempowered form of protest. The promise of compassionate dissent is that it provides a powerful, and in fact ever-deepening, motivation – for media activism, peace activism, human and animal rights activism, and environmental activism – in the understanding that compassionate thought and action are also profoundly conducive to our *own* well-being.

We need political dissent, but we also need personal, emotional, philosophical – that is, fully human – dissent. The sage Master Aro commented: 'On this depends my liberation: to assist others – nothing else' (quoted, Zhechen Gyaltsab Padma Gyurmed Namgyal, *Path of Heroes*, Dharma, 1995, p. 72). To understand that this truly is the case, is to have all the motivation we need to act for the welfare of the world.

# Resources

The following is necessarily a non-exhaustive sample of websites that provide useful news, analysis and/or commentary.

Al-Jazeera <http://english.aljazeera.net/HomePage>
English-language site for the Qatar-based news service.

AlterNet <www.alternet.org>
'AlterNet.org is a project of the Independent Media Institute, a nonprofit organization dedicated to strengthening and supporting independent and alternative journalism. AlterNet's online magazine provides a mix of news, opinion and investigative journalism on subjects ranging from the environment, the drug war, technology and cultural trends to policy debate, sexual politics and health issues.'

ACIJ <www.reportage.uts.edu.au>
'The Australian Centre for Independent Journalism (ACIJ) is fully committed to the principle that democratic societies require independent, critical and investigative journalism of the highest standard.'

The Activist <www.theactivist.co.uk>
'Encouraging active participation in political and economic issues: globalisation, Western economic imperialism, oppression, injustice.'

Appeals Worldwide <www.appealsww.com>
'Appeals Worldwide specializes in producing appeals letters based on Amnesty International cases, for you to send to the authorities in the countries concerned. No two letters that we produce are identically worded, and you can further adapt them to your own requirements. Never before has it been so easy to act on behalf of human rights victims.'

Arab Media Watch <www.arabmediawatch.com>
'AMW was set up to tackle a proliferation of traditional bias, ignorance and misunderstanding in the British media regarding Arab issues. The need to restore a measure of balance to its coverage is as urgent as ever in view of the power of the media to shape and influence public opinion.'

Black Rhinoceros <www.blackrhinoceros.org>
'The largest directory on the Net of environmental actions in the areas of Biodiversity, Conservation, Energy, Environmental Justice, Habitat and Pollution.'

B'Tselem <www.btselem.org/English/index.asp>
'B'Tselem is the Israeli Information Center for Human Rights in the Occupied Territories ... established in 1989 by a group of prominent academics, attorneys, journalists, and Knesset members. It endeavors to document and educate the Israeli public and policymakers about human rights violations in the Occupied Territories, combat the phenomenon of denial prevalent among the Israeli public, and help create a human rights culture in Israel.'

Campaign for Press and Broadcasting Freedom (UK) <www.cpbf.org.uk>
'The Campaign for Press and Broadcasting Freedom is an independent voice for media reform. We work to promote policies for a diverse, democratic and accountable media.
'We campaign for:

- a media which is more accountable to the people it is meant to serve
- the breakup of media concentration to promote greater media diversity
- rights of citizens to redress for unfair coverage
- rights of journalists to report freely

'Our membership is made up of individuals who care about the media and democracy, and affiliated organisations. These include national trade unions, local trade union and Labour Party branches as well as media, cultural and educational organisations.'

The Campaign for Press and Broadcasting Freedom (Canada) <http://presscampaign.org>
'The Campaign for Press and Broadcasting Freedom represents a common front of readers and viewers, those working in the media industries, and labour and community groups concerned about the increasing concentration of media ownership in Canada.'

Chomsky Info <www.chomsky.info>
The official archive of articles, speeches and interviews by Noam Chomsky.

Civil Disobedience <www.civildisobedience.org.uk>
'You want to change the world, but no longer believe in demos and petitions. Here are some other ideas.'

Cold Type <www.coldtype.net>
'Writing worth reading from around the world.' Beautifully produced pdf documents of essays, book excerpts, photojournalism and e-books by John Pilger, Danny Schechter, Norman Solomon and others. Tony Sutton is the website editor.

Common Dreams <www.commondreams.org>
US-based site for progressive news and analysis.

Corporate Europe Observatory <www.corporateeurope.org>
'CEO is an Amsterdam and Madrid-based research and campaign group targeting the threats to democracy, equity, social justice and the environment posed by the economic and political power of corporations and their lobby groups.'

CounterPunch <www.counterpunch.org>
'Muckraking US leftist newsletter edited by Alexander Cockburn and Jeffrey St. Clair.'

Crisis Forum <www.crisis-forum.org.uk/index.html>
'We believe that humankind is in serious trouble due to an economic and political system which is destroying our ability to sustain our existence on this planet. Our aims are: to bring together committed people from diverse college-based, academic disciplines, as well as independent researchers; to analyse the nature of the crisis in a genuinely holistic way; to put that knowledge to positive use so that ordinary people can apply global knowledge to local contexts; to develop this initiative as an independent research-based "centre" through projects, publications and study programmes.'

Dahr Jamail's Iraq dispatches <www.dahrjamailiraq.com>
'News From Inside Iraq
Weary of the overall failure of the US media to accurately report on the realities of the war in Iraq for the Iraqi people and US soldiers, Dahr Jamail went to Iraq to report on the war himself.
His dispatches were quickly recognized as an important media resource and he is now writing for the Inter Press Service, The Asia Times and many other outlets. His reports have also been published with The Nation, The Sunday Herald, Islam Online, and the Guardian to name just a few. Dahr's dispatches and hard news stories have

been translated into Polish, German, Dutch, Spanish, Japanese, Portuguese, Chinese, Arabic and Turkish. On the radio, Dahr is a special correspondent for Flashpoints and reports for the BBC, Democracy Now!, and numerous other stations around the globe. Dahr has spent a total of 8 months in occupied Iraq as one of only a few independent US journalists in the country.'

Democracy Now! <www.democracynow.org>
'A daily news and TV programme on over 350 stations pioneering the largest community media cooperation in the US. Hosted by award-winning journalists Amy Goodman and Juan Gonzalez.'

FAIR <www.fair.org>
Fairness and Accuracy in Reporting, based in the US, has been offering well-documented criticism of media bias and censorship since 1986.

Federation of American Scientists <www.fas.org/asmp/index.html>
Arms sale monitoring project.

The Fire This Time <www.firethistime.org>
'A deconstruction of the Gulf war, revealing media propaganda and the devastating effect of sanctions.'

Robert Fisk <www.robert-fisk.com>
Website dedicated to articles by Robert Fisk, Middle East correspondent for the *Independent* newspaper in the UK.

Foreign Policy in Focus <www.foreignpolicy-infocus.org>
US journal with many in-depth articles and much analysis of American foreign policy. 'Working to make the U.S. a more responsible global leader and partner.'

Glasgow Media Group <www.gla.ac.uk/Acad/Sociology/units/media.htm>
The Group consists mostly of people who have worked in the unit at Glasgow University, plus broadcasters and others who have published with them. The purpose of its work is to promote the development of new methodologies and substantive research in the area of media and communications.

Global Echo <www.globalecho.org>
UK-based progressive site with news and current affairs from around the world.

Global Issues <www.globalissues.org>
Progressive analysis of 'global issues that affect everyone'.

Globalvision News Network <www.gvnews.net/html/index.shtml>
'News and information from the inside out.'

Green Books <www.greenbooks.co.uk>
Publishers of books about the environment, ecology, politics, organics, conservation and green issues. Publishers of *The Compassionate Revolution* and *Free To Be Human* by David Edwards.

Hacktivismo <hacktivismo.com>
Hacktivismo is a group of international hackers, human rights workers, artists and others who seek to further the goals of human rights through technology.

Indymedia UK <http://uk.indymedia.org>
'Indymedia UK is a network of individuals, independent and alternative media activists and organisations, offering grassroots, non-corporate, non-commercial coverage of important social and political issues.'

Information Clearing House <www.informationclearinghouse.info>
'News you won't find on CNN or Fox (or the BBC).'

International Human Rights Seminar
<www.oxfordunivhumanrightsseminar.org.uk>
'IHRS is based at the Centre for Socio-Legal Studies at the University of Oxford and organised by students and foward-thinking academics and headed by Dr William Pepper, an International Human Rights Lawyer.'

Islam Online (in English) <www.islam-online.net/english/index.shtml>
'In this site, we strive to provide you with all the information you need about Islam and its civilizations, the universe and its changes, current affairs and their analyses, and general information and services that one cannot do without in the 21st century.'

Islamic Association for Palestine <www.iap.org/index2.html>
'The Islamic Association for Palestine (IAP) is a not-for-profit, public-awareness, educational, political, social, and civic, national grassroots organization dedicated to advancing a just, comprehensive,

and eternal solution to the cause of Palestine and suffrages of the Palestinians.'

Jewish Friends of Palestine <www.jewishfriendspalestine.org> 'The largest online collection of Jewish links to Jewish organizations and individuals advocating true peace for Israel and freedom for our Palestinian brothers and sisters.'

Justice Not Vengeance <www.j-n-v.org> 'Justice Not Vengeance (JNV) is an anti-war group which has developed out of ARROW (Active Resistance to the Roots of War). JNV opposes the US–UK 'war on terrorism', and campaigns for a peaceful resolution of international conflicts, based on justice and equality.' Includes excellent media reviews and other articles by Milan Rai.

Robert McChesney <www.robertmcchesney.com> Website of Robert W. McChesney, the author of *Telecommunications, Mass Media, and Democracy: The Battle for the Control of U.S. Broadcasting, 1928–35*; *Rich Media, Poor Democracy: Communication Politics in Dubious Times*; and *It's the Media, Stupid*!

Media Alliance <www.media-alliance.org> 'Media Alliance is a 25-year-old nonprofit training and resource center for media workers, community organizations, and political activists. Our mission is excellence, ethics, diversity, and accountability in all aspects of the media in the interests of peace, justice, and social responsibility.'

MediaChannel <www.mediachannel.org> 'MediaChannel is a media issues supersite, featuring criticism, breaking news, and investigative reporting from hundreds of organizations worldwide. As the media watch the world, we watch the media.' Includes link to 'News Dissector' blog by Danny Schechter.

Media Studies <www.mediastudies.com> 'The purpose of MediaStudies.com is to help advance research and education in media studies and critical thinking. The site serves as a hub – providing links to educational guidelines, global news outlets and other resources for media educators, students, researchers, and the wider community.'

The Middle East Research and Information Project <www.merip. org> 'In the words of French journalist Eric Rouleau, "No person, specializing or not in Middle Eastern affairs, can afford ignoring

Middle East Report." Professor Rashid Khalidi, a leading American scholar, says "Middle East Report is the best periodical (in English) on the Middle East – bar none."'

Morning Star <www.morningstaronline.co.uk>
'The only socialist daily newspaper in the English language worldwide.'

Network of Activist Scholars of Politics and International Relations <www.naspir.org.uk>
UK-based site. 'The Network of Activist Scholars of Politics and International Relations is a community of scholars, research students, and taught students, as well as individuals outside of academia.'

News Alternative <www.asia-stat.com>
'Access to a diverse range of news media from around the world.'

The NewStandard <newstandardnews.net>
'*The NewStandard* is a unique, independent hard news website. Dedicated to current events reporting and investigative journalism, *TNS* provides up-to-date news from a journalistic perspective that emphasizes the public interest ... *TNS* is a reader-funded publication – that is what makes it truly independent. Because it receives no funding from government, corporate or foundation sources, *TNS* remains free from outside pressures and accountable to its readership.'

Non-Violence Help <http://nonviolencehelp.tripod.com/index.html>
'This site draws together some of the available on-line resources on the history, theory and practice of nonviolence. It is both an introduction to nonviolent social change and a resource for trainers and activists.'

Open Democracy <www.opendemocracy.net>
'An independent, not-for-profit magazine dedicated to free dialogue across the globe about the major issues in the world today.'

People and Planet <www.peopleandplanet.org>
'UK student action on world poverty, human rights and the environment.'

John Pilger <www.johnpilger.com>
Website dedicated to the films and writing of John Pilger.

Private Planet <www.private-planet.com>
Excerpts from David Cromwell's book *Private Planet: Corporate Plunder and the Fight Back* (Jon Carpenter, 2001).

www.prwatch.org <www.prwatch.org>
Investigative reporting on the public relations industry.

Real News <realnewsbar.com>
'Not so much a web site as a toolbar that gives you full and updated access to the best independent journalists on the web.'

Relief Web <www.reliefweb.int>
'ReliefWeb is the world's leading on-line gateway to information (documents and maps) on humanitarian emergencies and disasters. An independent vehicle of information, designed specifically to assist the international humanitarian community in effective delivery of emergency assistance, it provides timely, reliable and relevant information as events unfold, while emphasizing the coverage of "forgotten emergencies" at the same time. ReliefWeb was launched in October 1996 and is administered by the UN Office for the Coordination of Humanitarian Affairs.'

rense.com <www.rense.com>
'Web site of the Jeff Rense program – US radio show.'

Andy Rowell <www.andyrowell.com>
Articles by campaigning journalist Andy Rowell, author of *Green Backlash*, who has had many stories published in newspapers and magazine across the world.

Schnews <www.schnews.org.uk>
The weekly newsletter from Justice?, Brighton's Direct Action collective.

Scientists for Global Responsibility <www.sgr.org.uk>
'SGR promotes the ethical practice and use of science and technology. We develop and support initiatives which make science more open, accountable and democratic. Our work involves research, education, lobbying and providing a support network for ethically-concerned scientists. Links to Science and Ethics related web sites and organizations.'

Spinwatch <www.spinwatch.org>
'SpinWatch exists to provide public interest research and reporting on corporate and government public relations and propaganda.

Spin techniques are much more extensive than is generally realised, encompassing media management, lobbying, corporate social responsibility, investor relations and corporate dirty tricks and spying. We aim to foster greater public and political awareness of spin and to campaign against the manipulations of the PR industry in the public interest.'

SQUALL <www.squall.co.uk>
'SQUALL Magazine Online is a forum for radical quality journalism and photography. It presents accessible and factually reliable investigations into issues which the mainstream media dare not touch.'

Take Back The Media <www.takebackthemedia.com>
' ... our [US] media has abandoned their responsibility to the country. The view that gets advanced is no longer the view of the "little guy" – it's the view of ownership, of top management, of major corporations. Editorial decisions are made with one eye on the political slant that will best benefit the company, and one eye on the bottom line. The corporate view is tainted, in that it looks for the best way to advance the corporation's financial interests. The result is this – instead of behaving as the Watchdog of Democracy, the media has become the Lapdog of government.'

Tikkun <www.tikkun.org>
'A community of people who share a spiritual/political vision of how to create a world based not only on economic justice, peace and human rights, but also on love, caring, ecological sensitivity and an ability to respond to the world with awe and wonder. It's not just for Jews, but for anyone who shares our core vision and agrees with our founding principles.'

Truth Out <www.truthout.org>
'We do truthout for three reasons: Far too often, the mainstream television news media act as little more than commercial advertisers for their parent companies. This is not journalism, and we desperately need journalism in this day and age. We also do truthout because the mainstream print media, while retaining great credibility, requires an enormous amount of time to sift through properly. Our editors, who read between 10 and 30 newspapers a day, do that for you.'

UK Watch <www.ukwatch.net>
'Focusing on the United Kingdom, collects and presents comment, analysis and opinion pieces of interest to activists and scholars of the left.'

Union of Concerned Scientists <www.ucsusa.org>
'Citizens and scientists for environmental solutions.'

UN Observer <www.unobserver.com>
'An independent journal of international affairs.'

The Voice <www.voice-online.net/content.php>
'Britain's best black paper' – coverage of a wide range of stories from a black perspective.

Voices in the Wilderness (UK) <www.voicesuk.org>
'Voices in the Wilderness has been campaigning – both here and in the US – against US/UK policy towards Iraq since the mid-nineties. First, against the economic sanctions and US/UK military strikes on Iraq and, more recently, against the invasion of Iraq.'

Waking Planet <www.wakingplanet.com>
'The time has come for a New World Flag that transcends boundaries and stands for all that is best in us; our ability to wage peace, ensure social and economic justice for all, foster racial harmony, end world hunger, and create environmental sustainability.'

War In Context <www.warincontext.org>
Alternative perspectives on the 'War on Terrorism' and the Middle East conflict.

The White House <www.whitehouse.org>
'One of the best satirical web sites on the planet.'

www.brianwillson.com <www.brianwillson.com>
Writings by peace activist Brian S. Willson, a former United States Air Force officer who served in Vietnam.

World Socialist Web Site <www.wsws.org>
'The World Socialist Web Site is the Internet center of the International Committee of the Fourth International (ICFI). It provides analysis of major world events, comments on political, cultural, historical and philosophical issues, and valuable documents and studies from the heritage of the socialist movement.'

Worldwide Democracy Network <www.wwdemocracy.org>
'The WDN was founded in the belief that a just and sustainable future can be achieved only through a fundamental transformation of our systems of democracy and governance, and is therefore primarily a political problem requiring a systems-based approach. Our aim is to bring together people and organisations who share this belief and wish to contribute to this transformation.'

ZNet <www.zmag.org/weluser.htm>
*Z Magazine*'s website: an independent political magazine of critical thinking on political, cultural, social, and economic life in the United States and around the globe.

# About Media Lens

Media Lens is an online UK-based media watch project, set up in 2001, providing detailed and documented criticism of bias and omissions in the British media. The Media Lens team consists of two editors (the authors of this book) and a webmaster (Oliver Maw).

## OUR AIM

Public access to honest and accurate information is vital if the democratic process is to be meaningful. Mainstream corporate newspapers and broadcasters provide a view of the world that is fundamentally distorted by greed for maximised profits. The costs of this misinformation in terms of human and animal suffering, and environmental degradation, are incalculable. We aim to raise public awareness of this systemic distortion by indicating how facts and opinions are consistently 'filtered' by a corporate media system dependent on advertising revenue, parent companies, wealthy owners and government news sources. We encourage the public to email critical challenges direct to journalists and to engage them in debate. Our aim is to help democratise the setting and content of news agendas, which traditionally reflect establishment interests. Our broader goal is the promotion of a more honest, compassionate society in which people and planet are no longer subordinated to profit.

## WHAT MEDIA LENS DOES

Through our free email media alert service, we provide rapid and detailed analysis of news reporting in the UK media, concentrating on the 'quality' liberal print and broadcast media. We expose biases, inconsistencies, inaccuracies, omissions and untruths. We challenge journalists and editors by email and invite their response. We then collate and analyse the material and distribute a media alert to members of the public who have signed up for the service. To date, we have sent out around 300 media alerts. We have thousands of subscribers in the UK and further afield, including Canada, India, Brazil, Australia, the US, the Netherlands, Finland, Iran, Colombia,

Japan and South Africa. Our alerts reach many thousands, even hundreds of thousands, of other readers via websites like ZNet and ColdType, and numerous other friendly sites.

## WHAT IS A MEDIA ALERT?

A media alert compares the mainstream media and political view of the world with fact-based, referenced and credible alternatives. We often take a topic – for example, the publication of the 2004 *Lancet* report estimating nearly 100,000 excess Iraqi civilian deaths since the 2003 invasion of Iraq – and check media accuracy and honesty against the facts, and against the testimony of expert commentators and other credible sources. The idea is to present both versions of a particular argument as clearly and honestly as possible so that our readers can make up their own minds on which arguments are more credible. We then invite readers to make their views known both to us and to mainstream journalists through the 'suggested action' section at the end of each alert providing contact details for editors and journalists. We urge correspondents to adopt a polite, rational and respectful tone at all times – we strongly oppose all abuse and personal attack. We often then follow up our alerts with updates containing analysis of and commentary on mainstream responses to our alerts, our readers' emails, and so on. Media alerts are archived at the Media Lens website (www.medialens.org) for ease of public reference.

Visit the Media Lens website:
www.medialens.org

Subscribe for free media alerts and cogitations:
www.medialens.org/indexphp

Please consider donating to Media Lens:
www.medialens.org/donate.html

# Index